ENLIGHTENMENT?

WHO CARES!

Other Publications by Madhukar Thompson:

Books

- Enlightenment: An Outbreak
- Enlightenment May Or May Not Happen
- Teachings en Route to Freedom
- Enlightenment: Never Found — Never Lost*
- Gentle Hammer, Friendly Sword, Silent Arrow*

Post Card Books
(Sets of cards taking a light-hearted look at different aspects of spirituality and the search for Truth)

- Enlightenment by Airmail
- Enlightenment à la Carte
- Zorba 'n Buddha Your Way to Freedom
- Of Jewels, Pigs and Freedom
- The Seeker and His Search*
- Meditation*
- Enlightenment*
- Master!*

---

*Publication scheduled for July 1999

ENLIGHTENMENT?

WHO CARES!

*A Seeker's Quest for Enlightenment with
Ramesh S. Balsekar*

Edited by
Madhukar Thompson

All rights reserved. No part of this book may be reproduced or transmitted in any form or by any means, electronic or mechanical, including photocopying, recording, or by any information storage and retrieval system without prior written permission from the publisher or his agents, except for the inclusion of brief quotations in a review.

Copyright © 1999 by
Madhukar Thompson

Published in India by

NETI NETI PRESS

8 Sheetal Apts.
Kawedewadi - Koregaon Park
P. O. Box - 194
Pune - 411001, India
Tel./Fax: (91-20) 603338
E-mail: neti_neti@yahoo.com
www.neti-neti.org

Printed by:

MUDRA
383 Narayan Peth, Pune - 411030, India.

ISBN 0-9665245-2-7

Dedicated to Sujaani

The Neti Neti Press Logo

The logo of Neti Neti Press symbolizes the non-duality of subject and object. All objective phenomena — including all forms and concepts — arise from, and dissolve back into, pure Subjectivity. The words "Neti Neti" (literally "not this, not this") remind us that this Subjectivity is indescribable.

The scarecrow — a silent and ever-vigilant guardian — wards off all attempts to define It by "landing" concepts in Its immaculate, ineffable purity.

Drawing its life from mud and water, the lotus blooms untouched by both. It represents the flowering of objective, phenomenal appearance that is ultimately identical with the pure Subjectivity from which it comes.

The full moon's witnessing serenity symbolizes the one pure Subject, impartially illuminating and permeating all phenomenal appearances. In Its rays, the duality behind all conflicts and differences is dissolved; they are shown to be nothing but Its own expressions, and are therefore not other than It. The moon's cool light thus evokes the peace, fulfilment and contentment of enlightenment — the simple realization of one's own Self.

ACKNOWLEDGEMENT

This book appears as part of the impersonal functioning of Totality or Consciousness or God. For a book to be published, and brought to the world at large, Totality brings about interactions and cooperation between many different human instruments which prompt and assist each other according to their destinies. As part of this impersonal process, the body-mind organism called "Madhukar" has been made to feel deeply indebted to all those whose concerted reactions to "outside" (i.e. God's) impulses have culminated in the object which you, dear reader, hold in your hands at this present moment. Madhukar hopes that he may be forgiven if he mentions only a few of them by name.

Top of the list come Ramesh S. Balsekar — the guru and preceptor — and all the seekers whose incessant inquiries drew answers from him and thus occasioned the conversations contained herein.

Next comes Mohan, a true brother, who was so unstinting in his help and generosity; his organizational advice and unwavering support are deeply appreciated.

Especially heartfelt thanks go to Dominic Harbinson (a.k.a. Guruta) who carefully pointed out numerous mistakes, made many excellent editorial suggestions and offered honest and invaluable advice about all aspects of the work in progress. Madhukar feels very fortunate to have a sub-editor who is not only skillful and understanding but who also "feels."

Madhukar would also like to thank Harish, Sushila and Unclekote for refining the cartoons and lending them touches of artistry.

Special thanks go to Munish for his indomitable willingness to lend a helping hand in times of computer-generated distress at almost any hour of the day or night, seven days a week.

In addition, Madhukar would like to express his gratitude to Joji, Mahmood and Sudhir for their patient and painstaking help in shaping the text, graphics and cartoons into form.

Last but not least, Madhukar extends his love and gratitude to Sushila whose steadfast friendship, love, inspiration and enduring encouragement were inestimable.

Madhukar Thompson
Pune, January 1999

Contents

Biographical Notes	15
Preface	17
Introduction	19
God's Instruments	23

Chapter 1

1.1	The Seeker is Like a Potato Baked in Clay; The Teaching's Hammer Tap-Tap-Taps the Shell Away	25
1.2	Phenomenality is in God's Charge	26
1.3	How Much Money should I Give to my Guru? — A Question of the Working Mind	27
1.4	*Sadhana* and Enlightenment are Destined. *Sadhana* does not Produce Enlightenment	28
1.5	Past-Life and Enlightenment — Are all 10,000 Preceding Body-Mind Organisms also Enlightened?	31
1.6	Enlightenment: Destined not Programmed. Body-Mind: Programmed with Receptivity for Enlightenment	34
1.7	The Process of Disidentification and Enlightenment: Evolution in the *Leela* of Phenomenality	37
1.8	*Leela*: Life has no Meaning nor Purpose; Enlightenment: Realizing and Accepting *Leela*	41

Chapter 2

2.1	Spiritual Danger: Not Following One's *Dharma*	42
2.2	My Message to Pune: Acceptance of "Thy Will Be Done" = More Happiness	45
2.3	The Guru's Lie may be What the Seeker Needs — A Lie can be the Teaching	46

Chapter 3

3.1	My Way is the Only Way to Enlightenment: A Guru's Erroneous Notion	49
3.2	The Presence of a Living Master does Something; Exactly What is not Known	50

3.3 Given with the Authority of the Guru: A Mantra 52

Chapter 4

4.1 Waking State: the "Me" Exists for the Ordinary Person, but not for the Sage; Deep Sleep: No Awareness and No "Me" for Both .. 53
4.2 "Being in Lucknow with Poonjaji, Why Should you Feel Ramesh in your Heart?" 55
4.3 Truth is What-Is at this Moment 57

Chapter 5

5.1 The Living Dream Appears and Continues for the Dreamer Who is Everybody Who is Awake 59
5.2 Consciousness itself is the Bliss and the Misery; Consciousness cannot Enjoy Bliss or Suffer Misery 67

Chapter 6

6.1 No Control over the Arising of Thought, but No Involvement in Further Thinking: The Sage 70
6.2 A Two-Week, 18 Hours-a-Day Enlightenment Intensive Course: What Happens 2 Weeks after the 2 Weeks? 73

Chapter 7

7.1 In the Absence of the "Me," the Observer and the Observed are One 77

Chapter 8

8.1 What is Right with Witnessing and Wrong with Involvement? 79

Chapter 9

9.1 If *Gandha* — Then Smell 82

Chapter 10

10.1 The Complete Manifestation Exists already, and is Served out Bit by Bit, in a Self-generating Process — a Speculation 84

Chapter 11

11.1 Deep Sleep — No Awareness of the Body or the Manifestation
for Sage and Non-Sage Alike 87
11.2 The Personal Dreams of the Sage are Psychological Reactions
to Actions in the Waking State 90

Chapter 12

12.1 "If We Want Life to Continue as We Know it, We Should Try
Not to get Enlightened" 92

Chapter 13

13.1 Grace Happening in the Guru's Presence: The Grace of God 100
13.2 In True Meditation there is No Meditator 101
13.3 When Enlightenment Occurs, What Happens with God's Will? 103

Chapter 14

14.1 Enlightenment: The Peace of Acceptance is not
a Permanent Blissful State 106

Chapter 15

15.1 Even A Mindful Sage Can Break His Leg 108

Chapter 16

16.1 The Four States of a Sage: Working Mind, Witnessing,
Non-Witnessing, *Samadhi* 111

Chapter 17

17.1 Destruction of the World: Balance of the Universe 114

Chapter 18

18.1 Can one Have a Direct Experience of Deep Sleep? 116
18.2 Rebirth And Reincarnation 119

Chapter 19

19.1 A Terrible Obstruction: "I Am Enlightened" 122

Chapter 20

20.1 Lucid Dreams: The Dreamer is Aware that He is Dreaming; Enlightenment: No Concern with Lucid Dreams 124

Chapter 21

21.1 Enlightened or Not? What are the Criteria? 126

Chapter 22

22.1 Work is Meditation: What about the Workaholic? 128

Chapter 23

23.1 What was First, the Chicken or the Egg? 133

Chapter 24

24.1 The Guru and his Teaching: A Hope for the World 135
24.2 *Karma*, Rebirth and the Pool of Consciousness 139

Chapter 25

25.1 *Satsang* in the form of Gossip about Contemporary Gurus 141
25.2 "Lineage" Means: "My Lineage is the Best Lineage" 149

Chapter 26

26.1 "I am Sorry to Say You are not Enlightened" 154

Chapter 27

27.1 Thought is Connected with Consciousness and not with the Body-Mind Organism 158

Chapter 28

28.1 "I Love Food, so I Strive to Be a *Mahabogi*" 163
28.2 When All Questioning Stops: The Most Powerful Understanding 166
28.3 Initiation of the Thinking Process — an External Impulse; Cutting Short The Thinking Process — Understanding 167

28.4 "Fish or Chicken, Sir?" Are they in your Mind, or on the Menu, or on the Plate in Front of you Now? Working Mind — Thinking Mind ... 169

Chapter 29

29.1 My Mission Or Poonjaji's Mission? — Gangaji 174

Chapter 30

30.1 Enlightenment can be Bought with Money —
And the Fake Guru Takes it! 178

Chapter 31

31.1 Rajneesh's *Mala* and Balsekar's Sacred Thread 185

Chapter 32

32.1 Enlightenment: the End of Wanting......................... 198
32.2 Poonjaji said: "You are Enlightened!" —
And Then He Went Away 199

Chapter 33

33.1 "My" Action — God's *Karma* 202
33.2 Enlightenment: The Eruption of a Volcano or the Blooming
of a Flower? 209
33.3 Sex, the Sage and the Working Mind 216
33.4 Why Does God Create Misery? — Why Not! 220
33.5 Is Gratitude a Precondition for Enlightenment to Happen? 222
33.6 Enlightenment Happened in My Case 226
33.7 Grace or Practice? 229

Chapter 34

34.1 God has a Problem 238

Chapter 35

35.1 "I Hate Your Teaching!" — *Sadhana* is both Necessary and
Not Necessary for Enlightenment to Happen 241

35.2 Enlightenment Cannot be Enhanced in Any Way,
     Though Money Can Help 248
35.3 The Seeker's Earnestness for Enlightenment,
     Or Free Entertainment 256

Chapter 36

36.1 "Poor Fool, You Don't Understand the Teaching!" 261
36.2 The Seeker Leaves the Guru and Tells him Why 263
36.3 The Seeker's Last Question 264

The Final Understanding 275

Epilogue 277

Postscript: From Ramesh to Adi Shankara, and Back Again 281

**Glossary of Concepts — Ramesh's Teaching According
to Classical *Advaita* Vedanta** 291

Ramesh S. Balsekar with Madhukar Thompson in Bombay

Biographical Notes

Ramesh S. Balsekar was born into a devout Hindu *brahmin* family in Bombay, on May 25, 1917. After his studies at the London School of Economics, he joined the Bank of India in 1940. He rose to become the bank's General Manager, and retired after thirty-seven years of service. Sri Balsekar married Sharda in 1940, and they raised three children.

Although Sri Ramana Maharshi (whom he never met in person) was one of his most important spiritual mentors, his personal guru for more than twenty years was Sri Vithal Rao Joshi who lived in Pune, a city some 180 kms southeast of Bombay. Sri Balsekar met his second and final guru — Sri Nisargadatta Maharaj — in Bombay in 1978. One year later, during *Diwali* (the Hindu "festival of lights"), Sri Balsekar attained enlightenment in Maharaj's presence. On September 6, 1981, Maharaj passed away, and Sri Balsekar began teaching in his own right. Since 1987 he has taught at public seminars held in Europe, the USA and India. He has also written ten books on the teachings of *Advaita Vedanta*.

Sri Balsekar meets seekers and answers their questions every morning from 10:00 a.m. to 11.30 a.m. at his residence in Bombay (Mumbai). During the last half-hour of these sessions, devotional songs (*bhajans*) are sung in his presence. Sri Balsekar's address is: Gamadia Road — Sindhula Bldg. (off Warden Road, near the French Consulate), Mumbai - 400026 (tel. 0091-22-4927725). Sri Balsekar is affectionately known as "Ramesh," and is addressed thus by his devotees and other visiting seekers.

Madhukar Thompson's first-hand experience of Eastern spirituality began in the early seventies while travelling in India and South East Asia from 1971 through 1973. Eventually, in 1980, he devoted himself whole-heartedly to the search for enlightenment, and was initiated into neo-sannyas by Sri Osho Rajneesh. He spent the next twelve years in his guru's communes in Pune, India and in Rajneeshpuram, Oregon, USA, but when his master died in January 1990, Madhukar had still not found enlightenment.

In 1991 he travelled to Lucknow, India, to meet Sri H.W.L. Poonja and, soon after, became one of his close disciples and personal assistant. On several occasions, Sri Poonjaji declared that Madhukar was enlightened but eventually, in 1993, feeling that his search was still incomplete, he left Sri Poonjaji and spent the next three years travelling all over India in search of a guru who could help him to realize final and total enlightenment. It was during this period that he met Ramesh S. Balsekar, moved to Bombay and stayed with him until 1996.

Madhukar has lived in India for the past 10 years, and during this time he has compiled extensive audio and video recordings of his conversations and interviews with Sri Poonjaji, Sri Balsekar, and several other Eastern spiritual masters and teachers whom he met in the course of his search for enlightenment. This material is currently being prepared for publication by Neti Neti Press, a publishing company he founded in 1998, in the hope that the interviews and the close personal exchanges it contains will assist other seekers in their search for truth, peace, enlightenment, and understanding.

Preface

This book documents the *Advaita* Vedanta teachings of Ramesh S. Balsekar, as expressed in conversations with seekers who visited his residence in Bombay over the period from November 1995 through to March 1996. It follows on from its companion volume *Enlightenment May or May Not Happen* which was based on recordings made from July — November 1995. Both volumes contain Ramesh's responses to questions and comments voiced by myself and other seekers regarding the spiritual search, meditation, practice, the guru-disciple relationship and enlightenment.

Readers who are already familiar with the earlier volume *Enlightenment May or May Not Happen* can skip the rest of this Preface (it doesn't contain the story you might be looking for — that's in the Introduction below). This section is intended for new readers only, and ends with a few words on laughter. First though, "for the record," a few details should be noted.

The extracts contained in each chapter were all recorded on the same day and, like the chapters themselves, they are presented in chronological order. One chapter — Chapter 33 — features the complete unabridged transcript of one of the morning sessions in its entirety. On occasion, the names of certain participants have been changed so as not to impinge on their personal privacy. Throughout the book, for the sake of clarity, questions and remarks made by myself and other seekers have been set in italics, to contrast with the comments and answers given by Ramesh. Where essential, light editing of grammar and syntax has been undertaken to ensure that the text is readily comprehensible. Sanskrit words which occur in the text are explained in the *Glossary of Concepts — Ramesh's Teaching According to Classical Advaita Vedanta* given at the end of the book. This Glossary — written by Upanishad scholar and teacher Ananda Wood — gives a concise exposition of Ramesh's teaching from a classical *Advaita* Vedanta perspective. It enables the reader to gain a deeper understanding of the main tenets of Ramesh's *Advaita* teachings, and is expressed with such elegance and precision that it can also be read as a valuable guide and reference work in its own right.

The text has been illustrated by a series of cartoons in which I express my personal views and understanding (and, at times, my misunderstanding!) of Ramesh's teaching. The ideas for each cartoon arose spontaneously while I was transcribing the talks, and at first I paid them little heed. As the ideas accumulated, however, I began to realize their potential. Cartoons, after all, are excellent vehicles for swiftly conveying information, and are particularly suited for commenting on events and pointing up the humor underlying them.

The inclusion of these cartoons is intended to illustrate and underscore key aspects of the teaching they accompany. They emphasize and clarify, helping the reader's own understanding of Ramesh's *Advaita* teachings to evolve. And, of course, the cartoons are also meant to entertain, and to make the seeker (and hopefully the guru!) laugh. They provide light-hearted touches of humor, generating amusement and laughter without losing sight of the teaching that informs them. Indeed, the cartoons not only reinforce the teaching, they actually hit the bull's-eye, landing the seeker right in the Heart whenever they provoke an outburst of laughter. For it is not possible to think and laugh at the same time — the two events are diametrically opposed to each other. Either one is thinking or one is laughing. What happens when one laughs totally? In such laughter, mind evaporates. The "me," the ego, the one-who-laughs disappears and only laughter remains. No sense of a separate "me"-entity can accompany it.

Laughter is a sort of no-man's land — or better, a no-"me" land — where the seeker and his search, the doer and his goal, all cease to exist. There is no thinker, no thinking, no thought — time stops. Thus, in pure laughter we are granted a "free sample" of what we are all seeking: *Sat-Chit-Ananda* — Truth, Consciousness, Bliss.

So, dear reader, as you make your way through this book, I sincerely hope and trust that you will find something herein which resonates with your own experience and illuminates it with the direct recognition of Truth. While you read on, the cartoons are there for your enjoyment.[1] God willing, they may sometimes raise a smile or a laugh that transports you, albeit briefly, across the seemingly vast, disheartening (but ultimately illusory) distance which lies between you and the enlightened state that you long for.

---

[1] Selected examples of the cartoons featured in *Enlightenment Who Cares* and in its companion volume *Enlightenment May or May Not Happen* have been published separately in Neti Neti's postcard series under the titles *Enlightenment à la Carte* and *Enlightenment by Airmail*. Each collection consists of a set of 20 detachable full-color cartoon postcards which readers can send to amuse and "enlighten" their relatives and friends.

Introduction

Ramesh S. Balsekar teaches that all actions and events — including the search for enlightenment — are God's actions and events. For it is God (or Consciousness) that is functioning through all the billions of sentient and insentient beings. This functioning is all-pervasive and totally impersonal, and it is against this background that the illusion of "me" as a separate entity arises. As part of the process of manifestation, impersonal Consciousness identifies itself as personal consciousness, thereby creating the "me"-entity with its sense of individual free will and personal doership. The spiritual search is simply the reverse of this process, in which the apparently separate "me"-entity with the sense of individual free will and personal doership gradually weakens, finally dissolving back into the impersonal Consciousness from which it arose.

If we accept that, in common with all other events in manifestation, the spiritual search is merely part of an impersonal process that is moved entirely by the Will of God (or Consciousness, or Totality, or the Absolute — label It how you will), this has highly significant repercussions. For this teaching necessarily implies that neither the seeker nor the guru can in any way influence or determine the form the search takes or its outcome. The seeker's seeking is truly God's action. It was God's Will that turned a person into a seeker, and it is He who will decide what sort of spiritual practice or *sadhana* (if any) the seeker will do, and when (if ever) enlightenment will happen in that person's case.

Ramesh, therefore, does not prescribe any particular practice or advocate any method for attaining enlightenment. Rather, he teaches that the process of seeking (whatever the form it takes) can only be witnessed and, in due course, it will turn out that the one who witnessed — the individual — never existed. The witnessing is and has always been impersonal. The one who is seeking is that which is sought. The seeker and the sought are "this-here-now" — that which is always present: the sense of presence, Consciousness.

So, dear reader, if you are looking for a "how to" guide giving some kind of method or "recipe" for enlightenment, you are bound to be disappointed. Ramesh maintains that nothing can be done to speed up the spiritual process — no personal efforts by the seeker, nor the guru's support, teaching or power will help. For some seekers this understanding brings about a sense of relief and freedom — freedom from the sense of responsibility, failure and guilt. For others, the opposite effect occurs: a sense of helplessness, defeat and fatalism arises with the understanding that, as mere puppets in God's hands, our fate is not ours to control.

However it affects you, the good news is that it may be possible to gauge your progress along "the pathless path." Certain indicators or signs may be witnessed in the here/now of the Present Moment, because the process of disidentification has certain discernible stages through which the spiritual seeker passes before enlightenment occurs. These stages, or rather the seeker's attitudes towards enlightenment which underlie them, may be summarized thus:

> 1. "Enlightenment must happen!" — a conviction that enlightenment is something which can be achieved; its attainment depends solely on the intensity of my own personal volition, efforts and deeds to accomplish it.
> 2. "Enlightenment may or may not happen" — the recognition that the occurrence of enlightenment is not actually in my hands, but in God's hands alone.
> 3. "Enlightenment? Who Cares!" — the individual seeker (the "me"-entity), the seeking and the sought (the goal of enlightenment) have dissolved; only the impersonal What-is remains. At this stage, it is recognized that the one who is seeking is and always has been that which was sought: Consciousness itself.

Ramesh admits — and this is probably the best news for the spiritual aspirant at large — that a seeker might not need to pass through each and every stage of the disidentification process. During the process quantum jumps are possible; enlightenment may happen at any time, from any level, without any precondition. Again, it all depends on God's Will. And Ramesh offers further comfort by pointing out that, "Out of billions of people, only a few are spiritual seekers and you are one of them. God's grace has already descended on you." He often quotes Ramana Maharshi's saying: "Your head is already in the tiger's mouth," and explains: "You are already on your way to enlightenment. The tiger may take his time. So what! The tiger will surely snap his jaws. There is no need to worry or hurry."

In fact, he declares that, "The greatest sign of 'progress' is the lack of concern about progress, and the absence of anxiety about enlightenment. When the seeker, in his deepest core, has intuitively understood that he does not exist as an individual entity and that, according to destiny or God's Will, enlightenment may or may not happen in the case of this particular body-mind organism — in such a 'state' enlightenment may actually occur at any moment. The seeker's attitude in this penultimate state prior to enlightenment is: 'I don't care whether enlightenment happens or not. And I really don't care even if I do care!'" By way of illustration, Ramesh often tells the following story:

> The desire for enlightenment once drove an earnest and highly-determined individual to spend several years in the company of a spiritual teacher. During these years he proved himself a devoted

disciple who was totally committed to the attainment of spiritual realization. When the time came for him to leave and return to his native place, his guru made him promise that he would write every month, reporting on his spiritual progress. The disciple gave his promise and received his guru's blessing. They said their farewells and parted.

The disciple had been gone just over a month when his first letter arrived. "I am experiencing the Oneness with the Universe," he wrote. The master said nothing, but crumpled up the letter and dropped it in the bin.

The next month's report came promptly and stated: "The Divinity present in all things has been revealed to me. I behold It in a flower, in a stone, in the very air, everywhere." Again the master read the letter, crumpled it up and tossed it into the bin without a word.

For four months the letters arrived regularly. In his third message the disciple declared: "The mystery of the One and the Many has been revealed to me. I now know and truly comprehend there is no difference between you and me or anything else." Once read, this missive also ended up in the guru's waste-paper basket. In the fourth letter the disciple said, "No one is born, lives or dies, because there is no one who exists." This letter too was read without comment and followed its predecessors, slipping with a rustle into the trash.

After the fourth month, however, no further letters arrived. No letter in the fifth month, no letter in the sixth month, no letter for a whole year! As the time passed and brought no news, the master became increasingly curious as to what had happened with his beloved disciple. Eventually, he wrote to him inquiring about his spiritual progress, and reminding the disciple of his promise to keep him informed.

Some time later, the guru was handed a letter addressed in a familiar hand. It was from his distant disciple. The guru opened it and read, and laughed out loud with obvious delight. His attendant disciples were puzzled as to what had prompted this outburst of joy. Beaming gladly, the guru passed them the letter. They saw that it contained just three words, and the three words were: "Enlightenment? Who cares!"

This book will probably not find its way into the hands of many people who share the total lack of concern for enlightenment expressed by the disciple in Ramesh's story. This is right and fitting, since the book is intended for readers who *do* still care about enlightenment, and for all those who remain perplexed about life and its purpose and who yearn, however sporadically, for peace, for final existential clarity. So if you experience this perplexity, this yearning, and if you believe that enlightenment exists, and if you entertain the (mistaken) notion that, once attained, it can be enjoyed by "you" as permanent, uninterrupted happiness, you are advised to read on. As you do so, you will be struck by the gentle persuasiveness of Ramesh's reasoning, and come across many valuable and profoundly transformative insights which, I trust, will benefit you greatly.

As the discussions unfold, you will also catch glimpses of the bitter-sweet and painful predicament in which I, the editor, found myself as my time with Ramesh drew to an end. Certain aspects of his teaching troubled me deeply, and you will witness how my growing disquiet leads to a series of highly charged encounters in which Ramesh — of course, as God's instrument — appears unable or unwilling to dispel my doubts. Eventually, I find myself left with no option but to kneel one last time before my guru, telling him that I was leaving him for good and spelling out the reasons why.

(*Ramesh S. Balsekar)

CHAPTER 1

1.1 The Seeker is Like a Potato Baked in Clay; The Teaching's Hammer Tap-Tap-Taps the Shell Away

Madhukar: *Is the sleep state, during which nothing happens, still in phenomenality?*

Ramesh: Of course it is part of phenomenality!

Madhukar: *Is the deep-sleep state the same as the "I-I" state?*

Ramesh: Yes, but it is not the "I-I" state. It is similar to the "I-I" state.

Madhukar: *Is the deep-sleep state the most similar state to the "I-I" state one can know?*

Ramesh: Yes. But even sleep cannot be experienced, because there is no awareness of sleep while sleep happens. We know about it only after waking up. Memory supplies us with the information about how we slept.

Madhukar: *But we cannot know the "I-I" state at all, not even as a memory, right? The "I-I" state can be known only conceptually, and it can therefore only be described as a hearsay concept.*

Ramesh: The "I-I" state is what you were before you were born, a hundred years ago. The "I-I" state is what you will be in a hundred years from now. The "I-I" state is that which exists when this body-mind organism is dead. As long as the sage is alive, his body-mind organism will need to go through all three stages. But he is not concerned with them.

Nikos: *Because he knows he is not the body-mind organism. The seeker, on the other hand, believes he is the body-mind organism, and is identified with it.*

Ramesh: And that is why the seeker suffers.

Nikos: *And the guru tells the seeker the real situation. And even though the seeker listens to the guru's words and understands them intellectually, he can't yet grasp the truth existentially. And what is worse, he can't do anything about it on his own account.*

Ramesh: And the guru repeats himself a thousand times.
    I'll tell you a story. During one of my seminars in the States, I was taken to

THE HAMMERING OF THE TEACHING

*Nobody knows how many taps it takes for enlightenment to happen—
the Last Supper may never end*

a restaurant which had a dish called "baked potato in clay." When it is served, the waiter carries along a tiny hammer and, in front of you, he keeps tapping the clay shell gently until the clay breaks, and the potato is there for you to eat.

That's what this teaching does — gently hammering at the clay. That's why I call this teaching a self-destructive process. The constant hammering of the teaching destroys the identification of Consciousness with the particular body-mind organism.

1.2 *Phenomenality is in God's Charge*

Francesco: *What do you mean by "God"?*

Ramesh: You can use the expression "Supreme Power," "Totality," or "Consciousness" for it. It is an abstract, impersonal concept. "God" is the personalized concept for the same Supreme Power.

Francesco: *You mean to say God is not a personal entity, but the impersonal Totality.*

Ramesh: God is both, namely: Consciousness-not-aware-of-itself, and, when it begins suddenly to stir, it becomes aware of itself as the manifesting phenomenality. Phenomenality is in God's charge.

God is a concept created by the human mind, because the human mind thinks, "I am separate." The concept of separation creates the concept of God, to whom the human being can refer and pray, asking for the good things which he cannot will himself. So, the concept of an individual, as a separate part of the manifestation, necessitates the concept of God, the whole. If there is no concept of an individual, there is no concept of God.

1.3 How Much Money should I Give to my Guru? — A Question of the Working Mind

Mary: *I was figuring out this morning how much money to give to you, how much I could afford to give to you. For me this is not so much a matter of making you happy. I have to go inside of myself and find out the amount which I can afford. I have to do this in order to feel settled.*

Ramesh: Quite correct. Now, that is being done by the working mind. If your flight is at midnight, then the working mind has to say: "I have to be at the airport at 10 p.m., I have to leave my hotel at 9 p.m., and I have to inform the cab-driver to be at the hotel by 8:45 p.m." All this is thinking done by the working mind. It is not involvement by the thinking mind. The thinking mind says, "Supposing the taxi driver doesn't come, suppose there is a puncture in the tire, suppose in the middle of the night there is no other taxi, suppose, suppose, suppose..." That is thinking and involvement. But this working out of the amount of your donation is the planning of the working mind.

Planning for enlightenment—with the working mind?

But I am not thinking of the thinking or the working mind now. What I am saying is that what an average person calls an action is really nothing but a reaction of the brain to an outside impulse — which may be something you see, hear, or think about — over which you have no control. There is truly no "your action," but only a reaction to an impulse. And the outside impulse comes from God. You have no control over what you will hear, and therefore you have no control over how the brain will react to what you hear. You will react according to the programming.

1.4 Sadhana and Enlightenment are Destined. Sadhana does not Produce Enlightenment

Michael: *I heard you say that no sadhana or discipline is needed for enlightenment to happen, and that all one can do is to follow one's inner guidance and keep doing whatever one does anyway already.*

Ramesh: No. For understanding to happen it may be necessary for one seeker to do *sadhana*, and for another seeker it may not be so. Whether *sadhana* is necessary or not depends on how a particular body-mind organism is programmed.

Michael: *We have to find that out. How can we come to know? Will we find out by chance?*

Ramesh: If the body-mind organism is programmed for it, *sadhana* will happen.

Sushila: *Do you mean to say that in the seekers who are programmed to do* sadhana, *something can be done for achieving enlightenment?*

Ramesh: No. That is exactly the point. Nothing can be done. You have just to follow...

Sushila: *If a seeker-organism is programmed to do* sadhana *he will do it, and enlightenment may then happen through him. Doesn't that mean that a particular seeker can do* sadhana *in order to become enlightened?*

Ramesh: No. It only means *sadhana* has to happen through that particular seeker, and therefore it will happen. And if enlightenment is destined for him it will happen with or without practicing *sadhana*.

Sushila: *So,* sadhana *is just a happening like a storm or an earthquake, right?*

Ramesh: That is correct. But the individual who is doing *sadhana* thinks, "I am doing *sadhana* and therefore I am entitled to become enlightened."

Sushila: Sadhana *is just an impersonal happening through a seeker, and the consequent result of enlightenment is not in his hands. That will also be an impersonal happening.*

Ramesh: Yes, *sadhana* is just a happening which will have just a certain consequence. The consequence will be that the *sadhana* will be part of this tapping of the clay. *Sadhana* is a happening. But the individual who is doing the *sadhana* thinks that he is practicing and therefore entitled to become enlightened.

Madhukar: *It could be that one clay-potato needs a lot of tapping and another one could open as soon as the waiter puts it down and taps it only once.*

Ramesh: Oh yes. Any amount of tapping is a possibility.

Sushila: *That is not what I am hinting at. Most seekers I know are involved in* sadhana *and practice. My question is the result of two contradictory statements of yours, Ramesh, regarding* sadhana. *On the one hand, I hear you say, time and time again, that nothing can be done and that no amount of* sadhana *can achieve enlightenment. On the other hand, I hear you say what you are telling us today. Namely, that* sadhana *is an impersonal happening and therefore it actually cannot even be avoided by the seeker if he is programmed for it.*

Ramesh: I am saying that no individual is doing the *sadhana*. *Sadhana* happens if practicing *sadhana* is destined. In some seekers *sadhana* may be necessary and such a body-mind organism is therefore programmed for it. Two seekers might be so programmed that *sadhana* is necessary. But *sadhana* may only happen in one of the two, depending on the respective destiny.

Sushila: *So, the point is that the seeker thinks he has personal volition and therefore is doing* sadhana *with the sense of individual doership.*

Ramesh: If a seeker is destined to do *sadhana* and if he is destined to be successful in his *sadhana*, then he will be sent to a particular ashram where practices are being done. The seeker will then practice for the destined period of time. After some time he may feel that this particular *sadhana* has not done him any good. The same power will then send the seeker to another ashram or guru where another *sadhana* or teaching is available and this may be more suitable for him. It may also happen that no *sadhana* is necessary anymore for the seeker. His *sadhana* has already been done according to his destiny.

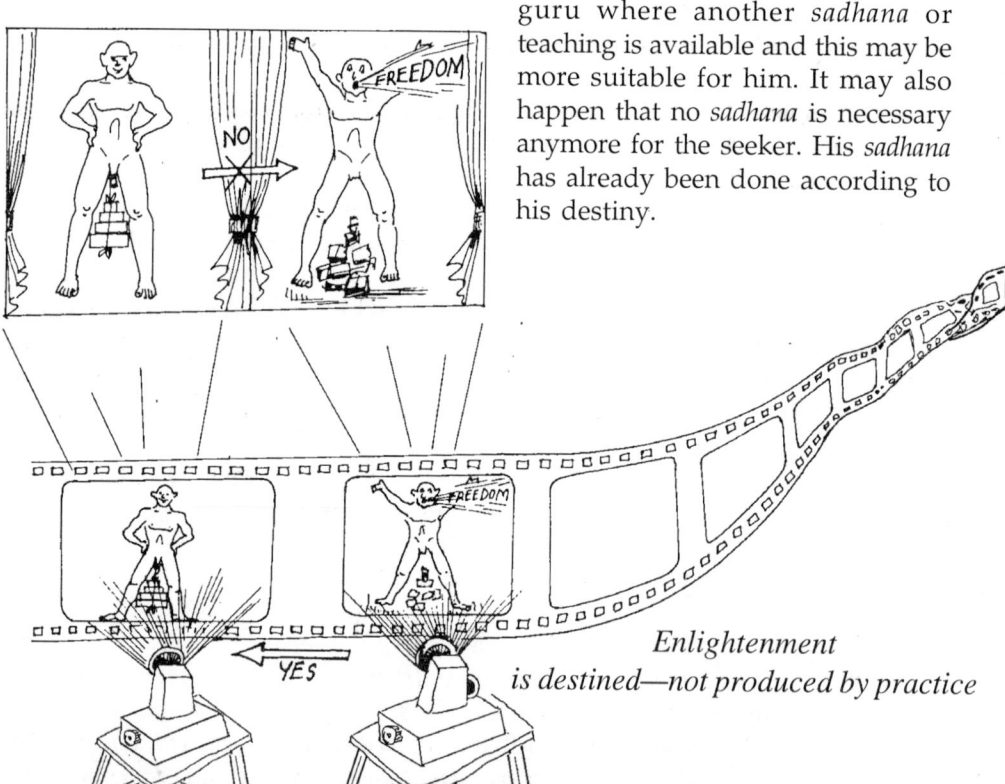

Enlightenment *is destined—not produced by practice*

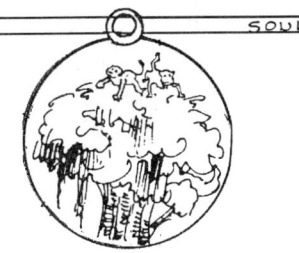   

1.5 Past-life and Enlightenment — Are all 10,000 Preceding Body-Mind Organisms also Enlightened?

Michael: *At present, reincarnation-therapy is very popular in Germany. During these sessions one experiences pictures and events from what are called past lives. Are these experiences just conceptual? And are past lives merely concepts?*

Ramesh: They are just concepts.

Michael: *Is it necessary for the spiritual aspirant to get information from past-lives?*

Ramesh: I would say, "Why bother? Why take the trouble to undergo such sessions?"

Michael: *You think such sessions bring trouble for the seeker?*

Ramesh: If past-life sessions are included in the treatment and therapy you are undergoing, then you will be doing them. They will be part of your therapy.

Michael: *I am really more concerned here with the question whether past-life experiences are based merely on concepts, or if they are real and the experience of them is helpful for the spiritual aspirant. I want to ask really if there is a soul which continues to live after death and reincarnates time after time.*

Ramesh: It is a concept.

Michael: *It is just only a concept?*

Ramesh: Yes, it is only a concept.

Michael: *But we are told by many gurus that the way we are living in this present life depends karmicly on our past life or lives. I was told in my reincarnation therapy that we are making some clearances during this present life which will influence the next life to*

come. In the next life we will undergo further spiritual growth experiences.

Ramesh: That is not correct. That is a concept. This concept is also believed in by the Hindu and Buddhist religions. But Buddha himself is reported to have said, "There is no soul and therefore there is no soul to be reincarnated." And he says further, "Deeds are being done, events happen but there is no individual doer thereof." To me, those words of Buddha mean everything.

Madhukar: *At some point in my life several past-life experiences literally came over me out of the blue. Those experiences were as strong and intense and real as the experience is at this very moment here — sitting with you and others in your living room in Bombay and hearing myself speaking these very words.*

Ramesh: Sure.

Madhukar: *During these experiences, one doesn't know that the actual deeds and events in which one is actively participating are actually part of a past-life experience. During a past-life experience one doesn't know that, while the events in the past life are happening, one's physical body-mind organism actually exists (in this present life), outside of the past-life events. One becomes aware of this fact only after one has come out of the past-life experience and realizes what has actually happened.*
    The interesting thing is that during the past-life experience one has the same sense of a "me"-entity that "occupies" one's body in this actual physical life. It seems to be the same "me" that inhabits the character in the past-life scenario.
    However long the past life experience lasts, at some point one comes back to this life and one recognizes one's surroundings and the people in it. It is as if one wakes up from the past life into this life. It is as if one wakes up from a past-life dream into this living dream.
    Such an experience can come over us as an event, like any other event in the normal life of this waking dream. It just happens. Therefore, does it have a meaning at all?

Ramesh: It is an experience in somebody's life. You say, "It is my life, it is my experience." That is where it is wrong. An experience was, of course, there, because that experience is an event which leads to something else.

Whose enlightenment?

Madhukar: *You mean to say that such an event may lead one then to wanting more of such experiences and therefore one may then subscribe to past-life sessions or reincarnation therapy?*

Sushila: *Would you say that that past-life experience or past-life vision of Madhukar has no connection with his body-mind organism which is sitting here?*

Ramesh: You see, when the body-mind organism dies, it is finished. I often ask, "If enlightenment happens in the body-mind organism called Sushila, who is enlightened? Is Sushila enlightened and all the 10,000 organisms of the previous lives?" Do all those previous organisms now say, "I am enlightened because of Sushila's enlightenment?"

Sushila: *I heard you say that the process of enlightenment advances over many life times. Could you explain which kind of evolution is going on regarding enlightenment?*

Ramesh: Yes, there is an evolution.

Sushila: *But it is not the evolution of an individual who may have lived the last time some hundred years ago in another life with another body-mind organism.*

Ramesh: Correct. There is causation. So, the *karma* theory is correct in this sense: God creates actions and events which have consequences. For those consequences to happen God creates new body-mind organisms which have nothing to do with the earlier ones.

Sushila: *These actions and consequences must, then, just be happening impersonally.*

Ramesh: Absolutely correct. And that's why you don't need to feel guilty for the consequences of your actions, because really they are God's actions and his planned consequences commissioned through his instrument called Sushila. God has merely programmed this body-mind organism in such a way that its brain would react to a particular event and produce God's desired action.

1.6 Enlightenment: Destined not Programmed. Body-Mind: Programmed with Receptivity for Enlightenment

Nikos: *The words you have told her just now, do they refer to her as a "me" or to her as Consciousness?*

Ramesh: They refer to a body-mind organism.

Nikos: *That means to the "me"?*

Ramesh: No! They refer neither to the "me" nor to the Consciousness. They refer to the body-mind organism which is an instrument. If you have 10 differently programmed computers and you want a specific output from one of them, you will need to input that particular one in a fashion that will guarantee you the desired output.

Nikos: *But aren't we computers created and programmed by God? Aren't we producing his desired outputs as reactions to his inputs? And the computer (the hardware), and God's program (the software), are the "me"?*

Ramesh: No. The computer is a computer. There is no "me."

Nikos: *Isn't it the "me" who has the illusion that it is the computer and that it is responsible for its hardware, the programming, the inputs and the outputs? And isn't that called identification or separation?*

Ramesh: Yes. That's why I say there is no "me" but only a living computer programmed by God in such a way that only certain actions will happen through it.

Nikos: *To whom do you speak? Whom do you address?*

Ramesh: I am speaking to the person who comes to me to ask questions.

Nikos: *To the person?*

Ramesh: I speak to the person who comes here and asks questions. I tell that person then, "You are truly not a person. You are merely a body-mind organism, an instrument, a programmed computer through which God or Totality creates such actions as He wants it. And therefore you are not an individual doer." Is it clear, Nikos?

Nikos: *I probably need to be hit with a bigger hammer.*

Ramesh: No. A bigger hammer will break your body. A gentle hammer it is. More strokes you need.

Madhukar: *Are the computer and the program different in the billion cases in manifestation?*

Ramesh: Yes. Every programmed computer is unique. Every thumb-print, heartbeat, voice, DNA is different.

Madhukar: *Originally a computer has been fabricated. Then a program or programs were put in. In your case something changed at some point in the life of the computer called Ramesh. Can the computer itself change? Or has it changed? Or does the programming change? And has it changed?*

Ramesh: No. What happens in a case like mine is that the destiny of the body-mind organism — which is the programmed computer — was stamped at the moment of conception. Let me repeat, the programming and the destiny of the computer, is stamped at the moment of conception. The destiny includes the length of life.

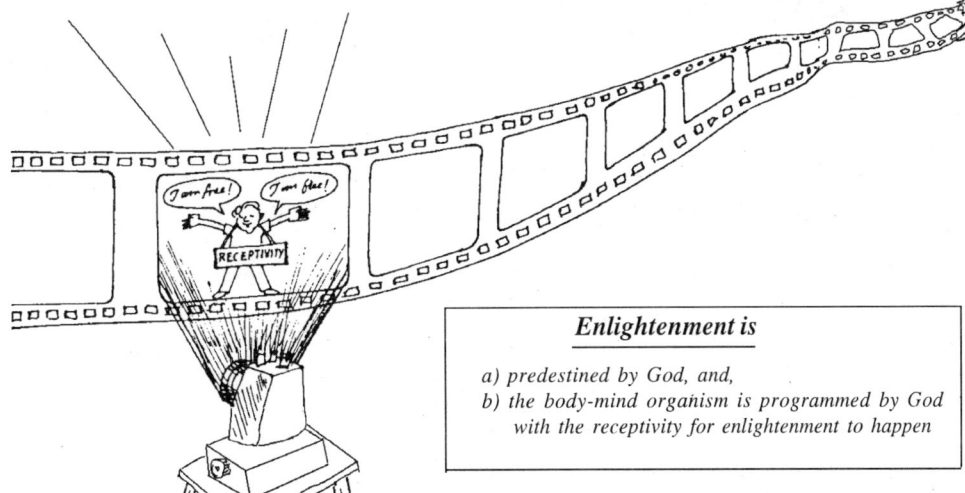

> **Enlightenment is**
>
> a) predestined by God, and,
> b) the body-mind organism is programmed by God with the receptivity for enlightenment to happen

Madhukar: *Does the computer evolve from moment to moment? Or are the programs rewritten via a self-generated process which is fed by the experiences of life?*

Ramesh: The computer doesn't evolve.

Madhukar: *Or change? According to the destiny, of course.*

Ramesh: If it is destined that the computer program changes with the event of enlightenment that change will happen.

Madhukar: *So, you are saying that the programming changes if it is destined to change. That change would be according to how God has programmed events to happen. Does the computer stay the same before and after enlightenment?*

Ramesh: Basically yes, but anything can happen according to God's Will. But, by and large, the basic programming will continue after enlightenment.
    Ramana Maharshi kept being a quiet organism after enlightenment while Maharaj kept his short fuse and kept becoming angry very quickly. The programming of the organism has nothing to do with enlightenment.

Madhukar: *You repeat quite often that a seeker can take it as a token for his spiritual progress if he finds himself to be more generous and to be more forgiving of others' weaknesses and mistakes than before. Isn't such a change in attitude a change in the programming? Is spiritual progress also part of the programming?*

Ramesh: That change is not part of the programming. That change is the result of the understanding of the teaching, Madhukar.

Madhukar: *But wasn't that programmed by God long before to happen at a certain point?*

Ramesh: That was destined by God to happen to that seeker. Make no mistake, Madhukar. The programming is one thing. Destiny is another.

Madhukar: *But don't destiny and programming come to be the same at some point?*

Ramesh: No. Not at all.

Nikos: *Is the programming according to the destiny?*

Ramesh: The programming is according to the Will of God.

Sushila: *Then the programming must be before the destiny, right?*

Ramesh: The destiny of what happens to the body-mind organism is also according to the Will of God.

Madhukar: *Destiny and the programming both are the Will of God then.*

Ramesh: But destiny is not programming. Let me put it this way: No two body-mind organisms can be programmed identically. Each is unique. But they may be similarly programmed, as in the case of twins. The appearance, as well as the programming, may be very similar. But the destiny of the two may be totally different. One of the twins may die at five. That's his destiny. The other one is destined to die after a 100 years.

Madhukar: *But we could say that the programming of each body-mind organism is also destined by God. So, both are destined by Him, the destiny and the programming.*

Ramesh: Yes, both are in God's hands and stamped at the moment of conception.

Madhukar: *That's what I meant earlier when I said both are the same at one point.*

Nikos: *For the destiny of a body-mind organism to happen, its programming must be also destined in a specific way in order that God's intended actions or outputs can be produced after He inputs the impulses into the computer.*

Ramesh: No. The destiny depends on what output God wants to happen through that body-mind organism. And that output depends on the programming. Destiny depends on the output. Destiny depends on the input and the output. Destiny has nothing to do with the programming. Programming means merely that a certain input produces a certain intended output.

1.7 The Process of Disidentification and Enlightenment: Evolution in the Leela of Phenomenality

Sushila: *I must ask a further question on evolution. I heard you say that there is evolution but no individual evolution.*

Ramesh: That is correct.

Sushila: *Couldn't we say that the understanding sinking deeper in a seeker is an evolution of Consciousness in a particular individual body-mind organism?*

*Hitler **Ramana Maharshi ***Enlightenment Building

What-is: Constant r-evolution of the Present Moment;
Enlightenment: Accepting What-is

Ramesh: It is a process of Consciousness, yes. It is a process in phenomenality exactly as the evolution from morning to afternoon to evening to night. That is an evolution in time.

Sushila: *But this kind of evolution is the same in time for everybody on earth. The evening arrives for everybody at the same time if one's watch is adjusted correctly to the standard time.*

The process of Consciousness, on the other hand, is not happening at the same speed and during the same time span in every body-mind organism. In some organisms enlightenment happens quickly, in others not at all.

Ramesh: The process starts with Consciousness identifying itself with a body-mind organism and creating a personal sense of "me," the sense of personal free will and personal doership. This identification continues sequentially in time through thousands of body-mind organisms. In a certain few organisms the mind turns inwards and the process of disidentification begins and, in even rarer cases, ends. But this identification goes on all the time.

Sushila: *Let me explain my question. You say,"All there is, is Consciousness."*

Ramesh: All there is, is Consciousness, but the evolution refers only to the phenomenality and not to Consciousness.

Sushila: *That's what my question was.*

Ramesh: Consciousness doesn't evolve. Two million years ago it was the same Consciousness as exists now and will exist two million years from now.

Sushila: *I see. Phenomenality evolves and not Consciousness. And phenomenality is part of the* leela *which evolves and keeps changing. And the process of disidentification, and the event of enlightenment, are still part of phenomenality.*

Ramesh: Evolution is *leela*. In your personal dream, evolution happens also.

Sushila: *With the event of enlightenment, the process from identification to disidentification is complete. In the enlightened organism the same pure Consciousness prevails then in phenomenality, as prevails before phenomenality appears.*

Ramesh: That is correct. Who thinks of all these questions? Who wants to know? It is the individual entity, the human mind, the "me." When the "me" has disappeared no more questions will arise because there are no doubts left. Everything is accepted as part of God's Will.

Sushila: *Enlightenment is actually simply part of, or a point in, the* leela *or the phenomenality process.*

Ramesh: Yes. Enlightenment is a process in phenomenality. Before the manifestation appears there is no question of enlightenment nor bondage. Both are interrelated concepts in phenomenality. Evolution is in phenomenality which exists in the personal dream and in the living dream.

Madhukar: *But phenomenality keeps existing for the enlightened one as well, but without identification and separation as an individual person with the sense of "me" and the sense of personal volition and doership.*

Ramesh: Absolutely correct. The body-mind organism of the sage continues as far as the destiny of his organism exists. If it is destined that the organism called Ramesh is to die in six months, it will be finished. His death has nothing to do with enlightenment, but with the destiny of his organism. In my case, enlightenment has produced a body-mind organism which is used by God or Totality to play the role of a guru. And that's what it is doing. Through this instrument certain books had to be written, seminars had to be held and talks are being given. The book-writing and the seminars have stopped. But the talks will most probably continue until this organism dies.

Madhukar: *And all of these actions and events have been destined? This particular destiny refers to the body-mind organism called Ramesh. And the programming for this particular organism is or was what?*

Ramesh: The programming in a body-mind organism in which enlightenment will happen is such that there is tremendous receptivity, total receptivity. And that has nothing to do with destiny. You can call the programming destined only to the extend that enlightenment had to happen as part of the destiny of this body-mind organism. Enlightenment happens because it is destined. And if the body-mind organism is programmed in such a way that, according to the organism's destiny, the process can proceed only to a certain stage, then that process of disidentification will stop at that destined point and will not end in enlightenment.

Madhukar: *So, the programming relates to the characteristics of a body-mind organism — the DNA and the environmental conditioning.*

Ramesh: Yes. The programming relates to the natural characteristics — physical, mental and temperamental — which are stamped at the moment of conception.

Madhukar: *And according to God's Will. And that's why those must be destined as well.*

Ramesh: Sure.

1.8 Leela: Life has no Meaning nor Purpose; Enlightenment: Realizing and Accepting Leela

Enlightenment: Accepting life without a purpose

Francesco: *If one gets enlightened, does one then understand the purpose of life? Or is there just acceptance of life as it presents itself and that's all there is?*

Ramesh: One understands that there is no purpose for all this. Life has no purpose or meaning. It is just *leela* — a play in God's hands.

Francesco: *And enlightenment is just realizing this and accepting it?*

Ramesh: That is correct. If it is not accepted all kinds of questions arise.

CHAPTER 2

2.1 Spiritual Danger: Not Following One's Dharma

Nikos: *You cited the example from the* Bhagavad Gita *in which Krishna tells Arjuna that he should follow his prescibed* dharma, *otherwise he will be in spiritual danger.*

Ramesh: You cannot but act according to your *dharma*. Lord Krishna tells Arjuna, "You may not want to fight, but you are born, trained, and programmed to be a warrior. And the energy inside you will make you fight, whether you want to or not."

Nikos: *But what happens if one doesn't know one's* dharma? *What does one follow then? One may be in conflict of wanting to become two things — to be a doctor and to be an accountant, for example.*

Ramesh: The natural characteristics may make one fit for both professions, in one and the same body-mind organism.

Nikos: *But I am talking about the person who doesn't know his* dharma *and doesn't know what to do.*

Ramesh: Even for a person with that kind of problem something will happen, won't it?

Nikos: *How is it possible for anybody not to do his* dharma?

Ramesh: It is not possible not to do one's *dharma*. The *dharma* Lord Krishna is talking about is not the *dharma* of becoming a doctor or an accountant. That is just another example. The whole *Bhagavad Gita* is addressed to Arjuna. It is therefore a special case. Lord Krishna tells him, "Your *dharma* is to fight. And if you don't want to fight, if you would rather be passive like a *brahmin*, then you will be in spiritual danger."

Madhukar: *Why? How so?*

Ramesh: Because Arjuna would not be following his *dharma* if he acts like a *brahmin* instead of like a warrior. But Lord Krishna also tells Arjuna that, ultimately, he cannot do what he wants to do, because his programming will make him fight anyway. It is Arjuna, the identified individual with a sense of personal doership, who says, "I don't want to fight. I would prefer to be a *brahmin* and be passive." Lord Krishna tells that individual, "It is easier and safer for you to follow your *dharma*."

Nikos: *In Arjuna's case, it is clear that he is a warrior. But what about a kid in high school? How can he or she find out what his* dharma *is?*

Ramesh: Today one can discover one's *dharma* with the help of aptitude tests.

Nikos: *But many pupils study in fields which are not suited for them.*

Ramesh: That means it is his or her destiny to be a failure.

Not following it ...

Nikos: *To be a failure is then that person's* dharma?

Ramesh: No. That is his or her destiny.

Nikos: *Destiny is different from* dharma? *Can one contradict the other?*

Ramesh: Yes, the one is contradicting the other. But Lord Krishna is telling Arjuna to follow his *dharma*, not his destiny. And he tells him further that if he doesn't follow it, he will be in spiritual danger.

Nikos: *But let me ask you one more time: how can we follow our* dharma *if we don't know it?*

Ramesh: If you know your *dharma*, follow your *dharma* and don't try to do something else. That is the point Lord Krishna is making. Lord Krishna is not talking about the situation in which one doesn't know the *dharma*. If you don't know your *dharma*, then you may do something which is against your programming, and you may come to harm. And if you come to harm, that is your destiny.

But if you are asking about a body-mind organism which doesn't know what it is meant to be, then an aptitude test can help it to find out what its *dharma* is.

Inge: *Could you explain one more time what, in short,* dharma *is?*

Ramesh: Basically, the *dharma* is your natural characteristics: mental, temperamental, physical. The *dharma* of a flower is to smell sweet. But the flower also has a destiny. Everything has a destiny. It can be the destiny of the flower to grow and bloom in an isolated location, where nobody will smell its fragrance. It will just be born and die without any meaning or purpose. But since the flower has no intellect, no "me," the flower is not concerned where it blooms.

Nikos: *It just enjoys its blooming.*

Ramesh: Yes. Blooming is part of its nature. Blooming is its *dharma*.

Madhukar: *And the destiny is where it will grow, and if and when it will bloom.*

Ramesh: That is absolutely correct.

2.2 My Message to Pune:
Acceptance of "Thy Will Be Done" = More Happiness

The bottom line for peace

Inge: *How do you feel about people who come from Pune (Osho's disciples)?*

Ramesh: What do I feel about them? Nothing. Whether they come to visit me from Pune or from Switzerland makes no difference to me. From Pune, from Lucknow, from Kerala — for me it makes no difference.

Claire: *The question is, how do you feel about people who come from the Osho ashram?*

Ramesh: I know. That's why I said Lucknow.

Claire: *Lucknow... oh, Poonjaji!*

Ramesh: That's why I said Pune and then I said Lucknow and Kerala.

Inge: *Do you have any message for the people in Pune?*

Ramesh: Do I have any message? Certainly! A very simple message: if you are able to accept that everything happens according to the Will of God, then you will be a happier person. That is the message. But it is not in your hands as to whether you are able to accept that or not. That is what the Americans call the bottom line. Is it your will or God's Will? It is God's Will! That's the bottom line.

2.3 The Guru's Lie may be What the Seeker Needs — A Lie can be the Teaching

Nikos: *Is mental illness an obstacle to the final understanding, enlightenment?*

Ramesh: I think it is the biggest obstacle. Because, as I told you, a psychopathic organism is so programmed that it produces only murder, rape, and other crimes — only bad actions will happen through it. And if the programming is to change, that change has to be part of God's Will.

Nikos: *But normally a murderer commits his crime only once. The murderer is not always murdering, like breathing, or like practicing a profession from 9 a.m. to 5 p.m.*

Ramesh: Are you asking me, "Can a psychopath be enlightened?"

Nikos: *In the* Yogavasishta *and other scriptures, we have examples of body-mind organisms being murderers first and then becoming enlightened.*

Ramesh: The *Yogavasishta* is still a concept written by an individual.

Nikos: *But can a sage like Vasishta be wrong? Would he dare to put down an incorrect statement in a spiritual book which is otherwise considered the highest of its kind?*

Ramesh: Well, some other sage will say something different. For each sage, it is a matter of interpretation and concept. Ten sages may have ten different concepts.

Nikos: *All contradicting each other?*

Ramesh: Yes. Each one uses his concepts for his own reasons. The *Yogavasishta* contains the advice and teaching given by the sage, Vasishta, to his disciple, Rama. Vasishta's concepts were what the disciple Rama needed at that time.

Nikos: *So, are you saying one sage can say one thing, and another sage can say the opposite? And even if one of them is lying, both are doing their job of imparting the teaching according to the seeker's need at that time?*

Ramesh: Correct. Sure.

Nikos: *What you have just explained to me must be correct, because you, as the sage, are saying it. That's why I can believe you now. Before, I had the notion that sages who are no longer individuals, who are fully realized, always spoke the truth, although what they*

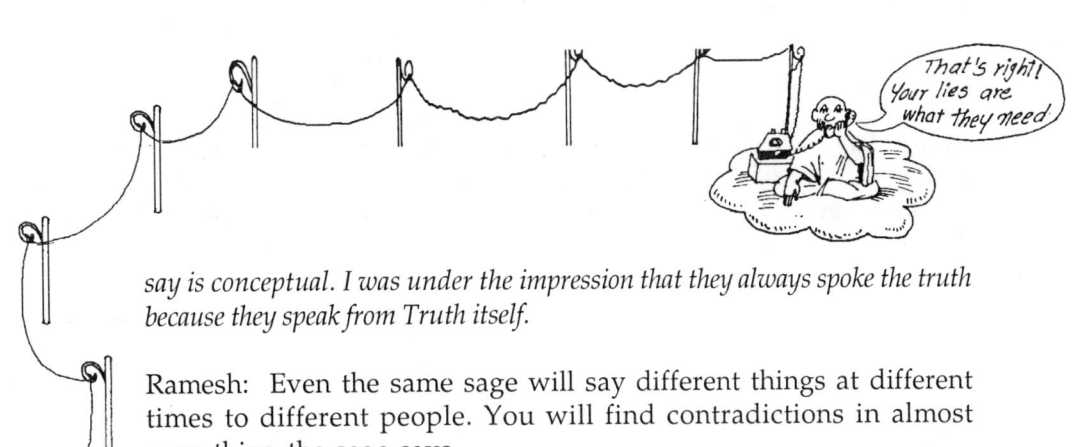

say is conceptual. I was under the impression that they always spoke the truth because they speak from Truth itself.

Ramesh: Even the same sage will say different things at different times to different people. You will find contradictions in almost everything the sage says.

Nikos: *Is that because the sage wants to help the seeker, and he knows that the seeker will not be helped in any other way?*

Ramesh: Exactly. So, in order to help Rama, the sage Vasishta used those concepts at that time.

Madhukar: *Could all sages in the world agree on one single concept about what enlightenment is? Is there one single true concept for everybody?*

Ramesh: No, on a concept they can't agree. No sages can agree on one or any concept, because a concept is still an intellectual understanding.

Lies, truths and teachings

Madhukar: *Could one say, "In phenomenality, conceptually, such-and-such is the truth?" And then could everybody, including all sages, agree to that conceptual truth? Is that possible?*

Ramesh: A concept is a concept. And a concept may be used to understand something. Ramana says one thing about *sadhana*, for example, and Vasishta says something else.

Nikos: *Ramana mentions the* Yogavasishta *very often, and cites from it freely.*

Ramesh: I know he does. And yet on the point of the concept of enlightenment, the two are different. When you go into individual concepts, you get into problems. Why bother with individual concepts? Why bother with the mechanism of phenomenality? But that depends on what you really want — a conceptual understanding, or one beyond conceptualizing? If the final understanding is beyond concepts, why bother with what one sage or another says? Whatever any sage said or says is a concept.

Nikos: *But doesn't conceptualization stop by itself when it is supposed to?*

Ramesh: The final understanding means abandoning all concepts.

Nikos: *But to stop conceptualization is not in our hands. That's what you said earlier.*

Ramesh: Sure. Therefore, the seeking goes on until conceptualization stops. So, if you want to continue conceptualizing, that is your destiny.

Madhukar: *The conceptualization on the part of the seeker includes the images he forms about the guru, and the guru's behavior and conduct.*

Ramesh: Yes. Sure. Of course, the seeker's image of the guru is a concept. "Consciousness is all there is," is still a concept. "All that prevails is God's Will," is still a concept. It is a concept because the opposite concept also exists.

Nikos: *But the seeker has first to stick to the concepts of his guru, until the intuitive understanding arrives.*

Ramesh: But the concept has to be used only for that occasion, the concept is not to be carried forward. It has to be discarded after its use.

Nikos: *So, as we said earlier, a disciple has to judge and test his guru until...*

Ramesh: If the seeker has to judge, then he is still very much an individual who judges. That judging will stop only when it is time to stop. Until then, the seeking will continue. The judging is the whole problem. Why bother with concepts at all? The only concept to be used for the final removal of the thorn of individuality is the concept that Consciousness is all there is, and that whatever happens is according to God's Will. No other concept is necessary. With these concepts, all other concepts can be removed. With this thorn, all the other thorns embedded in the foot can be removed.

CHAPTER 3

3.1 My Way is the Only Way to Enlightenment: A Guru's Erroneous Notion

Nikos: *If two sages look at the same painting, will they have different reactions?*

Ramesh: Certainly! Why? Because the different reactions are strictly according to the particular programmings of the two body-mind organisms.

Nikos: *So, the observation of the same picture by two sages will make their brains react differently. But wouldn't the two sages continue to see the same picture because they are purely witnessing it, and therefore their minds wouldn't be reacting at all? This is my impression of sages.*

Ramesh: In the *Bhagavad Gita*, Lord Krishna makes it clear that in a sage the same energy functions as in an ordinary person. The energy functions according to the natural characteristics of the body-mind organism, regardless of whether enlightenment has happened or not. One of the sages may say, "I like the green in the painting," and the other will like the blue in it — according to their programming.

Seekers are under the wrong notion that all sages think and act alike. No! Their behavior and conduct and preferences are different. What is common in a thousand sages is the total annihilation of the sense of personal doership.

Madhukar: *But can an enlightened sage declare, "I did such and such tapas and sadhana for so many years, and because of my sadhana I became enlightened?" Wouldn't that be a wrong notion?*

Ramesh: No, no. They are not wrong if they say, "In my case, enlightenment happened by following such and such practice."

Madhukar: *But are they mistaken in saying to their disciples, "If you do the same practice as I used to do, then enlightenment will happen in your case also?"*

Ramesh: No. They are wrong only if

"My way's the only way"

they tell the seekers that their practice is the only way for enlightenment to happen. For instance, if they say, "Unless your *kundalini* is aroused, enlightenment cannot happen," — that is not correct. The arising of the *kundalini* is only one path. And which path will produce enlightenment in which organism depends on the programming and the destiny.

Nikos: *So, the seeker who is destined to have his* kundalini *rise will go to a guru who became enlightened through that method.*

Ramesh: Quite right. I just want to correct one thing: "he" will not go. That Power, or Consciousness, will send him to that guru. And in addition, he may not be sent directly to that guru, but may find himself in various ashrams before reaching his final guru.

The other day, a Swiss couple came to visit me. The wife was a newcomer to spirituality. She came here without having seen any other guru before me. She just came, she just felt like coming. How it happens nobody knows.

Claire: *She saw the video of yours called "The Guru-Disciple Relationship." It moved her a lot.*

Ramesh: Yes. You see, there is always an obvious cause. Somebody mentions something. Somebody else reads a book. She saw a video. She was in search of a guru. When she came, I wasn't her guru. When she left, she accepted me as her guru. How this works, nobody knows.

3.2 *The Presence of a Living Master does Something; Exactly What is not Known*

Inge: *Does a seeker need a living master?*

The Master's presence

Ramesh: The answer is definitely yes. The first thing to point out is that the guru-disciple relationship is an Indian and East-Asian tradition. The second thing is that it is understood that the presence of a living guru does something. One does not know what.

If a hypnotist can produce a hypnosis by his own power, why shouldn't a kind of hypnosis happen in the presence of a living guru? If asked how that works, the guru will say he doesn't know. He says so because it is not he who produces something. Effects get produced.

Nikos: *Is it produced in his presence?*

Ramesh: Yes. And even if he is not present. A tremendous sense of presence is still felt today in the Ramanashram — in the meditation hall in which he used to live — fifty years after Ramana's death. Some kind of presence is present. And all kinds of presences exist, good and bad, everywhere in the world. That is part of the functioning of Totality.

Nikos: *Even if a seeker knows that the presence of a guru is helpful and does something for him, it may be that the disciple doesn't actually meet the guru until much later in time.*

Ramesh: Yes. It can happen that way. The time and the place and the length of the meeting between guru and disciple is destined.

Nikos: *In Ramana Maharshi's case there was no living guru, or was there?*

Ramesh: Ramana also held the view that a living guru is necessary for the seeker, even though he didn't have one himself in this life. "I didn't have a guru in this life, but in previous lives there must have been gurus," he used to say.

3.3 Given with the Authority of the Guru: A Mantra

Mantra Power

Given by the guru:
1,000 × 10,000,000 spiritual units

Nikos: *Does a mantra need to be given by a living guru? Is it only effective then?*

Ramesh: A *mantra* must be passed on to the seeker from a person with authority. The guru has such authority. A *mantra* picked up from a book will have comparatively very little effect. If a *mantra* given by a guru and repeated a hundred thousand times produces a certain effect, a *mantra* picked up from a book will have only a small fraction of that effect, even if it is repeated ten million times. A *mantra* has to have the authority of a guru behind it. I repeat, a *mantra* is a concept, and an Indian tradition.

Inge: *Is that why the seeker needs a living master? To profit from the authority and power of the master?*

Ramesh: That is correct.

Taken from books: 1 spiritual unit

CHAPTER 4

4.1 Waking State: the "Me" Exists for the Ordinary Person but not for the Sage; Deep Sleep: No Awareness and No "Me" for Both

Chuck: *May I read a quote from Ramana Maharshi. I do not understand it.*

Ramesh: Oh, sure.

Chuck: *He says, "There are only two things, sleep and creation. There is nothing when you go to sleep. When you wake up, there is everything. If you learn to sleep when awake, you can be just a witness. This is the real truth." Can you say something about this?*

Ramesh: What is sleeping? Sleep happens when the "me" is absent. Ramana says somewhere else, "You should be in the beingness throughout the day, even during work." And a verse in the *Bhagavad Gita* says, "When you know that you are not the doer no matter what you are doing, then you are in the beingness." The sage has no feeling of personal doership. He is in the beingness all the time. In deep sleep, the "me" is not present. In the waking state, the "me" is not present during witnessing. In witnessing, judging doesn't happen. During the waking state, judging doesn't happen when the identified sense of personal doership doesn't exist. If whatever happens is merely witnessed as part of the Will of God, or as part of the functioning of Totality, then you are sleeping — the "you" sleeps. And that is sleeping while you are awake. Here, "sleep" means: the absence of the sense of "me."

Chuck: *Does the sage's waking state feel like sleeping?*

Ramesh: That is correct. But in deep sleep you don't feel anything. The reference to deep sleep during waking is to the absence of the "me." The "me" is absent in deep sleep. But that awareness which is present in deep sleep, which knows whether one slept well or not, is Consciousness. In witnessing, there is no feeling of "me." Compassion arises, giving happens, actions happen, and all is merely witnessed. But there is never the feeling, "I am feeling compassion, I am doing something, I am giving something."

Madhukar: *But sages talk also about the opposite possibility. They say that they are awake while they sleep, unlike ordinary persons who sleep while they are asleep.*

In each case, in both states: as they are—part of the What-is

Ramesh: While the ordinary persons are awake, what does that mean?

Madhukar: *They live with the sense of personal doership during the waking state.*

Ramesh: So, the sage has no sense of doership during his waking state. And that is similar to the state of deep sleep, you see?

Madhukar: *Yes. But what is meant by being awake during the sleeping state? The sage is awake while others sleep or snore — or so the sage says.*

Ramesh: When the ordinary persons are asleep, the sage is awake but still in deep sleep. The ordinary person has no sense of "me" in the deep sleep state. The sage has no sense of "me" even when he is awake.

Madhukar: *That is understood. But can you explain how the sage is different from the ordinary person during deep sleep? I understand that in deep sleep the sage is the same as any other ordinary person.*

Ramesh: That is correct.

Madhukar: *Why, then, does the sage claim he is awake during deep sleep?*

Ramesh: Because for the sage the same state prevails, whether he is awake or asleep. In both states, the sense of personal doership doesn't exist for him.

Madhukar: *Poonjaji says that while others snore, the sage, in his sleep, is totally awake.*

Ramesh: According to my understanding, that interpretation is not correct. Or, if you want to say that the sage does not snore, that is also not correct. Or rather, the sage does not snore, but the body-mind organism of the sage may snore, if it is so programmed.

Madhukar: *I have read in the scriptures, and I have heard Poonjaji say, that the deep sleep state of a sage and an ordinary person are not the same.*

Ramesh: That is not correct. The deep sleep state is the same for both. And therefore, the state of death is also the same for a body-mind organism in which enlightenment has happened, and for one in which it hasn't happen. Who is concerned with death? The body-mind organism. Whether a body-mind organism belongs to a sage or not, death destroys it.

4.2 "Being in Lucknow with Poonjaji, Why Should you Feel Ramesh in your Heart?"

Ramesh (to David): So, you and Madhukar met in Lucknow?

David: *We have met many, many times in different parts of the world.*

Madhukar: We have met each other over the course of the past sixteen years.

David: *During several life-times, I guess.* (laughter)

Ramesh: So, what can I do for you?

David: *I just wanted to say hello to you. I visited you here two years ago, for just one meeting, which was very nice. I have been living in Lucknow for more than three years. I also sent some friends of mine to see you.*

Ramesh: So, you spend most of your time in Lucknow?

David: *Yes.*

Ramesh: Well, if you spend most of your time in Lucknow with Poonjaji, what

questions could you have?

David: *I don't have any questions. I just came to meet you.*

Ramesh: Oh, I see. Fine. Thank you. I appreciate the honor.

David: *I feel you in my heart very much.*

Ramesh: Oh, I see. Why? When you are in Lucknow with Poonjaji, why should you feel me in your heart?

David: *I don't know. These are the mysteries.*

Ramesh: If you are in Lucknow, you should feel Poonjaji in your heart.

David: *I feel Poonjaji in my heart. I feel you in my heart. I feel many, many people in my heart.*

Ramesh: Oh good. I see.

4.3 Truth is What-Is at this Moment

Ramesh: What are you by profession?

David: *I am an architect. I retired from my profession when I was thirty in order to spend all my time in search of Truth. I have lived in Japan, the USA, and in India, and wherever I was, I always made just enough money to live by. Or, enough money just came in somehow. In this way, I am looked after quite nicely.*

Ramesh: And that is the truth, isn't it?

David: *That's what happens. That is the truth?*

Ramesh: What is the truth? Truth is what happens. Truth is What-is at the moment. Whatever will happen tomorrow will be a conjecture.
   What happens in Lucknow with Poonjaji these days?

David: *Well, he is having* satsang *every morning.*

Ramesh: But somebody told me that he doesn't answer any questions these days. Is that correct?

David: *That's right. During the past three months he has been reading scriptures in* satsang.

Ramesh: He reads the scriptures and comments on them?

David: *No. He is just reading them.*

Ramesh: He just reads them?

David: *Yes, he just comes in, reads them, and goes out.*

Ramesh: What does he read? In Sanskrit?

David: *No, he reads the translations of the scriptures in English.*

Ramesh: Who has done the translations? Different people?

David: *Yes.*

Ramesh: And what do you mean by scriptures? What is the latest one, the current one which he is reading?

David: *It is the* Ribu Gita. *He is reading it actually for the second time. It doesn't seem to matter what he is reading, because most people can't follow his English. And the content of what he reads is too foreign for his disciples, who are foreigners.*

Ramesh: So, he just reads it without commenting on it.

David: *Yes. But the energy in the room is wonderful, no matter what he reads or does.*

Ramesh: How long a time does he spend reading from the *Ribu Gita*?

David: *An hour and a half.*

Ramesh: Is he keeping reasonably good health?

David: *Yes. He is fine again after he broke his arm in a car accident. I saw him two days ago, on the day I was leaving for Bombay. He was watching a cricket match. He usually cuts* satsang *short when a cricket match is shown on TV.*

Ramesh: Why not.

David: *In his community of disciples in Lucknow, there is a big baby boom happening currently. I don't know if that is because of his encouragement or not.*

Ramesh: I see.

~*~

CHAPTER 5

5.1 The Living Dream Appears and Continues for the Dreamer Who is Everybody Who is Awake

Chuck: *Would you explain to me what Ramana Maharshi could have meant in saying, only two things exist — sleep and creation? The mystics tell us that we create the world; the modern scientists maintain that the moon only exists when we actually look at it.*

Ramesh: The scientist now confirms what the mystic has been saying for thousands of years: nothing exists "out there," before it is observed. They say, objects exist only in your mind. Without mind-consciousness, objects cannot exist. If everybody on earth were to fall into a coma or into deep sleep at the same time, who would be left behind to confirm that the manifestation exists at all?
  What is your question anyway?

Chuck: *I just can't believe that only sleep and creation are supposed to exist.*

Ramesh: Let us presume that you are the only sentient being on earth, and you fall asleep. During your sleep, then, no manifestation exists. What exists boils down to sleep and creation and that's what Ramana means to say. Waking up, and the appearance of the creation, are synonymous. The manifestation arises or is created when you wake up. To that extent, it is you who generates the manifestation, including your own body-mind, in the split-second of waking up. And furthermore, consciousness appears also at this very same moment.
  Consciousness is dormant in deep sleep. Through the body mind organism, Consciousness creates consciousness and the manifestation. Manifestation exists only in the waking state.
  You may object and say, "I know, that manifestation doesn't exist for me in deep sleep, but surely it must exist for other people who are awake at the time I am asleep." I repeat: imagine that you, as the only sentient being on earth, are in deep sleep, or that all sentient beings are asleep together simultaneously. In both scenarios, no manifestation exists.

Madhukar: *But the fact remains that not all sentient beings are ever awake or asleep at the same time. That means, manifestation simultaneously exists and doesn't exist for different beings at one given time, depending on being awake or in sleep.*

Ramesh: The persons who are awake and see the manifestation are part of manifestation.

Nikos: *Wouldn't it be better to use the term "appearance of manifestation" instead of "creation of manifestation"?*

Ramesh: OK. You create what appears. Nothing exists unless it is observed. And what is observed is an appearance.

Nikos: *A creation has a beginning and it keeps creating further, while an appearance seems to be momentary.*

Ramesh: You can also create an appearance — a movie. Creation and appearance are just words. You can use whichever you like.

Madhukar: *Doesn't creation keep existing in time, visible and cognizable for the sentient beings who are awake, but not perceivable for the ones who are asleep?*

Ramesh: So is appearance which comes and goes with wakefulness and sleep.

Madhukar: *That is true if we consider the perception of only one single sentient being. But I am not the only sentient being. My question really is whether manifestation exists permanently — independent of any waking or sleep state of one or many sentient beings who are awake or asleep at different times from each other.*

Ramesh: Again, just imagine that you are the only sentient being on earth.

Madhukar: *In that case it is clear that no manifestation exists while sleeping. But I am not the only sentient being on earth, and all sentient beings are not asleep at one and the same time.*

Ramesh: The point is that all the others who are awake or asleep are part of that manifestation which is created when you wake up.

Madhukar: *The scientist also speaks of the Big Bang theory which happened in time and space billions of years ago. In the scientist's manifestation time is running non-stop, maybe into eternity.*

Ramesh: But time and space exist in your personal dream too.

Madhukar: *But the personal dream appears and disappears.*

Ramesh: In a split second, the personal dream is created and the mountains and rivers are billions of years old. There is no difference between the personal dream and the living dream.

Madhukar: *Does the living dream appear and disappear at least once a day for everybody? If the answer is yes, does that mean existence or manifestation actually doesn't continue for billions of years, solid like a rock in one piece of uninterrupted time?*

Ramesh: Manifestation exists in the personal dream to the same extent as it exists in your living dream. On waking up from your personal dream, you realize that the events in that dream were an illusion and nothing actually took place or ever existed in it.

Madhukar: *For the ordinary human being, the physical manifestation seems to continue independently of the individual's deep-sleep, dream or waking state. This notion is generally held as reality.*
In any case, nobody can really know if the so-called reality continues while one is asleep. But the fact remains that "we" wake up from our personal dream into the living dream every morning and depart from it every night.

Ramesh: I repeat, the same thing happens in your personal dream. During deep sleep your eyes start to flicker, which indicates, that you have started dreaming. In an instant, time and space and creation appear.

Madhukar: *Why do we have the notion at all, that the living dream is reality?*

Ramesh: That is exactly the concept of *maya*. *Maya* causes the hypnosis which makes you behold as real what in reality is unreal. An average hypnotist can produce the same illusion in you.

Madhukar: *And to come out of the hypnosis can only happen...?*

Ramesh: The living dream can only really end when you are dead. Death is the same as deep sleep.

Madhukar: *We seven of us are sitting here in this room as part of the manifestation. We participate in the same dream at this very minute. You are absolutely convinced of the dream-like nature of this dream, while I believe it is reality, right?*

Ramesh: But this dream is as real to me as it is for you. I see different people and objects, just as you do. But, yes, I definitely know that the living dream is as much of a dream as the personal dream.

Madhukar: *Both the personal and the living dream cannot be changed. We cannot enter or exit our own dream, nor anybody else's dream, nor can we hinder others from entering or exiting our personal dream. In short, there is no volition.*

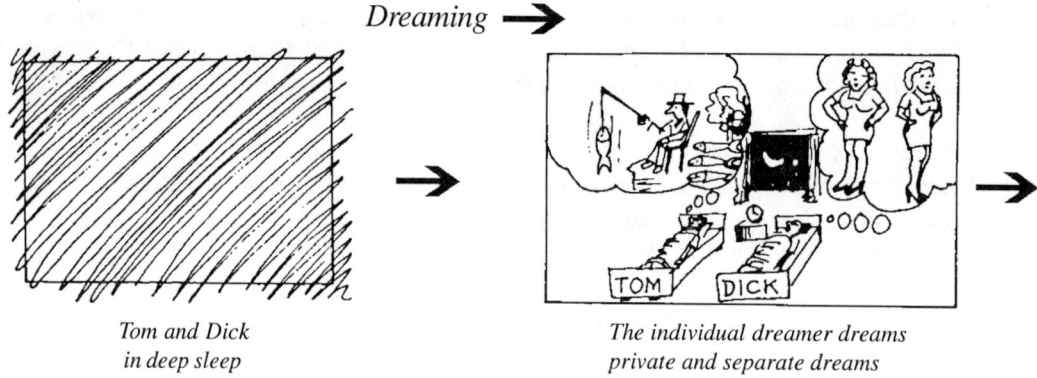

Tom and Dick
in deep sleep

The individual dreamer dreams
private and separate dreams

Ramesh: There is no volition, neither for the sage nor for the ordinary person.

Madhukar: *It seems that the knowledge of the dream-like nature of phenomenal manifestation may not make much of a difference to a life which is led in such knowledge, or does it?*

Ramesh: The dream will keep going. If you watch a movie and you know it is a movie, then you will not react as emotionally to the ongoing dramatic events as a child does, who believes the drama to be real.

Madhukar: *But a movie can be switched off, the living dream cannot.*

Ramesh: You can walk out of the movie, but as long as you are present in the theater, the movie carries on. If a child watching it gets angry or starts to cry, you console the child in saying, "Look, it's only a movie; it's not real."
  That's what the guru tells the disciple, "Life is not real, don't get too much involved in it."

Madhukar: *The guru doesn't have a switch either to stop the movie, or does he?*

Ramesh: The only switch is death. The switch is put on and off by God.

Madhukar: *The living dream continues uninterruptedly and the sentient being is switched "on" in the morning and "off" in the night. Is that correct?*

Ramesh: No. The living dream goes on only for that person who is awake. If all people sleep at the same time or all were dead, where would the manifestation be?

Madhukar: *Day or night don't occur for the entire earth at one time. That's why, I think, the sentient beings click into and out of the continuous large living dream through sleep.*

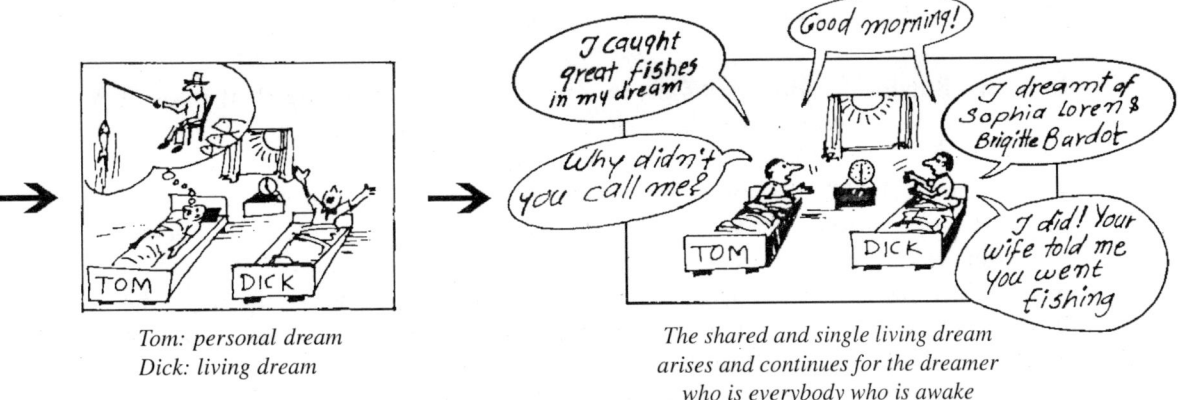

Tom: personal dream
Dick: living dream

The shared and single living dream arises and continues for the dreamer who is everybody who is awake

Ramesh: Even if that were so, the manifestation is still unreal and of the nature of a dream. The dream goes on only for those people who are dreaming. When one wakes up from the personal dream, one still keeps dreaming the living dream. For a dreamer, the personal dream continues. For an awake person the living dream continues.

Madhukar: *Does the cosmos and the manifestation continue to exist and unfold independently of the dreaming person? That's the question.*

Ramesh: It continues for the dreamer, who is awake to this living dream.

Madhukar: *Isn't the living dream one large dream which we all share?*

Ramesh: The continuous living dream is a single one for all awake dreamers. But your personal dream is a private one and for you alone, because you are an individual dreamer. The living dream appears and continues for the dreamer, who is everybody who is awake.

Madhukar: *Are all of us assembled here in this room dreaming the same dream? In truth, the dreamers are all one, aren't they? Each of the dreamers may entertain different notions and thoughts about their shared situation — which is part of the dream of Totality or God.*

Ramesh: That is correct.

Madhukar: *If one of us fell asleep right now, the living dream would stop for him, while it would continue for the rest of us...*

Ramesh: ...for us dreamers.

Claire: *Isn't that what Madhukar meant with the off- and on-switch?*

Ramesh: But the movie carries on for those who are watching it. It doesn't exist for someone who has fallen asleep. For them, the switch is off, for the former ones it is on. Only the operator can switch the movie on and off. The watcher can't. The watcher of the living movie is part of the movie. That is why he will disappear from it or walk out of it only when he dies or commits suicide.

After waking up from the personal dream, you realize that it was an illusion and you are no longer involved in it. Similarly, once you wake up from the illusion of the living dream, you don't get involved in it anymore. Although the dream continues, albeit without an entity "me."

The dreamer is God or Consciousness. The script of the dream is written by Consciousness. All objects and characters in it are Consciousness. And what is aware of the dream is also Consciousness.

Claire: *The living dream seems real to me, because I can watch a human being or a plant grow in time. In the personal dream I cannot see anything develop in time.*

Ramesh: In your personal dream and in the living dream exactly the same happens. Babies are born and they grow up. People are sick and old and die.

Claire: *But you can't watch a body grow in a personal dream; you can't measure it.*

Ramesh: You can! Growth happens.

Madhukar: *Please, may I repeat a question I asked you earlier? The sage tells us that we create the manifestation in a split second on waking up. What about the Big Bang theory, which explains that the universe is billions of years old?*

Ramesh: When you wake up, you become conscious. So, it is Consciousness which creates the manifestation at that split second you mentioned.

Nikos: *Isn't it better to use the word appearance instead of creation?*

Ramesh: OK, an appearance is created. What's the difference?

Nikos: *Do others exist separately from me?*

Ramesh: It depends what you mean by "me." The "me" is consciousness and not Nikos. Only when you are awake, consciousness exists; only then does manifestation — including yourself and others — exist. The others are the manifestation. The others are part of it. Even when enlightenment has happened, the living dream continues. Waking up from the personal dream is a physical phenomenon. Waking up physically from the living dream happens with death.

Madhukar: *Within deep sleep, a dream arises. The sleeping body-mind organism has absolutely no control over the content of a dream, including participating people, its beginning or end, its duration and the time of its occurrence, etc.*
The same happens actually in the daily living dream. We don't know, when we wake up, what will happen during the day or night, nor do we know when we will go to sleep. Similarly, we didn't decide when to be born, nor do we know what will happen during the span of our lives, or when we will die. It is absolutely clear that we don't create the dream.

Ramesh: Consciousness creates the dream. On waking up, consciousness appears along with the body mind organism, and the manifestation and the living dream is "on." The individual consciousness which creates the feeling of being the entity "Madhukar" is part of the dream. In this living dream, Madhukar is an object in the dream, like all other objects.

Madhukar: *Could we say Consciousness creates this body-mind organism and, through it, this living dream at the moment of waking up? The dream can be shared, as it is by the seven people here at this moment in this room. But is the consciousness in all of us the same?*

Ramesh: This sharing is part of the functioning of Totality. The questions and answers are one event amongst billions of events which occur simultaneously throughout the universe.

Claire: *Is that the* "leela"?

Ramesh: Yes. We are part of that play or dream.

Jayshree: *The* Bhagavad Gita *says, "When everybody is asleep, I am awake, and I am asleep when everybody is awake." Is that Consciousness speaking?*

Ramesh: The sage is awake when everybody else is sleeping in darkness. Awakened from sleep, the ordinary people consider the manifestation as real. For the sage it is unreal, a dream. He stays untouched and unaffected by the dream. To that extent, he stays in deep sleep.

Nikos: *How can one move from the dream to* samadhi? *Could you explain?*

Ramesh: You, as a "me," get involved in this manifestation. In deep sleep the "me" and the world don't exist. That happens also when you are in *samadhi*. Coming out of *samadhi*, or waking up from deep sleep, is the same, because the living dream starts in both cases.

A story about a *yogi* has been told, in which the *yogi* asked for his meal after he had just come out of a week-long *samadhi*. He fell into *samadhi* again before the meal was served. When he next returned from the *samadhi* state, he once more asked for his meal. The *yogi* was back to where he started from. Of what use is a *samadhi* state then?

Madhukar: *Samadhi seems to be a kind of a wakeful sleep; the body is awake but the consciousness is asleep. Is that correct?*

Ramesh: That is correct

Heiner: *For me, the importance of this aspect of the teaching lies in the recognition that the phenomenal manifestation is dream-like and not real. This realization will stop the suffering. As long as the living dream is taken as real, suffering will continue. For me the technicalities — such as waking up from the sleep dream into the living dream, or if the living dream stops when I fall asleep, or the nature of* samadhi *— are unimportant.*

Ramesh: You suffer in your personal dream because the dream-character is involved. And you suffer in the living dream because the character called Heiner is involved. Once you know this fact, you don't get involved so much anymore in the living dream. Less involvement — less suffering. The rest of the discussions refer only to the mechanics of manifestation. I entirely agree with you.

Heiner: *The personal involvement as a "me" in what happens in manifestation makes us suffer. And that suffering is driving us to find a way out of suffering.*

Ramesh: And if the deeper main basics of the teaching are understood then you will not be concerned and involved anymore, once you totally accept that only and exclusively God's Will prevails and all deeds and events happen as part of the functioning of Totality. That is the ultimate understanding. Let me repeat: the degree of suffering depends on the degree of involvement.

Sumitra: *Involvement in anything — politics or family or anything.*

Ramesh: Involvement is involvement. Whether you are involved in seeking money or enlightenment makes no difference. In both there is a seeker, the sought, and the seeking, and therefore the involvement — which means suffering. Enlightenment hasn't happened yet to the seeker, but he still wants it; therefore, he suffers. The money hasn't accumulated yet and the person still wants it, and therefore he or she suffers.

Nikos: *But if a seeker is in touch with a guru and he at least gets this kind of first-hand information, then this information becomes knowledge — part of the seeker's being. Does the seeking then continue, with the involvement becoming less and less for the seeker?*

Ramesh: Involvement means the "me." When the seeker listens to the guru the involvement decreases and becomes weaker, which means the understanding deepens. And as the involvement becomes less, the suffering becomes less.

5.2 Consciousness itself is the Bliss and the Misery; Consciousness cannot Enjoy Bliss or Suffer Misery

Nikos: *It is said that Consciousness is bliss. I presume that this bliss must be reflected in a body-mind organism through which enlightenment has happened.*

Ramesh: The moment you use the word "bliss," there is somebody who enjoys that bliss. So, Consciousness itself is bliss. But Consciousness is not something which enjoys the bliss.

Nikos: *But does Consciousness reflect itself as bliss in a body-mind organism in which enlightenment has happened?*

Ramesh: If you mean to ask whether such a body-mind organism is always in bliss, the answer is no.

Nikos: *Maybe the sage doesn't think that his body-mind organism is in bliss at all times. But for the seekers who are still in duality, it must appear as if the sage is always in bliss.*

Ramesh: The sage's body-mind organism is not always in bliss because it continues to function according to its natural characteristics; because the same energy, or *prakriti*, functions through all organisms, independently of enlightenment.

Nikos: *But what, then, is the difference?*

Ramesh: In the ordinary person there is involvement and the feeling of personal doership, and in the case of a sage there is no involvement. That is the only difference.

Nikos: *So, an ordinary person has no way to know for certain if a sage has the feeling of*

*Consciousness cannot enjoy bliss.
Consciousness itself is the bliss (and misery)*

personal doership, if he is enlightened or not, right?

Ramesh: Quite right. That's why you will find ten different sages conducting themselves in ten different ways. The energy is functioning through those ten organisms in ten different ways because of the different programming. But none of them have a sense of personal doership. In all other respects they are exactly like all other ordinary persons.

Madhukar: *The existence of the state in which there is absence of personal doership can only be known directly to the sage himself. A seeker cannot really know if his guru is enlightened.*

Ramesh: That is correct.

Madhukar: *The state of enlightenment exists as such in a sage, and deeds happen through him — he is part of events — because his brain reacts naturally to impulses from outside. But these reactions don't have the sense of personal doership. Summing up, it seems that there is not much meaning in the absence of personal doership.*

Ramesh: The difference between the sage and the ordinary person is that, in the first case, there is nobody involved to suffer, because there is no involvement and therefore no suffering.

Madhukar: *Therefore, the sage doesn't suffer either misery or bliss. And that seems to be good for the sage himself, but for others, and the world at large, his enlightenment makes no difference. That's how it is perceived by me.*
   I was reading in a book of Meher Baba's lately. What he seems to know about spirituality and avatarism is outrageous! Where does he get all this knowledge from? But it was Consciousness that brought all this writing and knowledge forward, and it was Consciousness which made use of the characteristics of the body-mind organism called Meher Baba, right?

Ramesh: That is what Consciousness or God has produced through that organism, according to its programming. And that happening was only for that moment.

Madhukar: *But what God produced through that body-mind organism only means that the writings were happening, and that some disciples were present at that time. For the world at large, there is no use or meaning in his writings. Most of what is written in his books regarding the future of the world never happened.*

Ramesh: And it didn't happen! I have told you about Aurobindo. In his case, it was similar. He said, among many other things, that his physical body will exist eternally because he knows God's secrets.

Madhukar: *How can somebody like Meher Baba declare to the world, "I am an* avatar, *and this and that is going to happen?"*

Ramesh: How can you prevent such people from declaring what they do? How can you prevent it? That is part of the show.

Madhukar: *But I have never heard about anything like this except in India. How can these people puff themselves up so big, write numerous books, and make millions of people believe this kind of crap?*

Ramesh: Because that is exactly what is supposed to happen. It is part of the functioning of Totality. Whatever happens is the Will of God. Who are you or who am I to question the Will of God? You could as well ask, "Why are wars happening and millions of people being killed all over the world?"

Sumitra: *I can't understand how an intelligent nation like Germany could believe Hitler, and make him its leader. Here in India we do the same, oftentimes, in believing in what the gurus say. And we make them our spiritual leaders. And they turn out to be frauds. But that must also be the Will of God, I suppose.*

Ramesh: Yes. Whatever happens is the Will of God. It is only the human mind which wants to know, "Why should this happen, and why should that happen?" Anything can happen.

CHAPTER 6

6.1 No Control over the Arising of Thought, but No Involvement in Further Thinking: The Sage

Madhukar: *In deep sleep, the personal sense of presence as "I am Madhukar" does not exist. It is said that the sage is aware in deep sleep. But I understand that nobody, including the sage, can be aware of the impersonal sense of presence in deep sleep. However, some awareness must have been present during deep sleep, because we remember after waking up, that we slept well. I hold that deep sleep is the same for the sage and the non-sage.*

Ramesh: If the sage says, he is awake in sleep, he means, that the "me" doesn't exist.

Madhukar: *But is he aware that his body sleeps?*

Ramesh: Who?

Madhukar: *I know. I understand that the "me" is not there. So, how could the sage be aware and awake in deep sleep?*

Ramesh: Nobody can be aware of being "awake" or asleep in deep sleep. The sage cannot be aware, because there is no "he."

Madhukar: *Is this the fact for everybody, enlightened or not?*

Ramesh: Yes. The ordinary person thinks he — the "me" — is asleep. But the sage understands that the "me" does not exist in deep sleep...

Madhukar: *...and in the waking state. That's why it is said that the sage sleeps while others are awake to the phenomenal manifestation, believing it to be real.*

Ramesh: That is correct. Deep sleep, anesthesia, coma, mean the same thing — the absence of the "me." Being awake in deep sleep means being aware that there is no "me" to be aware.

Madhukar: *But don't we all become aware of having slept after waking up?*

Ramesh: Sure, that happens to everybody, irrespective of enlightenment.

Nikos: *Could one say, that for the common person the split mind is in suspension in deep sleep but it still exists? How is it for the sage?*

Ramesh: For the sage there is no split mind, either in deep sleep nor in the waking state.

Nikos: *Does a sage dream?*

Ramesh: Personal dreams are the result of the reaction of the brain to outside impulses or events. According to the *Bhagavad Gita*, the *prakriti* functions through every body-mind organism, including the one of the sage. The brain keeps reacting to outside events after enlightenment also. Personally, I do not agree with the claim that the sage does not dream. Of course, some people, enlightened or not, may just not dream. The non-occurrence of dreams is not a valid proof of enlightenment.

Ramana Maharshi is reported as having told Arthur Osborne that he had a vision of his congregated devotees. A vision is in fact no different from a dream. When asked what the vision meant, Ramana answered that he didn't know its meaning.

A dream, a vision, a thought, a feeling — they occur, and nobody has any control over them, sage or not. Therefore, that dream or vision occurred to Ramana. Nobody — sage or not — has control over a dream, a vision, a feeling, or a thought. The sage knows that what happens through his body-mind organism is not his action.

Madhukar: *One of the greatest misunderstandings during one's quest for enlightenment must be the widespread notion that enlightenment means a state of absolute no-thought. Even most Ramana disciples who wrote about their personal encounters with Ramana report that Ramana considered enlightenment to be a state of absolute no-thought. His disciples misunderstood him completely on this point. It didn't seem to help them to hear him talk in person, and get the answers from him directly.*

Ramesh: What you are saying is correct. Ramana was misunderstood here. I often warn that the use of any word will have its implications, and the interpretation of such words may be misleading. Ramana Maharshi used to say, "What is the 'me'?" The 'me' is nothing but a bundle of thoughts. The mind is nothing but a bundle of thoughts." My interpretation of those words is, "Mind is nothing but a series of thinking."

Nikos: *A thinking process.*

Ramesh: Yes, a thinking process which is based on a thought which arises by itself. Neither a sage nor an ordinary person has control over a thought arising, nor over what thought will arise. But the result of that thought will be different.

Nikos: *Different for a sage and for an ordinary person?*

Ramesh: Yes. The ordinary person becomes involved with the arisen thought and starts thinking, and therefore becomes involved as a personal "me"-entity. And the personal involvement with a thought, resulting in thinking, is what Ramana Maharshi calls a collection of thoughts. For this process, I use the words, "The mind is nothing but a series of thinking." The mind is a series of involved thinking which is a reaction to an arisen thought, over which nobody has any control.

Madhukar: *So, we could say that the thoughtless state is a state in which thoughts may happen, but there is no personal involvement with these thoughts by a "me"-entity.*

Ramesh: That is correct.

Madhukar: *Poonjaji reported something quite different when, in* satsang, *he told us of the event of his enlightenment in Ramana's presence. He said that his hair stood on end, that indescribable bliss and love prevailed, and that his mind stood still, never to stir again. For months he didn't have a single thought. I could never buy what he was saying. In my own experience, I have never known a thoughtless state to last longer than a few seconds.*

Ramesh: You are quite correct. And that is what this verse in the *Bhagavad Gita* says: not a split second will pass without energy, or *prakriti*, producing something — some thought, some word, some action.

Madhukar: *Yes. That is the experience of this body-mind organism, called Madhukar.*

Ramesh: When words are used, they are likely to cause confusion because of their implications. I am absolutely sure that, by "the mind is nothing but a collection of thoughts," Ramana was speaking of involved thinking as a reaction to an original thought, over which nobody has control.

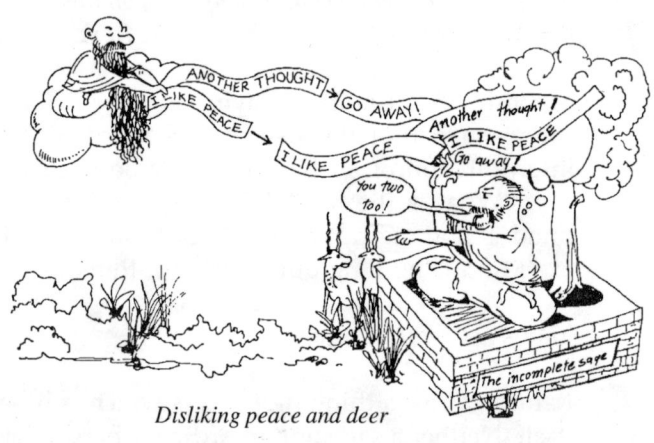

Disliking peace and deer

6.2 A Two-Week, 18 Hours-a-Day Enlightenment Intensive Course: What Happens 2 Weeks after the 2 Weeks?

Ramesh: You live in Maui. And what are you doing in Maui? Fire-walking?

Ken: *Yes, that is one of the things I do. But mainly, I am involved in a process called "Enlightenment Intensive" which uses the question, "Tell me who you are," as its basis. I do that all over the world. As I said, I also open people up for the fire-walk. And then we go into the fire in here* (Ken points to his heart), *which is more difficult to walk through. And then I support people. And I am discovering folks like you, and hanging out with people like you. Hanging out in* satsang. *So, that's about it, that's about what I do.*

Ramesh: So, hanging out in *satsang* is a kind of entertainment, isn't it?

Ken: *Hardly. Well, entertainment for the heart. But that can hardly be called an entertainment, like going to the movies.*

Ramesh: Well, a different kind of entertainment. Some people like classical music and others like rock and roll.

Ken: *I must say I feel eternally entertained in here* (Ken points to his heart) *with that presence which isn't born and doesn't die.*

Ramesh: I see. You said you do an intensive course of Self-inquiry.

Ken: *Yes. The Self-inquiry, "Who am I?"*

Ramesh: Can you tell me more about that? What do you mean by an intensive "Who am I?"

Ken: *Well, for eighteen hours a day, from six o'clock in the morning till eleven o'clock at night, we sit opposite each other in pairs, and we go back and forth every forty minutes in asking the partner sitting opposite, "Tell me who you are." And the partner shares whatever he thinks he is or has become identified with at that moment. This sharing and telling empties out the consciousness very quickly, and also the overlays.*

Ramesh: And how long do you do this?

Ken: *For three days, or for two weeks.*

Ramesh: Three days or two weeks, all right. What happens after two weeks? Or what happens two weeks after the two weeks?

Ken: *What happens during the process...*

Ramesh: Two weeks after the two weeks you are back to normal. Is it not back to normal? Isn't that what happens?

Ken: *For some people, yes. Not so for others. Some people actually have a direct experience of Self.*

Ramesh: A direct experience of Self. A direct experience of Self — even that disappears, does it not?

Ken: *Yes, that disappears. It does.*

Ramesh: So, of what worth is anything that disappears? I mean, any experience...

Ken: *The experience of "direct" — it is a bad term. This experience is like* anubhava. *It is the experience of no experience. All experiencing and processing stops.*

Ramesh: But it is still an experience. Does that experience remain?

Ken: *No.*

Ramesh: My point is, any experience that does not last all the time is not worth a thing.

Ken: *Yes, I agree with that.* (laughter)

Ramesh: So, what is it that would enable this experience to remain all the time? That experience remains all the time when it is no longer an experience. When you call something an experience, it is an experience. But an experience that lasts all the time is not an experience.

Ken: *Do you know the Sanskrit word* anubhava? *It means the union of opposites. That is the closest word in Sanskrit I know for the kind of experience*

I am talking about.

Ramesh: But *anubhava* is really used for an experience. It is synonymous with the word "experience." If you explain something to a person, that person may ask you, "Did you have an *anubhava*, an experience, of it?"

The basic point I am making, Ken, is that there is a Ken, a "me," who has had a certain experience, and who wants that experience to last for all time. Is that not right?

Ken: *That's the way the mind has set it up.*

Ramesh: So long as there is a mind, so long as there is a "me" wanting a continuous experience, that continuous experience cannot happen. That continuous experience you are thinking of is a lack of experience. It is no experience. Who has an experience? There is a "me" who has an experience. If there is no "me," who is there to experience it? There is no one to experience. As long as one is in search of an experience, there is a "me" that seeks and the experience being sought. Whether you are seeking a million dollars, or you are seeking enlightenment, there is no qualitative difference. In both cases, this triad exists: the seeker, the object sought, and the process of seeking. As long as this triad exists, the continuous experience of that state cannot happen. That state called enlightenment is merely the total acceptance of the fact that there is no "me," as an individual entity, to want any experience. That is enlightenment. That state can only happen. No one can achieve that state by sitting for eighteen hours a day for two weeks — or for two years — in an Enlightenment Intensive program.

When I was visiting the States in 1987 for my first seminar, I was asked what I thought about meditation. I answered that I believed meditation to be a good way to start. The man who asked me said that he was meditating for eighteen hours a day. I didn't need to ask him what he was doing for a living!

If I want to play golf, I have to go to a professional. He tells me how to hold the clubs and how to hit the ball. But when I actually play golf and I try to remember the details of the training, I will not be able to play golf. So, the golfer is a good golfer to the extent to which he can forget the basics of his training

To me, meditation begins with a meditator meditating with an object in view. But the true meditation does not happen unless the meditator disappears. As long as there is a meditator wanting to achieve a certain object, that is not true meditation. Enlightenment cannot be achieved by a "me." It can only happen if it is meant to happen as part of the functioning of Totality, and therefore its happening is destined for a particular body-mind organism. The penultimate state before enlightenment is the state in which there is total acceptance that enlightenment may not happen in this body-mind organism. There is the submission, "OK, God, if you don't want this body-mind organism to become enlightened, don't let it become enlightened." In such submission there is truly no "I," no "me."

What does enlightenment mean to you, Ken?

Ken: *The union of opposites. No more duality.*

Ramesh: Yes, no more duality.... Is there a duality at all?

Ken: *No, there isn't.*

Ramesh: So, where is the question of one meeting the other? Consciousness is all there is. For you to know someone or something, there has to be a "you" and there has to be an object, isn't that so? If Consciousness is all there is, how can Consciousness know itself? If you are Consciousness, how can you know Consciousness? Therefore, I don't like to say "I am That" or "I am *Brahma*." I prefer, "All there is, is Consciousness." If all there is, is Consciousness, then there is no "me" to do anything, to seek anything.

Ken: *There is no "I" to be That.*

Ramesh: So, the total acceptance of this is enlightenment.

Don't you think you are strengthening people's egos when you tell them in the Enlightenment Intensive course that they can do something, that they can achieve something, that they can practice and thereby become enlightened? "You" are capable of being enlightened. To me that is a contradiction. No "you" can become enlightened. For me, enlightenment means the total annihilation of the "me." So long as there is a "me" thinking he can be enlightened, enlightenment cannot happen.

Ken: *All that you are saying comes out and becomes clear to the people in the work I am doing with them. People usually come to that observation on their own.*

Up until being with Papaji, I also did some process-oriented work. But I just stopped that work, I threw it out of the window during these last three weeks. I am not doing that anymore. But I feel there is still value to the Enlightenment Intensive process. I feel like continuing with it, and seeing what happens now that I've had this new opening with Papaji. I don't want to be feeding people something that is going to hinder them, or that is a lie. It is cleaning out, here (Ken points to himself). *It's coming around.*

Ramesh: I see. Good.

CHAPTER 7

7.1 In the Absence of the "Me," the Observer and the Observed are One

Chuck: *The observed is the observer. This concept of yours is difficult for me to understand. Could you explain it?*

Ramesh: The observer is the observed when witnessing takes place. But when the observer thinks he is the subject, and that what he observes is an object, then it is the "me" who is the observer. But when you truly understand that there is no "me," then there is no subject/object differentiation by the split mind. If the "me" does not observe something as a subject observing an object, then only observing happens. And in that impersonal observing, there is no separate observer, no separate something observed. The observer and the observed are the same in the absence of the "me." This impersonal observing is called witnessing. In impersonal observing the subject and the object become the same thing, which is pure Subjectivity.

Witnessing, or, "we are one and no 'one' knows it"

If you work on a problem, then there is a "me" working on that problem. You work all night but no solution arises. Then you take a rest. On waking up from that rest, a solution to the problem comes to you in a flash. That answer has come intuitively, and not through the effort of an observer searching for an observed answer. There was no "me" which produced that answer. The answer happened.

Chuck: *So, the truth of the statement, "The observed is the observer," is only experienced during witnessing?*

Ramesh: There is only experiencing, observing, without the division into subject/object by the split mind. In witnessing there is no individual witnesser. Therefore it is ridiculous to be told by a scripture or by a guru, "Observe your thoughts!" Who observes the thoughts? The mind observes its own workings. And when the mind observes its own workings, the nature of the mind is to judge: "This thought or that thought was good or bad." But if a thought arises and it is merely witnessed, then that thought will either be cut off and disappear, or it will convert itself into action. If the thought arises, "I am thirsty," I pour some water in a glass and drink it. The thinking mind will not be there, and so the thought will convert itself into action. But an involved mind — the "me" — will say, "I am thirsty; should I drink Pepsi or Coca Cola or beer or water?"

Madhukar: *That's why it is said that the sage always performs the action which is appropriate to the prevailing situation, because he acts without the thinking mind, the "me." His brain might react to a thought, and his body-mind organism may then produce an action. But that action is understood to be impersonal and part of What-is, and therefore part of the functioning of Totality.*

Ramesh: You see, I don't like the words "perfect" or "good" or "right," because the moment you say "right," there is also "wrong." I would prefer to say, "Whatever action happens had to happen at that moment." What-is is not necessarily perfect. A war happens, a bomb kills 20 people. And that "is" is not perfect. I prefer to say that What-is is exactly what is supposed to be at that moment. And the human mind, the society, decides what is good or bad.

So, all there is, is Consciousness. What-is is exactly what is supposed to happen in the functioning of Totality, and according to the Will of God.

Chuck: *As long as there is an observer and the observed, there is misperception.*

Ramesh: That is correct. As long as there is an observ-*er*, there is the observed. But in observing, there is neither observed nor observer. The observer/observed relationship arises when the observing results in some judging.

CHAPTER 8

8.1 What is Right with Witnessing and Wrong with Involvement?

Parso: *What is the non-witnessing state?*

Ramesh: Ramana Maharshi calls that state the *sahaja sthiti*, or the natural state. The natural state is not *samadhi*.

We are sitting here in this room and we are talking. Supposing all of you leave, and I continue to sit here without doing anything. Now, it is the witnessing state if there is something to witness. When there is nothing to witness, it is the non-witnessing state. In the non-witnessing state, my eyes will probably close, and I will continue to sit in this chair. But in this state, consciousness still exists. I will still hear the sounds from the street. And I will still smell the smells from the kitchen. In this state consciousness is in a very passive state, which the Zen Buddhists and Taoists call the vacant or no-mind state, and Ramana calls the *sahaja sthiti*.

The non-witnessing state is the state in which there is nothing to witness. If there is nothing to witness, the change from the witnessing to the non-witnessing state happens like the shifting of automatic gears, very smoothly and by itself. When I sit there in the non-witnessing state and somebody calls for me or somebody comes in, then I witness that in the witnessing state. But if the non-witnessing state is not disturbed for a while, then the non-witnessing state can go deeper, into *samadhi*, in which there is no consciousness. Sounds will not be heard, smells not be smelled.

The normal state of an average person is one of continuous involvement. If there is some understanding, even only on the intellectual level, the stages are witnessing and non-witnessing.

Madhukar: *Is the non-witnessing state a natural state?*

Ramesh: The non-witnessing state is what Ramana Maharshi calls the natural state.

Madhukar: *Is* samadhi *also a natural state?*

Ramesh: *Samadhi*, therefore, is not a natural state.

Madhukar: *But before the state of* samadhi *happens, the witnessing and non-witnessing states happen first, right?*

Ramesh: Yes. Sure.

Druve: *To call the non-witnessing state the natural state is also a concept. What is not natural?*

Ramesh: It is a concept. Anything a sage says is a concept. *Sat-chit-ananda* is a concept. But that is not understood, and the individual says, "I want *sat-chit-ananda.*" But *sat-chit-ananda* is not an object to be had by an individual. It is not an object to be achieved by a subject.

Druve: *And even this underlying feeling that involvement is something bad and should be overcome, that the witnessing state should be reached, that too is a concept. What is wrong with involvement, or what is right with witnessing? Both are willed by God to happen at a particular time, for certain body-mind organisms.*

Involvement—Witnessing

Ramesh: That's why I am suggesting that you do not fight your ego. The ego came with the body-mind organism, it is not your fault or sin which has produced the ego. Therefore, accept the ego as part of the functioning of Totality, and as a creation of God. Who is to fight the ego? You are the ego! The ego can disappear only through understanding, not through any effort by an individual — which is the ego.

Parso: *The ego just disappears and a non-entity remains? Or how is that?*

Ramesh: The ego disappears in the sense that it merges with the "I-Am." "I am Parso" — when Parso disappears, what remains is "I-Am."

Druve: *And whether it merges or not doesn't really matter, because merging or not merging is destined by God, and therefore will happen or not.*

Ramesh: That is correct. Therefore, the total surrender to God is the acceptance, "Alright, God, whether or not Parso is to be enlightened, let that be according to Your Will." In that surrender, there is no Parso.

CHAPTER 9

9.1 If Gandha — Then Smell

Ramesh: Your name is what?

Gandha: *Gandha.*

Ramesh: How do you spell it? *(Gandha spells her name)* That is a name given by Rajneesh, isn't it?

Gandha: *Yes.*

Ramesh: And what is your own name?

Gandha: *This is my own name.*

Ramesh: What is the name given to you by your parents?

Gandha: *This is the name I have been using for nineteen years.*

Ramesh: Yes. But before that, what was your name?

Gandha: *Why do you want to know?*

Ramesh: Because that is the name I would prefer to use when I talk to you.

Gandha: *I would prefer that you use the name that I use for myself.*

Ramesh: Alright. Then we will use that name.

Gandha: *Thank you.*

Ramesh: Gandha, is that correct, yes?

Gandha: *Yes.*

Ramesh: Do you know the meaning of it?

Gandha: *It means fragrance.*

Ramesh: *Gandha* is not fragrance. *Gandha* means smell. *Sugandha* means fragrance and *durgandha* means bad smell. So, *gandha* simply means smell. But that is another matter. So, *gandha* is not a name. *Gandha* means smell and not fragrance. *Sugandha* means fragrance.

A name is a fiction, an illusion, a concept

Gandha: *The prefix, the forename Osho gave me is Prem. So, it is "smell of love."*

Ramesh: Prem is love, yes. What is this Gandha? There is no Gandha really. Your earlier name, or Gandha, both are just names. They are names given to you by your parents or by your guru. What is this "me," what is Gandha, or the earlier name you had which you are so reluctant to tell me? Your name is just a concept. All that exists is a body-mind organism with certain natural characteristics which were programmed at the moment of conception. And you had no choice in being born to particular parents who lived in a particular environment. What Gandha thinks she is, her personality, is nothing other than the genes inherited from her parents, plus the conditioning she has received. Gandha is only a concept, a fiction, an illusion.

And any action which you consider your action is nothing but the reaction of the brain to an outside event. Therefore your action is really God's action through this body-mind organism. God creates your action by putting in an input, like a thought or something you see, and your brain reacts to that input. You don't have free will to act. Nobody can act, the brain can only react according to the programming.

When I know that anything that happens is not your action, how can I ask you to do anything? How can I ask you to witness? How can I ask you to do any *sadhana*? I cannot tell anybody to do anything, because there is no one to do anything. And this is the only understanding which will produce what is destined to be produced.

CHAPTER 10

10.1 The Complete Manifestation Exists already, and is Served out Bit by Bit, in a Self-generating Process — a Speculation

Nanette: *Is destiny part of time?*

Ramesh: No. Destiny refers to the individual body-mind organism. Any action that happens is a reaction of a brain to an outside impulse. And the appearance of those impulses are willed and destined by God. The reaction of the brain, and the resulting deeds, are also according to God's Will.

Nanette: *But destiny has to do with past and future.*

Ramesh: Yes. And the future is already there. You believe that action A, cause A, has produced the effect B, and that effect B becomes the cause of effect C. What I say is that B had to happen and therefore A happened, and C had to happen and therefore B happened. We think in terms of cause and effect. But the cause has to be there if the effect has to be there. Something happens today which leads to something tomorrow. And something happens tomorrow which leads to something the next day. What I am saying is that what happens today has to happen, because what will happen tomorrow has already happened. So, cause A leading to B, and B leading to C, is the destiny of the body-mind organism through which A, B, or C happens.

Nanette: *I just can't believe that for every sentient and insentient being in the whole universe, the destiny, in every minute detail, is already fixed into all eternity.*

Ramesh: The moving energy produces A, B, and C. A, B, and C are different things at different times by the same moving energy. But the moving energy produces A, B, and C as a matter of destiny. Somebody may be A, and somebody else may be B. But it is the same moving energy producing them.

You see, you can't see a ten-mile long painting all at one time. You can only see portions of it at a time. In the same way, we are unable to see our whole past and future, or the past and future of the manifestation around us. But the whole picture is already there.

Nanette: *This concept of the picture already made by God is unacceptable for me. I believe that this picture of manifestation is created every moment. It forms itself every moment.*

Ramesh: No, the picture is already there. What is new for you is the new portion of the whole picture which you see at the present moment. You can't see the whole picture.

The ready-made world served out bit by bit

Madhukar: *Conceptually speaking, even if the whole picture, as you describe it, didn't exist, that would not make any difference anyway. Because the basic question is whether I as an individual have free will, or whether whatever happens is according to God's Will. If it is a total intuitive conviction that all happenings are according to God's Will, then it does not matter if He creates the picture at every present moment, or if the whole picture of the past and future manifestation exists already. In either case, it exists according to His Will.*

Nobody really knows if this picture-concept is correct, if it actually exists as something "real," like a glass of water. It is hidden from the human being's perception. In any case, first and foremost, the total conviction must arise that whatever is happening in manifestation is according to God's Will — that there is no free will. The concept of the whole picture, and all other concepts like destiny and programming, are based on this conviction, and are intuitively derived from it.

Ramesh: That is absolutely correct.

Madhukar: *But, truly, nobody knows if the whole-picture-is-already-there concept is correct.*

Ramesh: Nanette, once you accept that you have no free will then you also accept that you have no control over what happens.

Nanette: *I don't doubt that whatever happens is according to God's Will. I have to formulate my question in a different way.*

Ramesh: You have a difficulty in understanding?

Nanette: *Yes.*

Yogesh: *Maybe her question is, "Is the script set, or is it auto-generative?" Auto-generative means that events happen, and because of the interaction of them with the existing basic laws of manifestation, new events are happening by themselves; these again produce further new events, caused by the further interaction with those laws. So, her question may be: is the whole picture already there, or is the picture auto-generating itself anew every moment?*

Ramesh: The script, the movie, is there already. The characters are already there, which is why in the *Bhagavad Gita*, Lord Krishna tells Arjuna, "You think you are going to kill your teachers, friends, and relatives. But truly, as Time, I have already killed them. You are only the instrument through which they will be killed." So, the picture is already there. Whether you call it auto-generative is immaterial and irrelevant. Even if God's Will were to be executed in an auto-generative process, what happens would still be according to His Will.

Nanette: *I am still not able to follow what you are saying.*

Ramesh: Something happens today which leads to something tomorrow. And something happens tomorrow which leads to something which happens the day after tomorrow. What I am saying is that what happens today must happen, because what will happen tomorrow has already happened in time. And what will happen tomorrow must happen because what will happen on the day after tomorrow has already happened in time.

Nanette: *Again.*

Ramesh: For what has to happen tomorrow, something has to happen today. And what has happened today is the result of what has happened yesterday.

Nanette: *I just can't follow. You suppose the whole picture concept...*

Yogesh (to Nanette): *If you look at your life it is very obvious that God's Will must prevail, that our life-course is predestined.*

Ramesh: That is correct.

CHAPTER 11

11.1 Deep Sleep — No Awareness of the Body or the Manifestation for Sage and Non-sage Alike

Sushila: *In deep sleep there is no manifestation. That is true for the sage and the ordinary person. But some sages claim that they are awake and aware in deep sleep too. How can that be?*

Ramesh: That which is awake in deep sleep is awake for everybody and not only for the sage. The fact that we slept well or we didn't sleep well, is known to us only after waking up. Therefore there was something in deep sleep which knows in the morning about our good or bad sleep. That which exists in deep sleep is pure Awareness, pure Subjectivity.

Sushila: *I am totally unconscious in deep sleep.*

Ramesh: It is total unconsciousness of "me." "I-Am" is present in deep sleep. What is absent in deep sleep is "I am Sushila."

Sushila: *What then is awake all the time? What are the sages talking about? In my deep sleep I am not aware of anything remaining always aware and awake.*

Ramesh: Something is awake, but not Sushila.

Sushila: *Who then is aware that something is aware? How do we know that something? I don't understand.*

Ramesh: The pure Awareness, the impersonal Consciousness is aware. Sushila cannot accept any other consciousness than that of Sushila. So, what is present in deep sleep is that Consciousness which Sushila is not aware of. Sushila is only aware of consciousness in this body-mind organism on waking up. What is present in deep sleep is that awareness which is also present in all body-mind organisms in the waking state — impersonal Awareness.

Sushila: *Is impersonal Awareness also present in a general anesthesia then?*

Ramesh: Yes. Coma, and anesthesia are like deep sleep.

Sushila: *Are you saying that the impersonal Consciousness is always there?*

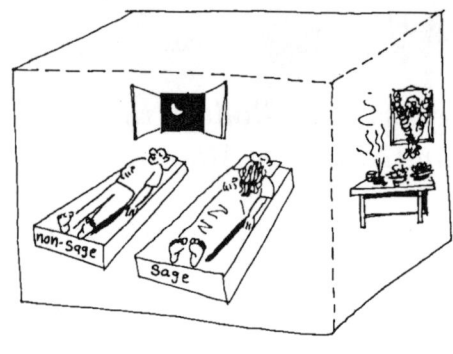 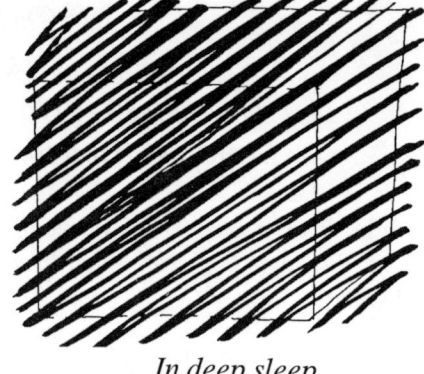

Both still awake *In deep sleep*

Ramesh: Correct. On the other hand, the personal consciousness is there only when you are awake. The manifestation appears only in connection with Sushila. Sushila is part of that manifestation. In deep sleep there is no manifestation.

Sushila: *But, then, what is the difference between a sage and an ordinary person?*

Ramesh: On the level of deep sleep, there is no difference.

Sushila: *Is there, then, absolutely no difference between the sage and the ordinary person in the event of death?*

Ramesh: Death is death for both. There is no difference whatsoever. Why? Because the physical body-mind organism dies.

Sushila: *Is the awareness during deep sleep, which the true sage speaks of, connected with the body?*

Ramesh: No. What is meant is that there is an impersonal Awareness which is present. It is not the personal awareness.

Sushila: *I want to ask again. In deep sleep, are sages aware of their sleeping body-mind organisms and the manifestation, and are they also aware of awareness itself? If the sage is aware of his body, he consequently must be aware of the manifestation around his body, too. How could that be?*

Ramesh: It cannot be.

Sushila: *Then it must be a lie when they claim that kind of awareness, isn't it?*

Ramesh: What they mean is one thing. What they say is something they should not say.

Sushila: *What is it that they mean? Is it the same as what you say?*

Ramesh: Yes.

Sushila: *But they are saying something else.*

Ramesh: They are saying something else. I don't know whether or not they say it with some purpose. I repeat what I am saying: in deep sleep, the same state prevails for both — for the sage and for the ordinary person.

   Now, you see that ceiling fan is not working; that lamp over there is also not working. But the electricity is present in the cables of both of them, and it is the same. Even though the gadgets are switched off and therefore not functioning, the electricity is still present. Similarly, impersonal Consciousness is present in deep sleep and during the waking state.

Sushila: *Some sages make one believe that, because of their enlightenment, there is something which they are aware of in deep sleep which I am not able to be aware of. That makes them special, and their claim makes me feel incomplete, wanting what they claim to have. And then I keep asking, "How can I reach that same state of awareness?" Furthermore, they make us believe that even in their death and beyond, they are going to stay aware.*

Ramesh: Yes, I know, some do say so.

Sushila: *On the other hand, you say in deep sleep and in death there is no manifestation. The Unmanifest prevails, in which awareness cannot be known, and in which awareness cannot be aware of anything, including itself. Is that correct?*

Ramesh: Absolutely correct. Therefore, you will not hear me say that "I" am aware in deep sleep. That is just not possible for anybody. I know some sages claim such awareness. Maybe they want to deliberately mislead the honest seeker. Mind you, even such a false teaching is part of the functioning of Totality, or God.

Sushila: *I have heard these false claims throughout my entire spiritual life.*

11.2 The Personal Dreams of the Sage are Psychological Reactions to Actions in the Waking State

Madhukar: *My question is about dream. In my own case, there is identification in sleep-dream. A body-mind organism exists which senses and reacts with the notion of a "me," just like in the waking dream.*

In your case, since there is no "me" in the waking dream, there shouldn't be a "me" in the personal dream either. Is that so?

Ramesh: In my personal dream there is a "me," because the body-mind organism called Ramesh is playing a role.

Madhukar: *When you wake up in the morning, do you also remember a body-mind organism called Ramesh having taken part in events which happened in the personal dream?*

Ramesh: Yes, I do remember.

Madhukar: *But is there identification? Do you have the notion of a "me" doing things in your personal dream?*

Ramesh: No.

Madhukar: *Or is it more like watching a movie, in which the character and the role of one's own body-mind organism is played?*

Ramesh: Yes. Exactly.

Krishnamurti said that he never dreamed. I don't believe him. What are dreams? Dreams are psychological reactions to the actions which happened in the waking dream through the body-mind organism. As long as actions happen through a body-mind organism of a sage, psychological reactions are bound to appear as personal dreams. Those psychological reactions in the personal dream will also depend on the programming of the body-mind organism, because all "primary" actions in the living dream depend on the programming in the first place. If the programming of this body-mind organism is to worry, then that worrying may produce personal dreams. Say, the programming is courage, fear, uncertainty or an inferiority complex, then those characteristics may prevail in the personal dream as well. If one consults an ayurvedic or homeopathic doctor who derives diagnosis and treatment according to one's dreams, one actually may be cured of such psychological diseases, because the content of a personal dream is directly related to what happened in the waking state. The doctor can make use of this fact.

Madhukar: *I need to ask one more time: just as there is no personal doership in your waking state, there is no notion of personal doership in your personal dream. Is that correct?*

Ramesh: There is no personal doership in the waking dream. In the personal dream, the "me" continues to play its role.

Madhukar: *But without the sense of doership?*

Ramesh: In the personal dream the question of personal doership doesn't arise.

Madhukar: *In my own case, there seems to be a sense of personal doership in my dreams. Perhaps, rather, I should call it the notion or the feeling of "me," or "me"-ness. The actions seem to be done by something else which simply uses this body-mind organism. But at the same time, the sense of "me" prevails.*

Ramesh: The sense prevails that this body-mind organism is playing a role. That role is also being played in the personal dream.

Madhukar: *As I said, identification as a "me" exists for me in both states, the personal and the living dream. After waking up from sleep, I feel that "I" have been involved in that personal dream as a "me"-entity. Is that the same for you?*

Ramesh: No, there is no feeling of involvement in my case.

Who would claim that he is not dreaming if he is not dreaming? "Who" is dreaming anyway?

CHAPTER 12

12.1 "If We Want Life to Continue as We Know it, We Should Try Not to get Enlightened"

Nanette: *Why doesn't everybody get enlightened?*

Ramesh: If everybody were enlightened the show of life, as we know it, couldn't go on. Life only goes on because Consciousness-not-aware-of-itself — called "I-I" — has become aware of itself, and as such is called "I-Am." This is the impersonal Consciousness. "I-Am" has become the personal consciousness, "Nanette," in this body-mind organism. And because billions of individuals interact with each other, life is what it is. Therefore, the interconnected opposites arise, like love and hate, etc.

Nanette: *So, if we want life to continue as we know it, we should try not to get enlightened, right?*

Ramesh: But that is also not in your hands.

Louisa: *But if everybody were enlightened, it wouldn't make any difference, or would it? Why do you say it would be the end of the show?*

Ramesh: Life would be a movie in which nothing happens — without a hero or a villain.

Louisa: *If we were all enlightened, we would all keep living. We would all keep following our destiny exactly the same way as we follow it now, except there wouldn't be any sense of personal doership.*

Ramesh: Ah! You said everybody would follow their destiny. But if everybody were to accept his destiny, there wouldn't be any interconnected emotions, such as love and hate, friendship and enmity.

Louisa: *Those feelings would arise, but surely the sense of personal doership would be lost.*

Ramesh: Therefore, nothing would happen on the stage, and the curtain would come down.

Louisa: *I don't know. I can't understand this.*

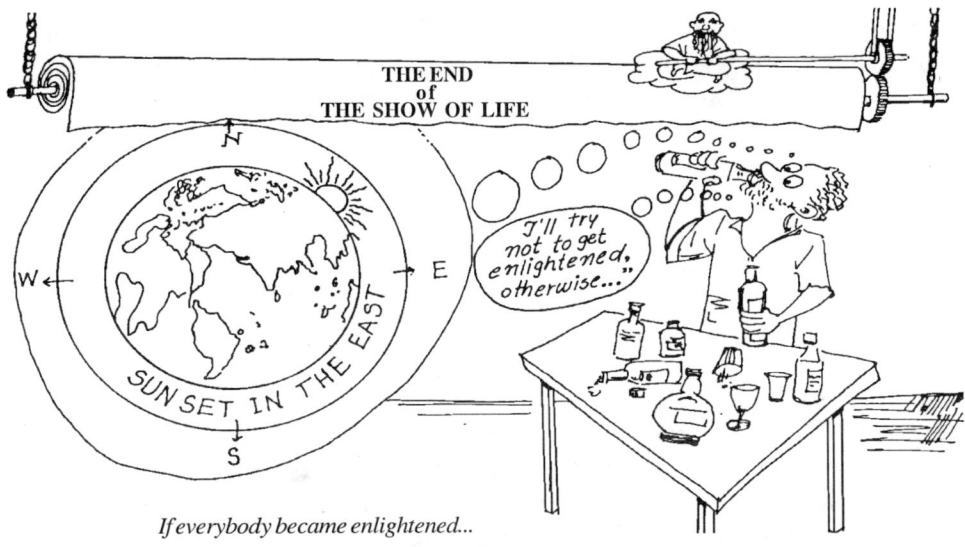

If everybody became enlightened...

Ramesh: Would you go to see a show in which people just moved about and did nothing? If everybody were enlightened, then that kind of a play would occur.

Louisa: *You are enlightened, right? Let's take it as a basic premise that you are enlightened. You have lost the sense of personal doership and yet, as a body-mind organism, you still act — or rather, react — to outside impulses, right?*

Ramesh: Yes. This body-mind organism continues to function according to its natural programming. Make no mistake, preferences are programmed, and continue as such.

Louisa: *So, preferences would continue to exist. The play would continue. Something would happen.*

Ramesh: But there wouldn't be any interactions between the enlightened people. You see, I can't consider anybody my enemy. There is no feeling of pride or disgust or frustration.

Louisa: *But you are not a vegetable, or are you?*

Ramesh: You see, if there are a lot of vegetables sitting around...

Louisa: *But you are not a vegetable.*

Ramesh: ...or, if the enlightened people just go about doing their own business, without interacting with other people, then there will be no interest in the show because there aren't any interconnected opposites anymore. What is life?

Louisa: *Relationships.*

Ramesh: And relationships are based on interrelated opposites, like love and hate, and friendship and enmity, etc.

Louisa: *So, you don't have friends anymore?*

Ramesh: I have friends as sort of a custom. If somebody does something for me I say, "Thank you very much" as a matter of social custom. I know that somebody who is my friend today can be an enemy tomorrow. He may think he is my friend, but I know that next week he may think I am his enemy. If he also thinks in the same way as I do, then there will be no relationship.

Nanette: *Then there wouldn't be any gurus anymore. The guru-disciple relationship would disappear because no teaching would be needed anymore.*

Madhukar: *I have the same problem as Louisa has. I can't buy that the show would just stop if everybody were enlightened. We have heard about the conduct of dead sages, like Ramana Maharshi and Maharaj, and we can witness the conduct of living sages, like you. So we know, therefore, that anger and other reactions still arise in a sage. In that way, life still goes on for the sage even without the feeling of personal doership.*

Ramesh: Why does anger arise for you? Because you think somebody has done something which you didn't like. But if the understanding is that nobody does anything, that everything happens by itself, then there will be no reactions.

Louisa: *Nisargadatta still became angry quite often, and intensely so, because of the programming of that body-mind organism. Everybody was afraid of him and his temper.*

Ramesh: But that anger arose because of inter-human relationships. If there are no inter-human relationships at all, if life just goes on, then even those feelings may not arise.

Louisa: *So, if he met somebody else who was enlightened, he would not get angry — ever?*

Ramesh: If three or four enlightened people were to get together, anger wouldn't arise.

Louisa: *Why?*

Ramesh: Because nothing would happen which could cause anger.

Louisa: *But the conditioning and programming in the four sages is still in place, still operating. If the body-mind organism of one of the sages absolutely abhors tobacco smoke, and Maharaj lights up a beedie, would the sage become angry? Or what would happen?*

Ramesh: Nothing would happen.

Louisa: *The sage would tell Maharaj that his body can't stand smoke.*

Ramesh: And that would be accepted.

Louisa: *What's the difference between that and being a vegetable, then? You have said that the sage is no vegetable.*

Ramesh: You see, anger arises out of something which happens in life. Life means inter-relationships. Without inter-relationships, the chances of anger arising are very small. Something which happens causes anger. But that something which happens is based on an inter-human relationship.

Madhukar: *We can go back all the way to the existential level and look at what life is. As long as body-mind organisms need to eat, drink, and go to the toilet, life must go on, at least at that level — even if everybody were enlightened. An enlightened person also says, "This is tasty food, and that is rotten stuff."*

Ramesh: But then, what would be the point in life? If everybody were enlightened there would be no interest in life anymore. God has created this living dream. And God would not be interested in it anymore, just as you would have no interest in a "live show" without the villains and heros.

Madhukar: *I feel this whole discussion is fruitless and purely speculative. Nobody knows, or can ever know, how life would be — or if it would continue at all — if everybody were enlightened.*

Ramesh: Make no mistake, what I am saying is a concept.

Madhukar: *In any case, I cannot imagine that life would just stop if everybody were enlightened, because we still would eat and drink and do the basics. The energy would still function inside all the enlightened body-mind organisms, causing them to continue to act according to God's Will.*

Ramesh: Life would not stop, but it would have no interest. Who has created this life? God. And He would have no interest in it anymore, and therefore He would bring the curtain down.

Madhukar: *That I don't know.*

Ramesh: Make no mistake, it is a concept.

Louisa: *Say, a body-mind organism which is an actor becomes enlightened. So, that organism is programmed to be an actor and most probably will continue to be an actor after enlightenment. His "act" would be seen for what it was, but he wouldn't care about that.*

Ramesh: What role would he play? His role depends on real life, with the opposites of hero and villain. Without them, the actor would have no role to play.

Louisa: *Say, a villain, a murderer, gets enlightened.*

Ramesh: A murderer cannot get enlightened.

Louisa: *Why?*

Ramesh: Or, rather, a murderer cannot get enlightened because a murder is usually committed by a murderer with a sense of personal doership, with a certain motive. Why is a murder usually committed? It is committed by an individual doer with a certain motive. Otherwise, the murder wouldn't happen.

Louisa: *I see.*

Ramesh: It is the destiny of a murderer to commit the murder. And it will be the destiny of the other organism to be murdered. The bringing together of the two organisms in life is the combined destiny of both organisms. The consequences of that murder will also be the destinies of those individual organisms.

Louisa: *So, if he were enlightened...*

Ramesh: You see... but the murder is usually committed because there is a sense of individual doership.

Louisa: *Because the unenlightened body-mind organism reacts. If he were enlightened he wouldn't react, right?*

Ramesh: If he were enlightened, he wouldn't react. There wouldn't be a personal doer, and there wouldn't be any enemy to murder. If everybody were enlightened, no murders would happen.

Louisa: *You have said that the body-mind organism is programmed in a certain way at the moment of conception; and that program is destined, stamped on the forehead. On the other hand, the ordinary person thinks he is causing what he does to happen, though this is actually the path he must follow. He is obliged to do it.*

Ramesh: If everybody were enlightened, enlightenment would then have needed to be the destiny of every body-mind organism.

Luisa: *Well, yes. That is, if we talk theoretically.*

Ramesh: But that destiny cannot happen in everybody's case. Not everybody can fall asleep at the same time. It is said this manifestation is an illusion because manifestation doesn't exist while you are in deep sleep. Only that which exists always is real. But while you sleep, the manifestation exists for those who are awake. So, if we would have the situation in which everybody were in deep sleep at the same time...

Louisa: *Then nothing would exist.*

Ramesh: Then nothing would exist. Who, then, would be there to say that something exists? Therefore, manifestation doesn't really exist, and is said to be an illusion. Even the scientist says that an object in manifestation arises only when it is observed. The object which is not observed does not exist. If everybody were in deep sleep, who would see what object? There wouldn't exist any object at all, then. But the fact is that not everybody is asleep at the same time. If everybody were enlightened, then the entire world would be seen as an illusion.

Louisa: *But the world would still be there?*

Ramesh: The world would still be there, but it wouldn't hold any interest for the One Who created the play. God would have no interest in this play.

Nanette: *How can you say both: that the world would still exist if everybody were enlightened, and that it would be the end of the show of manifestation?*

Ramesh: What I am saying is that the curtain would come down in a play without inter-human relationships, without love and hate. The hall would be empty.

Nanette: *I don't understand. If everybody were enlightened, the manifestation would continue to exist because it is observed. On the other hand, you say that the curtain would come down, that the play would end.*

Ramesh: The sages would still be there, but there would be no game. Without a game, nobody would be interested.

Juergen: *There is no reason for the children to be there.*

Madhukar: *The sages are already dead. Maybe that's why, in the scriptures, the sages are referred to as "dead while they are still alive."*

Ramesh: In any case, the whole thing is a concept. "What if" is a concept of the thinking mind.

Louisa: *The thing is, I don't want to go after enlightenment only to end up as a carrot, you know?* (laughter)

Ramesh: If that were to be the case, you would like to stop the seeking. But you can't. The seeking starts with the baby searching intuitively for the mother's breast. And from that moment on seeking continues, it becomes part of the organism's nature. The energy inside the organism will always seek something. And that something — be it God or Truth or whatever — will be strictly according to the programming. And even if that seeking means misery, you can't stop it.

Madhukar: *I am not able to believe in the concept which holds that the play of life would end if everybody were to become enlightened. How, and if, the manifestation would continue in such an extraordinary situation, nobody knows. And such a situation will most probably never happen anyway. Why to use concepts at all?*

Ramesh: Right. Why to deal with such a concept at all?

Madhukar: *But what can be done about it? Either these concepts stop appearing, or they keep arising in the form of thoughts, they keep nagging. Either way, nothing can be done about it.*

Ramesh: As long as you have a concept, it will nag you. Ramana Maharshi's answer to such nagging questions — which are nothing but concepts — was a counter-question: "Who wants to know? Is there a 'who'?"

Madhukar: *My question, therefore, is why do you talk about this what-would-happen-*

if-everybody-were-enlightened concept at all? Is it only because the question was asked that you entertain such speculations? Is that why? Because, really, nobody can give a valid answer to this question.

Ramesh: Yes, quite right. You see, if the seeker asks conceptual questions, the answers can only be conceptual. That's why the answer to a conceptual question is, "Who wants to know?" The seekers will then be brought back to the basic understanding that there is no "who."

Madhukar: *That's the end of the discussion.*

Nanette: *But if you were always to reply with the counter-question, "Who wants to know?", then the seeker wouldn't have the possibility of verifying that he understood correctly what the guru told him.*

Ramesh: Who understands what correctly or incorrectly, Nanette? Who gets anything?

Nanette: *I am here to understand what you teach.*

Ramesh: No, you are here to understand only one thing. You see, I bring you back to the basics. Yes, it is a concept. The basic concept is that you are not an independent entity. What you consider yourself to be — an independent entity with a sense of personal doership — is merely a programmed body-mind organism through which God or Totality creates certain actions. You believe those actions are your actions, but really they are God's. And the only final thing to understand is that there is no individual doer who is capable of any personal action. An action happens through a body-mind organism, and the consequences are to be borne by the same organism. It is the destiny of one body-mind organism to commit murder, and it is also its destiny to be punished, or not, for that deed. And it is the destiny of another body-mind organism to be murdered. There is really no murderer and no murdered. There is a body-mind organism through which a murder is committed, and another one through which a murder is received. So, if you truly understand that there is really no doer, then you know that what you think is "your" action is merely a reaction of the brain of the programmed body-mind organism to an outside impulse, which can be a thought or a sense object. That is the basic thing to be understood. Once this basic point is understood, no problems arise.

CHAPTER 13

13.1 Grace Happening in the Guru's Presence: The Grace of God

Whose grace for whom?

Ramesh: "*Satguru's* grace" is just a way of speaking. It is not in his power to confer grace to anybody. It is not correct to call it the *satguru's* grace when grace happens to somebody in the guru's presence. If it were his grace, then it should be in his power to give enlightenment to anybody at any time, as he wishes. A genuine guru will tell you frankly that he is not able to confer enlightenment to anybody. Enlightenment can only happen if that event is destined to happen to a particular body-mind organism. In truth, the *satguru's* grace is really God's Grace. I prefer the expression "God's Will" to "God's Grace."

Louisa was just reading one of my spiritual books and suddenly she was overpowered by a tremendous feeling. She had an experience just by reading a book. There was no *satguru* present, unless you consider the author of the book an indirect guru. She must have felt a tremendous sense of gratitude. How did you feel about the experience when it happened?

Louisa: *It just was what it was.*

13.2 In True Meditation there is No Meditator

Devesh: *What is the role of meditation?*

Ramesh: If you start playing tennis, you go to a professional coach who will show you what playing tennis is; and he will teach you what and how to practice. So it is with meditation. Meditation is spiritual practice for the beginner, to be done in order to come to know what this is all about. But if you keep practicing, if that is all you do, then you will never be able to play. At some point you have to start to play in earnest. And once you play well, your practice techniques will not come to your mind at all during play. Practice leads to good play.

Meditation is merely a means towards some end — call it: purifying the mind and the body. Or one could say that meditation is a way to prepare the body-mind organism for its programming to operate. Many gurus and many disciples consider meditation not a means but as an end in itself. So, if you keep on meditating with a certain objective in mind, the seeker, the meditator, will continue to exist.

But true meditation happens only when there is no individual meditator. Whenever true meditation happens, you will realize that the meditator is not there. So long as the meditator is there, thinking he is doing the meditation for a particular purpose, then that is only practice, not "play." But when the practice becomes more and more natural, then the principles and techniques are forgotten. The more meditation happens, the less the "me" will be there as the meditator. True meditation happens when the individual meditator is not present. True meditation may only be for a few minutes. But most of the time there is the meditator wondering whether his back is straight enough, or thinking about how much of the prescribed thirty minutes have passed. To whom do all these thoughts come? To the individual meditator. But if you practice meditation for a reasonably long period of time, the meditator disappears, and true meditation happens. Then you may find that you meant to sit for only half-an-hour, but you find yourself sitting for forty-five minutes. When that happens, that is true meditation in which there is no individual meditator. Then meditation happens.

The real role of meditation is only as a beginner's practice. But the trouble is that many practitioners consider meditation an end in itself.

Madhukar: *During my many meditation retreats in India, and in other countries, I was told that the goal of meditation is a state of thoughtlessness which can be obtained by ardently practicing* Vipassana *or Zen meditation for many years. However, a state in which no thoughts arise seems to be an impossibility. So, in having a wrong idea about the goal, the basic premise of my meditation practice was also altogether wrong. I was expecting the cessation of the arising of thoughts for more than twelve years. I am sure*

that I could have kept meditating until my last breath without success, because the goal is itself an impossibility.

Ramesh: What is impossible, Madhukar?

Madhukar: *No thoughts to arise. They cannot be prevented from arising.*

Ramesh: Because the not-arising of thoughts is not in your hands.

Madhukar: *Sure. But I was told that it was. I was told that it was — here in India and elsewhere. I was told that the arising of thoughts would cease at some point. But that point in time never came.*

Ramesh: You see!? *(laughter)*

Madhukar: *The content of thought — good, bad, etc. — had no importance in those meditations. The focus was choiceless awareness. It was the involvement in thinking, i.e., the breaking-down of the choiceless awareness, which one tried to avoid. I used to judge myself a lot for this.*

Ramesh: A thought arises from outside. The arising or not-arising of a thought is not in your hands. Nobody can prevent a thought from arising. But what happens once a thought has arisen? The brain gets involved in that thought and starts thinking horizontally. But if an arisen thought is merely witnessed, then it disappears.

But as Madhukar said, you are supposed to sit still; the intention of the meditation practice is that you have no thoughts. But it is not in your hands whether or not to have thoughts. Thoughts will occur. And the more you think you should have no thoughts, the more you are involved. And you think like this because you were told that in true meditation there are no thoughts.

What is the answer? Let those thoughts occur. Don't get involved in those thoughts. If you ignore those thoughts, then they become fewer and fewer. But if you try not to have thoughts, they will appear with more frequency. Madhukar is quite right: you are told that meditation is something you do in order to have no thoughts. Having no thoughts means that there is a "you" to have, or not have, thoughts. But it is not "you" who has the choice.

Meditation is something that happens. Let it happen. Anyway, it happens. That is the understanding with which you sit in meditation. When you truly understand that there is no "you" to do any act, that all actions are produced by the Supreme Power through each body-mind organism, then every action of yours is merely witnessed without getting involved in them; you don't judge them as good or bad. Then you don't feel guilty and frustrated if they are unsuccessful; and you don't feel proud when they turn out to be successful. And that makes life simpler. If you live with such an attitude for a long period of time, this attitude will become a habit, a life-style.

There is a difference between observing and witnessing. Observing means the mind, the "me," the ego, is observing its own working. The nature of the mind is to judge. And if the mind observes thoughts or actions, it will judge them as good or bad. And that is involvement. When whatever happens is not judged, witnessing happens. And only this understanding — that whatever happens is God's Will, and not your action — will prevent judging. It is this understanding which will gradually produce the cessation of judging. And then witnessing results. But "you" cannot use the understanding to produce witnessing.

13.3 When Enlightenment Occurs, What Happens with God's Will?

Wolfgang: I believe that it is a very common idea amongst seekers that an enlightened being has some special awareness.

Ramesh: The special awareness of the sage is the awareness of the absence of the sense of personal doership. This awareness is constant and permanent after enlightenment has happened. And there is also the constant awareness that whatever happens is part of the functioning of Totality, with which the sage is not in any way concerned.

Paul Brunton complained to Ramana Maharshi one day about the evils of the Second World War, when England killed ten thousand Germans in Hamburg in a single night's bombing. Paul Brunton considered Ramana to be an individual, and expected a reaction from that individual. But there was no individual to react.

Madhukar: *You were saying yesterday that the enlightenment process is a process in phenomenality, and that the event of enlightenment itself is therefore still part of phenomenality.*

Ramesh: What you are saying is correct.

Madhukar: *Could you explain one more time what you said earlier about that?*

Ramesh: Yes. What is enlightenment? Does the question of enlightenment arise during your deep sleep?

Madhukar: *No. Therefore enlightenment is something which is concerned with life. And enlightenment is a happening in phenomenality.*

Enlightenment—then what?

104

And once it has happened, the sage, with his enlightened understanding, is still part of phenomenality; his destiny and future are still part of God's Will, and are therefore unknown to the sage.

Ramesh: What you are saying is correct. Indeed, the sage is part of phenomenality.

Madhukar: *The sage's state of not having a sense of personal doership is also part of phenomenality?*

Ramesh: Yes, indeed.

Madhukar: *And will this situation continue for him until his death?*

Ramesh: Quite right. The functioning of the body-mind organism of the sage is still in phenomenality.

Madhukar: *And does life, with its ups and downs, contine for the sage, the only difference being that he has no feeling of a sense of personal doership and is therefore not involved in life as an individual entity?*

Ramesh: That is correct.

Madhukar: *And whatever happens through the sage is destined, right?*

Ramesh: Quite correct. Each sage has a different image and personality. But his body-mind organism continues to have disease or health strictly according to the destiny of the organism. A sage may have cancer and have a painful death. Or he may die comfortably in his sleep. Or a sage may keep on talking and suddenly die in mid-sentence. Either way, he knows he has nothing to do with his life or death, or with how he dies. All he knows is that in deep sleep he was not concerned with anything. And he knows that death is something like deep sleep, in which there will be no one to bother about anything.

CHAPTER 14

14.1 Enlightenment:
The Peace of Acceptance is not a Permanent Blissful State

Ramesh: Enlightenment or freedom or liberation means the total acceptance and understanding that there is no individual doer of any action or deed. Enlightenment means the total annihilation of the "me" and the total acceptance that whatever happens is part of the functioning of Totality. After enlightenment, the Supreme Power has a certain role for the enlightened body-mind organism to play. The role may be the same as before, or may slightly change. In a small village, the enlightened one may continue to live the same life. But the neighbors will realize that something has happened; they will see some changes in the person and start going to him with their practical or spiritual difficulties. That is how a guru is born, because Totality wants that person to play the role of a guru. Enlightenment does not mean that the sage can see everything that happens anywhere in the world. Enlightenment does not enable a sage to look into the future.

Nanette: *The examples of the lives of many sages demonstrate that they are not spared from physical ailments and diseases. Are they spared from mental problems? Or would a sage go to a psychologist if he had mental difficulties?*

Ramesh: If he has a mental problem.... if something causes him some mental unease, he will sit quietly. But, for the most part, the mental problems will not be there. A sense of fear may arise in him, which you could call a mental problem. Or a sense of dislike may arise in him as the reaction of the brain to an outside impulse. But that fear or dislike will be witnessed as something which arises and, because it is not taken delivery of, it will simply disappear.

Madhukar: *I think the greatest misconception of the seeker is the image he has of an enlightened being, namely that the sage is always happy and in bliss. The scriptures say it. And many sages and gurus I have met in person expressed their state with such descriptions; many pretended to be in a permanent, blissful state.*

Ramesh: That is a misconception.

Madhukar: *The main misconception. And it is also the biggest attraction for the seeker to want enlightenment.*

Ramesh: The misconception is regarding the meaning of the word which is used. The word one uses has implications. If you use the word "happiness," the implication is that an individual considers himself happy. And the word used to describe the state of a sage is "happiness," or even "bliss." To me, these words are misused. The word I prefer is "peace," rather than bliss or happiness. There is peace, yes. Totally.

CHAPTER 15

15.1 Even A Mindful Sage Can Break His Leg

Judy: *Recently, I tried to take a sauna in a friend's house. When I poured some oil on the heated rocks, a huge fire erupted. I was able to put the fire out and no damage was done. I learned afterwards that the oil needs to be put on when the rocks are not yet heated.*

Sometimes I watch an eruption explode out of a conversation or an interaction, just as that fire did. I observe the interaction going on and I see myself saying something, or doing something, and I tell myself, "Oh my God! Why don't I shut up?" And yet I can't stop what happens. I can't stop the thoughts. I can't stop the words. I am obviously not in control.

Ramesh: Do you want to say that you are sometimes absent-minded?

Judy: *No, no, no! That's not it. What I experience sometimes is that, even though the events and words are being observed while they happen, and it is known to me already at that very moment that what is going to happen next will be a fight or a "fire" erupting, there is no way it can be stopped from happening. Can those fires be prevented?*

Ramesh: You have no control. You can either be absent-minded — which means you are in the thinking mind — or you can be in the working mind — which means that you are really mindful of what you are doing. That's what the Zen-saying means: if you want enlightenment, wash dishes. The point is that you concentrate on the job, during which time your mind should not wander to something else.

Judy: *I can see how mindfulness applies to an action or an event, but how could it apply to a simple conversation?*

Ramesh: You were saying you did something wrong, and therefore the fire blew up. If you had followed the instructions, if you had acted with the working mind, the fire would not have erupted.

The Buddhists use the expression "mindfulness," which means being present and concentrated upon whatever you are doing. I know a quite well-known *Vipassana* meditation teacher who fell and broke her leg. Her friend asked her, "Ruth, were you not mindful?" She didn't like to be asked that question.

Judy: *But was she mindful?*

Ramesh: She was obviously not mindful, otherwise she wouldn't have broken her leg. (*laughter*) But my point is that she was not mindful at that moment because it was her destiny to fall and hurt herself.

Judy: *Can somebody who is absolutely enlightened also have such an accident?*

Ramesh: Certainly.

Judy: *Does that mean the sage was not mindful?*

Ramesh: Yes.

Madhukar: *At that point in time.*

Ramesh: At that point in time, it was not the sage's destiny to be mindful.

Judy: *Could one be mindful and something could happen over which one has no control?*

Ramesh: If you are mindful, the chances of an accident happening are very little. The chances for an accident to occur are higher when one is absent-minded. But an accident can happen even if you are mindful. Then the accident is destined for those who are concerned with the accident.

Madhukar: *According to some gurus, the sage is supposed to be in total awareness during his entire waking life. Let us not talk at this point about some gurus who claim to be aware even when they are asleep. We were talking about the event of the sage breaking his leg. Could it be that, at that moment, the sage was not mindful because a thought arose, or he saw something, and that is why his attention was diverted?*

Ramesh: Yes. That is correct.

Madhukar: *Say, a loud sound is perceived by his mind. Then his attention would be attracted towards the direction from where the sound came; he would look there instead of looking at the path, and at that moment he would step on a stone, fall, and break his leg.*

Ramesh: That is correct.

Madhukar: *It seems to me that this situation can happen to the sage or to an ordinary person — enlightened or not, it wouldn't make any difference, right?*

Ramesh: Correct.

Madhukar: *There is one more possibility for the ordinary person, but not for the sage:*

the ordinary person might have been in the thinking mind, and therefore his attention was not on the actual action of walking. And the occupation with the thinking mind made it impossible for him to be aware of the existence of the rock on the path, causing the fall.

Ramesh: Correct. But in the case of the sage, the attention being drawn elsewhere, and therefore the breaking of his leg, is part of his destiny.

Madhukar: *So, it is a misconception to hold that a sage has absolute and total awareness, and therefore an accident as described here couldn't happen to him?*

Ramesh: That is correct. Yes, that is a wrong concept. Accidents will happen to a sage. I told you that the *Vipassana* teacher who broke her leg didn't like to be asked if she was not mindful when it happened.

Madhukar: *But that dislike of that question shows her state of mind, doesn't it?*

Judy: *Ramesh, it wasn't the incident of the fire in the sauna I wanted to tell you about earlier. What I wanted to hint at is my total helplessness in stopping my talking or action, even when I am aware of them and I know disaster is brewing. Even my thinking mind comes in and says, "Now you should stop talking, Judy." But I keep talking. I am not able to stop at that moment.*

"I wish I could break my leg"

Ramesh: Whether your thinking mind is telling you something or not, what is going to happen is going to happen anyway.

Judy: *I can see my mind thinking, and I am absolutely unable to stop it, even though I feel absolutely tired of it. But I think the tiredness is part of the judgement.*

Ramesh: The tiredness being part of the judgement is part of the destiny.

Judy: *And that needs to be accepted.*

Ramesh: Correct. Everything that happens needs to be accepted.

CHAPTER 16

16.1 The Four States of a Sage: Working Mind, Witnessing, Non-witnessing, Samadhi

Nanette: *Is witnessing for you, the sage, always there? Can witnessing stop for you?*

Ramesh: Witnessing is there. The only way it gets stopped is when the "me" comes in, the thinking mind comes in.

Nanette: *But witnessing is still there, isn't it?*

Ramesh: Witnessing is always there, but it is covered up by your thinking mind. Consciousness-not-aware-of-itself, "I-I," becomes the impersonal "I-Am." And the impersonal "I-Am" identifies itself and creates an "I am Nanette." During the waking state, moments happen in which "Nanette" is absent. Whenever "Nanette" is absent, the impersonal "I-Am" is there. The impersonal "I-Am" is always there, even in your deep sleep. In the waking state, the impersonal "I-Am" is also always there, but it gets covered up by the personal "I am Nanette" whenever the thinking mind — the "me" — obscures it. In effect, the "I-Am"-in-action in daily life is witnessing. Witnessing happens whenever the thinking mind is not there.

Nanette: *We were talking about absent-mindedness and the thinking mind yesterday. I still have a question about that.*

Ramesh: Being absent-minded means you are not concentrated on what you are doing. In this context the Buddhists speak of "not being mindful."

Nanette: *I thought that in absent-mindedness the thinking mind was absent.*

Ramesh: No, it is not absent. Absent-mindedness is an aspect of the thinking mind. Anything that distracts from concentration on the work is the thinking mind. Concentration on the work is the working mind, or mindfulness. Either you are mindful of what you are doing, or you are not. That not being mindful can be either absent-mindedness or the thinking mind. The thinking mind can be active or passive. In absent-mindedness, the thinking mind is passive. But in any case, it is still the absence of concentration — or the absence of mindfulness — on the work you are doing. The more your working mind is in function, the less the thinking mind intrudes, and work truly becomes worship. Work is worship or work is happiness. So, the degree of happiness may depend to a certain extent on the nature of the work. An artist who is really working on something will be far more happy than somebody who works as a mechanic or a surgeon. But even for the mechanic, a certain job satisfaction is there when he works with full concentration.

Madhukar: *I heard you say earlier that the thinking mind obscures the impersonal "I-Am." Does that mean that at the moment in which a thought arises, the "I-Am" is obscured for a moment? Since nobody, including the sage, can prevent a thought from arising, would the "I-Am" be obscured for the sage as well at that moment in which a thought appears to him?*

Ramesh: No. What obscures the "I-Am"?

Madhukar: *The sense of a personal "me."*

Ramesh: Yes. And the sage, or enlightenment, what does it mean?

Madhukar: *The feeling or the sense of personal doership is annihilated.*

Ramesh: Yes. The total annihilation of the "me."

Madhukar: *I understand that. Since the arising of a thought is not part of the thinking mind, and therefore does not obscure the "I-Am," a thought as an original impulse from outside must be part of the "I-Am." Is this correct?*

Ramesh: In the sage, the "me" is annihilated. On the other hand, the average person — what I am going to say is again a concept — is most of the time in the state of involvement; he is in the thinking mind. In the case of a sage, involvement is extremely rare. So, in the case of a sage the stages are: witnessing if there is

The four stages of the sage

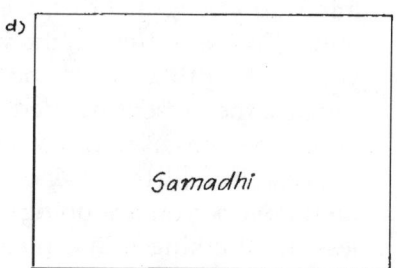

something to witness, and non-witnessing if there is nothing to witness. For him the shift from the witnessing state to the non-witnessing state functions as easily as the automatic gear-shift in a car. You see, I sit here, we are talking. That is being witnessed. After the talk, when you all leave...

Madhukar: *Witnessed while you are talking? Witnessing and talking happen at the same time for you?*

Ramesh: That is the whole point.

Madhukar: *So, a thought arising is also witnessed as part of What-is? A thought is also part of the "I-Am"?*

Ramesh: Whatever is happening is witnessed. To put it more specifically, you think you are Madhukar, that Madhukar is talking, and that Ramesh is listening. Or you think Ramesh is talking and Madhukar is listening. The way the sage understands this situation is that a conversation is taking place through two body-mind organisms, that nobody is talking and nobody is listening. The talking and listening is one movement which is happening at the present moment. And that is witnessed by the sage. But if you all leave and I sit quietly here, then there is nothing to witness. Then the non-witnessing state may occur.

Madhukar: *I think the misconception on my part is that I thought that the state of "I-Am" — the "I-Am"-ness or witnessing — was a totally pure state of no-thought, of emptiness, of silence and peace; an empty screen. And that whatever appears on that empty screen is obscuring the state of "I-Am"-ness.*

Ramesh: No. That's why when witnessing is not there, there is a state of non-witnessing in which consciousness still exists in a very passive way. Sounds are heard and smells are smelled, but there is no "one" to smell or hear. Listening and smelling happen.

Madhukar: *What you are saying cannot be understood by the mind. What you are saying is not my existential experience. So, I have to believe what you are saying until this experience happens in this body-mind organism.*

Ramesh: That is correct. It can only happen. As I have said, the shift from the witnessing to the non-witnessing state is extremely smooth; and when the non-witnessing state is for some reason not disturbed, then a deeper state occurs — which may be called *samadhi* — in which the senses don't register anything anymore.

CHAPTER 17

17.1 Destruction of the World: Balance of the Universe

Ramesh: Whatever happens in your personal dream is something you really have no control over.

Manshu: *But the Dreamer has control over this dream, right?*

Ramesh: No. He started the dream long ago and the dream is going on.

Sujeeta: *You mean to say He is not playing any part now?*

Ramesh: No.

Sujeeta: *How can that be?*

Ramesh: The dream was dreamed earlier and it is already there. The entire picture is already there.

Sujeeta: *But a lot of things which exist now were not there at the beginning, billions of years ago.*

Ramesh: Does the same thing not happen in your personal dream? There is no dream at all, and all of a sudden there is a dream; and in that dream there are things which are millions of years old. What happens in this living dream also happens in your personal dream. When you wake up from your personal dream, you realize that it was only a personal dream. And when you wake up spiritually you will realize that manifestation and life are only a dream, and that it really doesn't matter what happens.

Sujeeta: *When was the whole picture created?*

Ramesh: The Divine Novelist has written and completed the novel. But *you* can know the novel only page by page. In a novel, you can skip the pages and see how it ends. In the Divine Novel, you can't.

Manshu: *But can the enlightened one do that? Can he see backwards and forward?*

Ramesh: No.

Because the universe wants to continue

Sujeeta: *This novel has a beginning and an end. So, does...*

Ramesh: This novel never had a beginning, and will never have an end. The beginning and the end is a human concept, isn't it? The Divine Novelist has produced His novel, and it exists. How long it is, is a matter of concept. In order for new events to happen page by page, the Divine Novelist is creating new body-mind organisms through which whatever is to happen in the future pages is happening. All you can do is to accept your role in that novel, accept it as a role that is being played by God through this body-mind organism. All you can do is to understand that whatever is happening is part of the novel — also called the living dream — which doesn't really concern any individual.

Madhukar: *Was the novel created in one flash, in one Big Bang?*

Ramesh: Yes. It is created in one flash, exactly as your personal dream is created in one flash. During deep sleep your personal dream appears in a flash, complete with rivers and mountains which are billions of years old, with babies being born, and with all the rest of life in it.

Sujeeta: *Can the living dream also disappear as suddenly as it appeared?*

Ramesh: The living dream disappears suddenly when enlightenment happens.

Sujeeta: *Can manifestation disappear suddenly? That's what I want to ask.*

Ramesh: Yes, if that is the Will of God. God keeps balance in the whole creation, in the whole universe. Otherwise, it wouldn't have lasted for billions of years. And if, in order to keep balance throughout the entire universe, God needs to destroy this world, what is to prevent Him from doing so?

CHAPTER 18

18.1 Can One Have a Direct Experience of Deep Sleep?

Ramesh: Everything a scripture or a sage has ever said is a concept. A concept is something which people can either accept or reject. The only thing that is not a concept is something about which there cannot be two opinions. There cannot be two opinions about the fact that you exist. You are aware of your existence. The awareness of existing, of being alive, is not a concept. You don't have to ask anybody, "Do I exist?"

Jayanti: *What about* maya, *which says that everything is an illusion?*

Ramesh: *Maya* means that what is unreal is considered to be real. *Maya* is that hypnosis which makes the individual human being believe that the manifestation is real. The sages, on the other hand, say manifestation is unreal. Often, the question is asked, "But the objects are so real, I can touch them." The answer is again very simple. A mass-hypnotist...

Jayanti: *You were saying that there cannot be two opinions about the fact that I exist. I was wondering if that saying of yours is also part of* maya.

Ramesh: No, the fact that you exist is not part of *maya*. Part of *maya* is that you exist... your first name is what?

Jayanti: *Jayanti.*

Ramesh: So, that you exist, that there is existence — that awareness is impersonal. *Maya* is "I am Jayanti." "I am," "There is existence," that is not a concept, that is not *maya*. *Maya* is that which makes Jayanti believe he is a separate human being with intent, volition, and power to act. That is part of *maya*. *Maya* is that which makes this really unreal thing seem real. That which comes and goes is unreal, and that which always exists is real. That is the definition of what is unreal and real.

A mass-hypnotist can make two thousand people believe something exists when there is actually nothing. If a mass-hypnotist can do that, do you think it is difficult for the Supreme Power to create this hypnosis?

The manifestation, which you think is real, disappears and doesn't exist in deep sleep. The manifestation arises when you are awake and disappears when you are in deep sleep. It doesn't exist all the time. It is for this reason that *Advaita* says it is unreal.

Madhukar: *The impersonal sense — "I-Am" or "existing" or "being" — also disappears during deep sleep. That's why it must also be part of phenomenality. Is that right?*

Ramesh: No, "I-Am" does not disappear in deep sleep, Madhukar.

Madhukar: *I mean to say that we can neither be aware of being asleep nor of the feeling "I am, I exist, I am alive." During deep sleep, there is a total black out.*

Ramesh: You cannot be aware of it because "you" are absent.

Madhukar: *But isn't it true that nobody, not even the sage, can be aware of the feeling, "I am, I exist, I am alive," during deep sleep? Nobody can actually know that "I-Am" exists in deep sleep. One cannot have a direct experience of deep sleep.*

Ramesh: That is why the idea of "I-Am" is a concept. But it is not a concept to the extent that, when you wake up, you are able to say whether or not you slept well. If "something" had not been present during deep sleep, what would enable Madhukar to say, "I slept well," or, "I didn't sleep well?" Something was present and something was absent.

No sage or non-sage can have a direct experience of deep sleep

Madhukar: *But that something is a matter of speculation for us. It is a concept, because we can't know it. So, we can speak only conceptually about it, isn't that so?*

Ramesh: Yes. Therefore when you talk about it, it becomes a concept.

Madhukar: *Let me ask you the same question in another way. The sense of presence, of existing, of being — which is present right now at this moment in this room — disappears in deep sleep. It cannot be observed or felt in deep sleep.*

Ramesh: Wait a minute, wait a minute! What disappears is Madhukar. "I-I," the Supreme Power, Consciousness-not-aware-of-itself, becomes "I-Am," which is the impersonal sense of presence. So, the awareness that you exist, the awareness of existence, is impersonal. The impersonal sense of "I-Am" becomes "I am Madhukar." "Madhukar" disappears in deep sleep, but the "I-Am" remains. And that "I-Am" exists all the time, and that is why it is real.

Madhukar: *Well, we can suppose that it is the way you describe it, but nobody will really ever know. All of what you have just said is a concept, speculation. Yes, it's true we say in the morning, "I slept well," or, "I didn't sleep well." But as to why we know this, nobody knows.*

Ramesh: Yes, it is a concept. But when you wake up you *do* know that you slept well, don't you? If something was not present during deep sleep, how would you be able to say you slept well?

Madhukar: *I don't know how I am able to know how I slept. I just know it.*

Ramesh: Something was present. Or was it not?

Madhukar: *It must have been.*

Ramesh: And Madhukar was not present. That is also certain. So, if Madhukar was not present, something was present. So, the "I-Am," the impersonal sense of presence, was present. The identified sense of presence was absent.

Madhukar: *What you say can only be verified mentally, conceptually. We can observe and describe the sleep state like a scientist and say it seems to be like this and like that. But we truly don't know.*

Ramesh: No. No. Who doesn't know, Madhukar? Who doesn't know?

Madhukar: *The mind, the intellect.*

Ramesh: Therefore, this mind, this intellect, this Madhukar is unreal. The Madhukar who wants to know is unreal. Madhukar is only a concept. And Madhukar wants to know God. Madhukar wants to experience reality.
    There is a huge machine with billions of screws and nuts and bolts. And one tiny, little screw wants to know what the whole machine is all about. Is that possible? And that is what Madhukar says: "I want to experience that whole machine."

Madhukar: *If we could experience that impersonal Awareness, that would mean that we could know God as an object, which is not possible.*

Ramesh: That is correct. That is why Consciousness is all there is. No one can know Consciousness. If you know something, it means you are the knower-subject who knows the known object. But if Consciousness is pure Subjectivity, then there can be no object to understand the Subject. And what the human mind wants to do is to be a subject which can understand God or the Supreme Power or Consciousness as an object — which is not possible.

All that exists is Subjective Presence, the Supreme Power, which cannot be known by anything else whatsoever, because there are not two. If something can know the Supreme Power, there must be two. But all there is, is one Supreme Power. Otherwise, you wouldn't call it Supreme. So, no human mind can understand pure Subjectivity. And even this, the moment it is said, becomes a concept.

So, what is real and unreal? Only that is real which exists in deep sleep — the sense of impersonal Awareness which makes you say, "I slept well," in which the individual, identified consciousness is absent.

18.2 Rebirth And Reincarnation

Ramesh: "Events happen, deeds are being done, but there is no individual doer thereof," is what Buddha is reported to have said. If that is totally accepted, that is enlightenment.

Jayanti: *What has Buddha said about rebirth and reincarnation? All his boddhisatvas are said to have lived with him in previous lives.*

Ramesh: I don't know what Buddha has said about them. But rebirth and reincarnation are concerned with the mechanics of phenomenality. They are still phenomenality. Why to go into those mechanics? Why to bother about them? If you accept that phenomenality is unreal because it disappears in deep sleep, then the mechanics of phenomenality are irrelevant.

Jayanti: *Are you saying there is no rebirth?*

Ramesh: Rebirth is a concept concerning the mechanics of phenomenality. You can be for or against it. If you are truly concerned with transcending phenomenality — trying to understand the What-is, the Supreme Power — then the final understanding is that I, as an individual doer, cannot understand God. One little screw, in a big machine with billions of screws, cannot understand the working of the whole machine. But because all these screws have intellect, the screw wants to know. The final understanding is that it is impossible for the intellect to understand the Supreme Power. In trying to

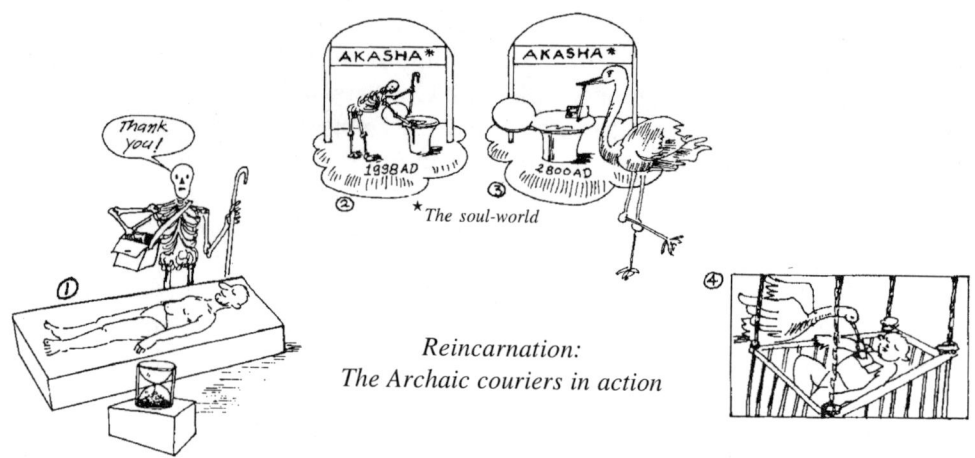

*The soul-world

Reincarnation:
The Archaic couriers in action

understand the Supreme Power, all we do is conceptualize. We create one concept after another. When it is finally understood that there is no individual doer, conceptualizing stops, and What-is is accepted as something which is the functioning of Totality or God. All events and actions concerning this body-mind organism are part of What-is at the present moment.

Madhukar: *Could we say that, at this very moment in the waking state, it is actually the impersonal Awareness which is aware as "I am, I exist, I am present"; but that this Awareness is misconceived as "I am Madhukar." The impersonal Awareness is identified as "I am Madhukar," while the actual, impersonal What-is is perceived through this personal "I am Madhukar." And because of that, the What-is is "Madhukar-ized." Thus, separation from the whole What-is — as a "me," as "I am Madhukar" — has taken place. Is that correct?*

Ramesh: That is exactly what is meant by *maya*, Madhukar.

Madhukar: *And it is this same impersonal Awareness which exists and is aware in deep sleep, and therefore enables one to know how one has slept.*

Ramesh: Quite correct.

Madhukar: *So, it is the same impersonal Awareness which is present in deep sleep and in the waking state. It is always there.*

Ramesh: It is the same impersonal Awareness which is there all the time. It is merely covered up by this identified consciousness. And this covering up of that impersonal Consciousness by the identified consciousness is exactly what is meant by the word *maya*. That is *maya*.

Madhukar: *So, truly, this talk here at this moment is an impersonal event.*

Ramesh: That is why I am saying that this talking and listening is an event which is part of What-is at the present moment.

Madhukar: *Just as this event is impersonal, in the same way deep sleep must also be impersonal.*

Ramesh: Certainly. That's why I say that you think there is one individual Ramesh talking, and another individual Madhukar listening. My point is, there is no individual doing the talking or the listening. The event of a conversation is happening through two body-mind organisms as part of What-is at this moment. It is one movement in What-is.

Jayanti: *This conversation is also* maya, *then?*

Ramesh: Indeed, it is *maya*.

There is a story about Adi Shankara, the founder *Advaita*. He used to say, "All this is *maya*." One day, when the king was riding through town on an elephant, he spotted Shankara. The king, who was Shankara's disciple, thought he would play a joke on him. He ordered the elephant to charge after Shankara, who swiftly ran for cover.

"If all this is *maya*, why did you run for cover?" the king asked Shankara. The answer was, "Nobody ran for cover. The body-mind organism has a natural survival instinct as part of its programming. As a reaction to the elephant's charge, the programming made the body-mind organism called Adi Shankara run for cover. The body-mind organism, with its natural reactions, is also part of the *maya*." In other words, there is really no Shankara. Who ran for cover? The body-mind organism.

CHAPTER 19

19.1 A Terrible Obstruction: "I Am Enlightened"

Ramesh: What, ultimately, does enlightenment really mean? It simply means the total acceptance that there is no personal free will, that nothing can happen according to your will unless what happens to be your will also happens to be God's Will. Then it will happen.

Then there are people who propound the philosophy of positive thinking. They believe that if you only want something intensely enough, it will happen.

Janine: *Only if it is the Will of God.*

Ramesh: There is no individual with free will. That is the only final understanding. The final understanding is that that final understanding is not in your hands. (*laughter*) And if it is not truly and completely understood that nothing is in your hands, then a certain kind of understanding happens. But that certain understanding is misinterpreted as a "me" having understood something. And in that kind of "final" understanding, there is still a "me" which has understood, or thinks it has understood. And if that is the case, a terrible thing can happen: "'I' have understood it completely. 'I' have the final understanding." And that kind of understanding gives rise to a feeling of wanting to be a guru. That is a terrible obstruction. It is a terrible obstruction. The person who thinks he or she has the final understanding wants the world to know it. You see?

Janine: *Yes, the person wants to start teaching.*

Ramesh: If someone has that kind of understanding, he or she is concerned that the world should know. But if the understanding is true and complete, he or she doesn't care whether the world knows it or not. In the true understanding there is no one who has understood anything. If there is no one who has understood anything, where is the one who wants to be a guru? Wanting to be a guru is a terrible obstruction. But that obstruction is also part of the process.

Janine: *No "me" can be enlightened.*

Ramesh: You are quite correct. Why, Janine?

Janine: *Because the "me" is part of the body-mind organism, the thinking mind. And the thinking mind cannot be enlightened.*

Ramesh: What you mean to say is that the "me" cannot be enlightened because enlightenment means the total annihilation of the "me." For that reason, no "me" can be enlightened. And when enlightenment has happened, there will be no "me" wanting to be a guru. There will be no "me" wanting the world to accept him or her and acknowledge that enlightenment has happened. But if there is a "me," that "me" wants a certificate from somebody that he or she is enlightened.

Janine: *And such a person can be very proud and think she or he is a superior person.*

Ramesh: Yes, sure. But let me go one step further. If there is a "me" who thinks he or she has understood, and therefore he or she is enlightened, then he or she will want the world to know. But even that fact is still part of the functioning of Totality. So, no "me" is doing anything wrong in wanting to be a guru. The "me" wanting to be a guru, and whatever happens subsequently because of that desire, is part of the destiny of that body-mind organism. So, whether the true understanding happens or not, is not in the hands of the "me" at all. Enlightenment means the total annihilation, the total destruction, the total disappearance of the "me." So, how could a "me" be enlightened?

CHAPTER 20

20.1 Lucid Dreams: The Dreamer is Aware that He is Dreaming; Enlightenment: No Concern with Lucid Dreams

Madhukar: *Some time ago, I heard you talk about lucid dreams.*

Ramesh: No. Some people were asking me about lucid dreams, and I told them that I had no personal experience regarding them.

Madhukar: *How do you define a lucid dream?*

Ramesh: I have no definition other than what I have been told by other people: a dream is called lucid when the dreamer is aware that he is dreaming, and he is aware of what he is dreaming.

Madhukar: *Is such dreaming really possible?*

Ramesh: I don't have any personal experience of lucid dreaming. There are people who are not enlightened, and yet they say they are aware of their lucid dreams. The experience of a lucid dream does not necessarily mean enlightenment.

According to science and research, lucid dreams do occur. There is no doubt about that fact. What makes you think lucid dreams could not occur? Anything can happen in this world.

Do spirits exist? Why not! If God can create beings with bodies, why shouldn't He be able to create ones without? Spirits are beings without bodies. What is not usual, people call a miracle. What was considered a miracle

"Sorry, lucid dreaming is not enlightenment"

a hundred years ago has today been explained and proven by science to be part of the natural laws.

Wendel: *You have spoken of the thinking mind and the working mind; what is the dreaming mind?*

Ramesh: As I said people talk and write about lucid dreaming. They say some people are aware that they are dreaming during the dream itself.

In deep sleep, the identified consciousness is not present. The impersonal Consciousness is present. When you wake up, you know how you slept because of the impersonal Consciousness, which was present during sleep. The only thing that is real is that which is present in deep sleep. Everything else is a concept, unreal.

Madhukar: *So, lucid dreaming would be something like witnessing during dreaming, wouldn't it?*

Ramesh: Yes, you are quite right, it would be something like witnessing during dreaming.

CHAPTER 21

21.1 Enlightened or Not? What are the Criteria?

Udo: In your case, are you sure that enlightenment happened and that it will not get reversed?

Ramesh: What you are asking is, what is enlightenment? Enlightenment has happened when there is no longer a sense of personal doership, and when there is a total understanding of the fact that whatever happens is not my action, but God's Will. Enlightenment happens only when the individual "me," with a sense of personal doership and volition, is totally annihilated. In my case, there is the total understanding that this is a body-mind organism which will be used by God, for His purposes, as long as it is alive.

Udo: But why are you so sure that it will not change, that it cannot change?

Ramesh: Because it hasn't changed for sixteen years. And if it is to be changed, fine. The "me" is dead forever. Until the "me" is dead forever, there will be ups and downs; which means that sometimes you have the feeling you have understood, while at other times you have the feeling that the understanding has disappeared. But that is not a reversal of the progress. That is still part of the progress of seeking. With enlightenment, there will be a constant feeling of peace, and a feeling of the lack of personal doership.

Sometimes I am asked whether a sage could murder somebody. My answer is: yes, murder by a sage can happen. Or rather, my answer is no, because the sage will not murder anyone; but murder could happen through a body-mind organism in which enlightenment has happened, if it is so destined. The reaction or the consequences of the act of the murder will also be according to the destiny of that organism. It is the destiny of the organism called Mother Teresa to perform good actions and to be respected for them. And it is the destiny of the psychopathic organism to commit a murder and to be punished for it.

Udo: Are there criteria which establish the fact that somebody is enlightened? Can one know from outside whether somebody is enlightened or not?

Ramesh: As I told you, enlightenment simply means the total absence of the sense of personal doership or desire. When enlightenment has happened, the body-mind organism will no longer care what happens. It doesn't care if the world knows that enlightenment has happened. But if enlightenment didn't truly happen, then there is still the desire of wanting one's enlightenment to be acknowledged.

The answers

Udo: *Can you know for sure if another individual is enlightened or not?*

Ramesh: Not really, except from the way in which he acts. If someone wants to be acknowledged as enlightened, then I know that such a person is not enlightened.

Udo: *Other than that, can one tell from the outside if enlightenment has happened or not?*

Ramesh: One cannot tell from the outside, because the understanding is always from the inside. So, the actions of the enlightened one will be more or less the same, but his attitude will be different. What the human mind does is to lay a great deal of importance on the sage's actions. But the real difference is that the ordinary person believes that he is the doer of his actions. In the case of the sage, there is the total understanding that actions happen through a body-mind organism, without personal doership. That is the only difference between the two. The existence of yogic powers is not an indication of enlightenment.

CHAPTER 22

22.1 Work is Meditation: What about the Workaholic?

Janine: Since my husband died two weeks ago, I have nothing to do anymore. What should I do now? According to you, even sitting in meditation will not be helpful for bringing about enlightenment. Having heard your teaching, and knowing the fact that whatever will happen, will happen as part of God's Will, makes me feel fatalistic.

Ramesh: What do you mean by fatalism? Fatalism is just a word, a label. The word fatalism, as I understand it, means that I shall not do anything. Isn't that it?

Janine: Yes.

Ramesh: Just sit quietly and do nothing. That's what you mean. But that can't happen. Because, if I can't do anything, I just sit idle. But you can't sit idle, because the energy inside this body-mind organism will produce some action. You may be physically idle, but thoughts will still arise. So, either physical or mental action is bound to happen anyway. The attitude, "There is nothing else for me to do," will soon disappear when you find that you cannot sit idle. My point is that you cannot be fatalistic.

Janine: You think it is impossible?

Ramesh: Fatalistic may mean that something is happening in which you don't take any interest.

Janine: But that isn't the same as what you call witnessing.

Ramesh: No. You can't sit idle. When something is happening, there is either the working mind or the thinking mind. The feeling of fatalism, of thinking, "Why should I do anything, why should I care about anything?", can happen to someone who doesn't have any work; someone who doesn't need to earn any living. Then this kind of attitude may take place. And that person loses interest in things because he doesn't need to work at anything.
   So, that's why I tell people, "You must work at something. Do something!" Because if you aren't doing something, your working mind will not be there. And if the working mind is not used, the mind will not remain empty. The thinking mind will come in. And it is the thinking mind which will get you into

trouble, into concepts. So, the feeling of fatalism can only arise if the working mind is not employed. But if you find something to do, if you apply your working mind, then this fatalistic attitude will not last.

Janine: *Are you saying if I don't need to work for a living, I should try to be busy with something...*

Ramesh: Do some social work.

Janine: *Some social work?*

Ramesh: Yes, certainly. Do some social work. Do some social work, any work in which your mind will be employed.

A young lady wrote to me saying that she was holding a regular, full-time job as a secretary. At the same time, she studied in an evening school to become a medical representative. She complained, saying that she now had to work twelve hours a day, and therefore didn't have much time for meditation anymore. I wrote back to her and told her that she didn't know how lucky she was! To work from eight o'clock in the morning until eight o'clock in the evening is a kind of meditation. If you still have extra time, sit and meditate. But if you don't have the time to meditate, don't think you are missing something. That's what I wrote to her. Because when you are working with your full attention, the working mind is operating. And that is a kind of meditation. When is there no meditation? When the thinking mind keeps coming in. So, what is meditation? Meditation really means the absence of the thinking mind.

Work: meditation for the masses?

That's why I always tell people to find something to do if they don't need to earn a living. Find some social work. If I have nothing to do, the thought may arise that I lose interest in life. And it could even be that you lose interest in whatever you are doing. But if you are doing something, and the work needs attention, then the working mind will be there. Therefore, the Zen master says, "If you want liberation, wash dishes. And make sure you wash them very well." If you concentrate your attention on what you are doing, that is a kind of meditation — perhaps one of the best kinds of meditation, especially for someone who finds it difficult to meditate.

Therefore, I say that, after you have heard my teaching, continue doing whatever you were doing. If you are meditating and you like it, keep doing it — even if you are a meditator meditating on something as an object, which is not true meditation. Having heard my teaching, you don't need to change your life in any way. If you change your life, that means you are saying, "I shall use this teaching to change my life, to improve myself." That cannot be done. Accept the understanding and accept the changes, if they happen. Changes in your daily life will be produced by the understanding, and not by "you." If, after listening to me, your meditation cuts itself back from two hours to one hour, accept the change and don't feel guilt or pride. "If I cannot do anything for my betterment, why should I do anything?" That is said by the ego. The ego has nothing to do with what happens through the body, because there is energy inside the body which will produce some change.

Juergen: *But it is my destiny if I have to suffer because of fatalism, right?*

Ramesh: That is absolutely correct. Whatever happens, happens because of the Will of God. That is the basis of my teaching.

Udo: *I like to play on my computer. Often I get involved in this activity for the whole night.*

Ramesh: That kind of involvement is not involvement with the thinking mind. If you are working with the computer and you get involved in what you are doing, it is the involvement of the working mind, which is exactly how it should be. Involvement is good when it happens to the working mind.

Udo: *Even if the computer carries me away and I get lost, is this good?*

Ramesh: The more you get lost in the working mind, the better it is, Udo.

Udo: *I seem to have the choice between reading your books and playing with the computer. You say I don't have the choice and, in any case, both activities are equally good because they involve the working mind.*

Ramesh: That is correct.

Udo: *I will choose between the two depending on which one gives me satisfaction at a given time.*

Ramesh: Quite right. Concentrate on what you are doing. That's all. Don't think of the computer while you read the books, and don't think you are not able to read the books while you are playing with the computer. Then there will only be the working mind.

Udo: *So, maybe moderation is good. That was the advice you gave me yesterday.*

Ramesh: Sure. Moderation is always good. But moderation may not be part of the programming of an individual. Why are there drug addicts or alcoholics? Biologists have now come to the conclusion that one becomes an addict because of the genes, the DNA. More and more, science is telling us what I have been saying for so many years. Whatever the human being thinks he does is really nothing but a reaction of the brain to an outside impulse. And that reaction happens according to the genes and conditioning of the body-mind organism, which is the programming. Today, science even attributes adultery to the genes and DNA.

Elke: *I think it doesn't matter whether I read your books or whether I do something else. To me, it sounded as if Udo was saying it is better to read Ramesh's books than to play with the computer. There may be a difference in quality. But there is no difference really, because you are doing whatever you are doing.*

Ramesh: That is exactly what I told Udo.

Elke: *Therefore, it is not better to read the books.*

Ramesh: Read the books, enjoy them, without thinking of the computer. But if you are working on the computer, don't think, "Oh, I am wasting my time on this computer. I could have spent the time reading the books, instead." Enjoy whatever you are doing.

Juergen: *Where is the borderline between working with the working mind and addiction to work?*

Ramesh: You see, the addiction to do something is part of the destiny. Therefore, you find people who are working sixteen or eighteen hours a day. In America, they are called "workaholics." These people are not happy unless they work. They are unhappy if they are not able to work for some reason. So, that is addiction. There is no difference between addiction to work and addiction to alcohol or drugs. And any addiction is a bad thing. But if that addiction is to happen, you can't get away from it.

But let us go back to basics of the teaching. Whatever happens is part of the destiny of the body-mind organism. So, addiction to work is destined. Some may be addicted to work because they make more profit if they work more. Because they are more successful. But there are people who still must work, irrespective of what happens. That is an addiction. Many social workers are addicted to their social work even though their hard work doesn't bring them more money. Addiction is entirely a separate matter. It is part of the programming of the body-mind organism. Which addiction it is, is really immaterial. Well, it affects your life, but basically, addiction is part of the programming. And you are lucky if your addiction is to something good, like reading books about *Advaita*. That is not a bad addiction. And it is a particularly good addiction for the author and the publisher. (*laughter*)

Udo: *Can an addiction continue if a person becomes enlightened?*

Ramesh: Certainly. Maharaj used to smoke. For him this addiction continued. If an addiction continues for an enlightened person as well, what is the difference between him and an ordinary person? Maharaj didn't think that the addiction of smoking was bad for him. The body was addicted. Let the body be addicted. Only when his smoking led to cancer did he have to stop smoking. And he quit not because it was an addiction, but because smoking gave him discomfort and pain. The sage doesn't deliberately say, "It is an addiction and I must give it up." But it may happen that the addiction just goes.

In this life, I myself had two addictions. One was playing golf and the other was watching horse races. My addiction to golf stopped by itself in 1974. After I had visited my son in England — he studied and worked there — I found myself without any of my four golf partners. All of them were posted to other cities in India. So, golf stopped at that time. I had played for thirty-five years, but I didn't stop it. I wasn't even concerned with *Advaita* at that time.

I used to watch horse races. Sometimes I would bet and I would lose. My betting was always in moderation because part of the programming of this body-mind organism is moderation. But somehow last year I didn't feel like going to the races anymore. So, that just stopped. Before that I used to go to almost every race. So, an addiction is part of the programming of the body-mind organism, and the destiny.

CHAPTER 23

23.1 What was First, the Chicken or the Egg?

Shiva: *Ramesh, could you answer my question about how an egg creates another hen? How does a hen create another hen?*

Ramesh: You want to know the mechanics of phenomenality, don't you? How does the manifestation work?

Shiva: *Can you tell me what Consciousness has to do with the creation of the hen?*

Ramesh: Consciousness is the ground of everything. Consciousness is not a hen coming out of an egg. Consciousness is both, the egg and the hen.

Daniel: *At the same time.*

Ramesh: Quite right, at the same time. So, the question of one producing the other doesn't arise. Everything is at this moment.

Shiva: *I have always had this question about which comes first, the hen or the egg. And how does an egg create another egg? How does Consciousness know what to do in order to get to know itself? Consciousness is creating another consciousness, isn't it?*

Ramesh: The "you" who wants to know is a small screw amongst billions of screws, nuts, and bolts in huge machine. This little screw wants to know how the whole machine works. And that is just not possible for the little screw.

So, the question of "how" is really irrelevant. It's only science which asks the "how" questions and produces answers. But the answer which is sought by asking "how?" is necessarily based on the existing knowledge. That is why what is happening today was considered a miracle a hundred years ago. Forget the television! Even the radio would have been considered a miracle then. So, the "how" questions of today might easily be answered by a child in a hundred years from now. If you ask a "how" question now, you will get an answer according to the existing present-day knowledge. But the existing knowledge is not the total knowledge, even from the point of view of science. However, it is because of the working mind of the scientist — asking all these "how" questions — that science has been progressing. But to ask "how?" when Consciousness is concerned, is like a tiny screw wanting to know the workings of a huge machine.

If God created the world, who created God?—Who wants to know?

Shiva: *So, it is just the "me" wanting to entertain itself when I ask the hen-and-the-egg question?*

Ramesh: Yes, it is just the mind wanting to entertain itself with such questions. And that is why when such questions were asked, Ramana Maharshi's stock answer was the counter-question: "Who wants to know?" The answer is: a tiny screw wants to know the workings of a huge machine. And that just can't be known to the screw. So, the little mind wants to know the Mind of God. And that is not possible.

CHAPTER 24

24.1 *The Guru and his Teaching: A Hope for the World*

Abe: *Can you remember a particular breakthrough in yourself with regard to the teachings of Maharaj?*

Ramesh: Yes, I remember two breakthroughs. There may have been more. There were at least two. The earlier one happened during a time when Maharaj was talking and I was the translator. During the translation, Maharaj and I were discussing a point in question. While that happened, I could feel a sudden silence in the room. It was more of a shock than silence. After the talks ended, the silence continued for a while. Later on, the friend of mine who was sitting beside me said...

Abe: *"You were in great form."*

Ramesh: No. That was at the second breakthrough. The first time, there was just this shock. But I couldn't understand what the shock was about. I wasn't aware of what I was saying. Since the talk was audio-recorded, I went with my friend to his residence to listen to the talk once more. And when I heard the cassette, I was shocked.

Abe: *Shocked by what?*

Ramesh: By the directness and equality with which I was discussing with Maharaj. Normally, I wouldn't talk with Maharaj with a sense of equality. Never! Never! That's why I was shocked. You could say I was talking to Maharaj with equal authority.

The more important breakthrough was the second one. That happened also when I was translating. The translation became so spontaneous that I almost knew beforehand what Maharaj was going to say. I was impatient. I almost couldn't wait for Maharaj to finish a sentence so that I could translate it. There was not even a split-second for the thinking mind to intervene and try to grasp what Maharaj was saying, and then interpret it into English. Immediately after Maharaj would end a sentence, my translation would begin.

After that talk, the same friend of mine said to me, "You were in great form this morning." I asked him in what way I was in great form. He said, "You made gestures which you normally don't. And you spoke with an authority which was quite uncommon." So, that was when this translation was spontaneous, without the intervening thinking mind.

Maharaj also understood that something had happened. Usually, if Maharaj wasn't sure whether my translation was correct or not, he would ask me, "What did you say? Tell me!" I would then repeat what I had said. And he would either agree with it or tell me that my translation was not correct. And then he would explain and tell me one more time what he meant for me to translate. This happened to me when I was the translator only once or twice. But even in these one or two cases in which he made me repeat to him what I had translated, he fully agreed with what I had said. Still, he felt a doubt about whether I had translated correctly or not. But from that day onwards, he never again asked me, "What did you say?"

And the occurrence of that second breakthrough led to another incident. It happened at a time when Maharaj was already quite ill. He was lying down. A group from Satara, a city some two hundred miles from Bombay, had come to visit. He told them, "Don't ask stupid questions. I don't have the energy to answer them. So, before you ask a question, decide if it is an important one. One of you will be the speaker for the group." In that manner they kept asking questions, which I translated. At a certain point, Maharaj had to go downstairs to the toilet. Before leaving he said to the group, "You continue the talks," and, pointing to me, he said, "He will answer." That was the first time Maharaj had authorized anybody to talk.

Before that incident, he used to say, "You don't talk, you merely translate what I am saying." So, this was the first time he said, "He is authorized to talk," or rather, he meant to say, "He is authorized to talk." But because there were no questions from the group, no talks ensued. Someone next to me said, "Maharaj is going to be very angry when he finds out that nothing has happened here." And he was. He asked, "What has been going on?" I answered, "Maharaj, there were no questions. That's why nothing happened." He grumbled. I said to him, "They want to hear the talks directly from you and not from me, for, to them, I am like a tape-recorder." Maharaj laughed at my joke.

I had understood that his authorization as a specific authorization for me to talk on the occasion of that morning only. What Maharaj said to me on that morning I did not take as a general authorization to talk. I did not talk unless Maharaj was present, and then I was merely translating. And Maharaj knew that. This is how it was until one day before Maharaj died. Maharaj was very ill on that day. When he wanted something, like a glass of water, his attendant had to bring his ear close to Maharaj's mouth to be able to understand what Maharaj said. Suddenly, Maharaj got up on his elbows and, with tremendous strength of voice, he said to me, "Why don't you talk?!" Then he fell back on his bed. This was on the ground floor, because Maharaj was so weak. He couldn't walk anymore at that time.

The attendant and I, we realized that Maharaj had thought at this moment of the occasion when he had authorized me to talk. Maharaj had known all along that I hadn't taken that occasion as a general authorization for me to talk. Thus far, I had not been talking yet. And he probably felt I would continue not talking unless he gave me a further authorization. That must be why he said to me, "Why don't you talk?!" Maharaj died the next day. So, I took this occasion as a very clear authorization that I should speak.

Abe: *For which we are grateful.*

Ramesh: Yes. Gratitude is something which arises. Just as this body-mind organism was grateful to Maharaj, there are some others who are grateful to this body-mind organism for something which is happening through this body-mind organism.

There was another occasion which Consciousness brought about in which, indirectly, Maharaj authorized me to speak. He told me, "Many of my co-disciples do not like what I am saying because I am not parroting my guru's words. They think I am talking without the authorization of my guru. They think I am not supposed to speak without his authorization." And then Maharaj added, "My co-disciples don't know the real truth. Therefore, they think an individual is talking. But the truth is, there is no individual talking here. The words which come out of my lips are spontaneous words which are needed by the people who come to see me."

To this, he then added something which surprised me at the time. He said, "When you talk, you will not merely parrot my words." I silently laughed. I said to myself, "That will be the day, when I am going to talk!" Somehow I knew this teaching would go forward, you see.

Abe: *I feel like a child who has heard a story many times from the parent, and who nevertheless says to the parent, "Tell me the story about..."* (laughter) *And one can hear the same story an endless number of times.*

Ramesh: And what is more, Abe, the child may have heard the story fifty times. But if, during the fifty-first telling, the story-teller is absent-minded and omits one point, the child will immediately point out which part was forgotten. (*laughter*)

Abe: *But this time you were not absent-minded. You told your story quite correctly. I have been wondering about one thing. It seems like Maharaj authorized only one person to teach. I have the impression that you have given rise to five or six or seven — how should we say? — "enlightened" disciples. Frankly, it seems that your teaching is even more clear than Maharaj's.*

Ramesh: Let me explain something at this point. You feel that what I am saying is more clear than what Maharaj was saying. That is because you never directly heard Maharaj speak. You know him only through translations which were done by five or six people. And those translations were according to the level of their understanding and their interpretation. And the English was subject to the limitations of each translator's vocabulary. Several books have been written based on those translations of Maharaj's talks, which were audio-recorded.

But here you are listening to me directly, and I speak English, which is your language. That's what makes you feel that my teaching is clearer than Maharaj's.

Abe: *That's an interesting point. But some of my thoughts go further than that, and may be a bit fanciful. I am thinking that, perhaps, in these apocalyptic times when we all feel the possibility of the planet coming to an end, Consciousness has arranged for a speeding-up of the general apprehension of wisdom.*

Ramesh: Yes, I agree with what you say whole-heartedly. If it is the intention of Consciousness that more people become enlightened, then things will happen which will make this teaching available to more persons.

*non-violence
**Satya yuga: the Age of Truth
"The year 2000 is heralding the New Age, the Age of Aquarius, or Satya Yuga"**

Originally, only a handful of people came to visit Maharaj, and they were Indians. Only after the book *I Am That* was published did Westerners begin to visit him. I went to Maharaj in November, 1978. The book was published two or three years earlier. So, it was only about two years before I came to him that foreigners arrived. The disadvantage was that Maharaj needed an interpreter for the foreigners. Ramana Maharshi also needed a translator. But he had some basic knowledge of English, and he could correct the translations when they were not correct. But Maharaj didn't know any English. That's why he would sometimes interrupt and ask, "What did you say?"

The Westerner of today is more interested in this sort of teaching, the *Advaita* type of teaching, than in earlier times. Earlier, in the 1960s and 1970s, Westerners who were concerned with Eastern teaching were more interested in yoga. They associated the word yoga with the Indian philosophy. Their interest in a pure teaching, like *Advaita*, started only fairly recently with Ramana Maharshi, who still had only a few Western disciples.

It is amazing how widely Mahesh Yogi's yoga and Transcendental Meditation has spread in the West, particularly in the United States. His teaching is basically concerned with the body. Tests conducted at Harvard University have proven that Transcendental Meditation, practiced twice a day for a period of twenty minutes, can cure many physical illnesses. Those results show the connection between the mind and the body. And those results made Mahesh Yogi well-known. Yoga is fascinating to the Western mind because of yogic feats like walking on water, which the Indian *yogis* have amply demonstrated. But only a very few people were interested in transcending these physical yogic feats. Out of ten thousand people who practiced with Mahesh Yogi, just a handful is inclined to go higher, to go further. But today, more and more people are interested in transcending phenomenality.

24.2 Karma, Rebirth and the Pool of Consciousness

The scientist is still concerned with phenomenality. Henry Swift had a wonderful experience in Hawaii during one of my seminars a few years ago. I think he really got the total understanding. He has gotten the understanding, but his interest as a scientist continues. He wrote to me and said that he is tremendously interested in rebirth. He has come across several stories of others' past-life experiences, and his interest in rebirth is very strong now. He wanted to know about rebirth.

I answered his letter by saying, "Either there is rebirth or there is no rebirth. Knowledge of a previous life may happen in one out of ten thousand people." My conceptual explanation is that nothing can be wasted — all there is, is Consciousness. So, each and every thought which appears in all the heads of all times — all the reactions of all the brains, all involvements, all thinking and doing — all of this goes into the pool of Consciousness. At the moment when a new body-mind organism is conceived, a certain memory is transferred to the new conception from this pool of Consciousness. It is not known what goes into the new conception. The memory of this new body-mind organism may consist of an assortment of small, partial memories from a total of ten thousand people, which now constitutes this single, new memory. Of the total, one per cent of the new memory may be much stronger than the remaining ninety-nine per cent of the memory. And it is this one per cent which is being remembered by the new body-mind organism. And remembering it, this person will say, "I was that person in a past life." But that is a presumption, because he doesn't remember the other 9999 past lives from which he got the rest of his memory.

In any case, I concluded my letter to Henry by saying, "Rebirth refers only to phenomenality. Rebirth concerns the mechanics of phenomenality. Why are you bothered about these mechanics of phenomenality?"

Claire: *When Henry was here, he talked about the hope for a better world. He believes that your teaching, together with the new idealistic physics of Goswami, gives hope for the world and its evolution.*

Ramesh: That was not Henry. Hope, his wife, said that.

Claire: *No, no, it was Henry. He spoke at great length about it.*

Ramesh: The scientist is concerned with the mechanics of phenomenality, but what the seeker is truly seeking is that which transcends phenomenality. Why bother with the mechanics of phenomenality?

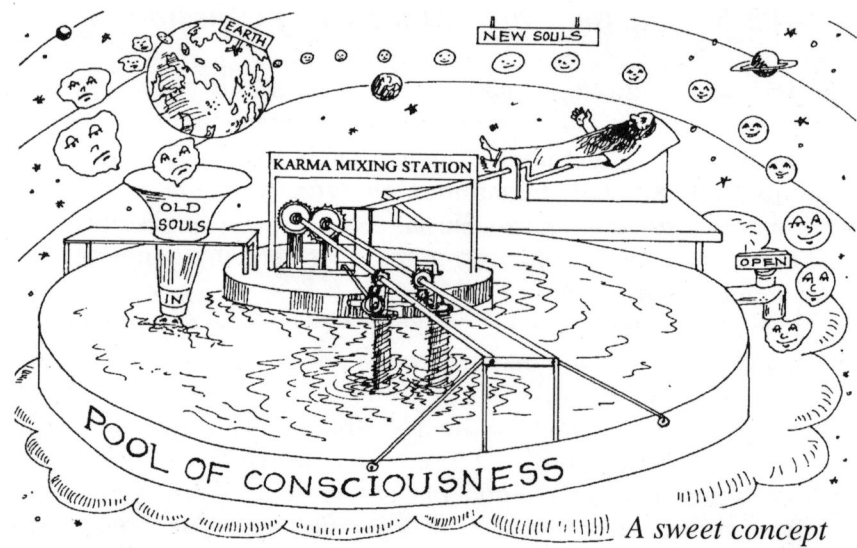

A sweet concept

CHAPTER 25

25.1 Satsang in the form of Gossip about Contemporary Gurus

Ramesh: Having read my books, do you have any questions?

John: *Nothing burning, really.*

Ramesh: But to start with?

John: *To start with?*

Ramesh: Yes. Does Linda have any questions?

Linda: *I would just like to listen.*

John: *I have realized a lot since the last time I was here. A lot of things have changed since then. It is very difficult to put it into words.*

Ramesh: But tell me, what has changed for you? A lot of things began to change since you visited me last time. Why is that? Is there a central theme in your thinking which changed?

John: *It has to do with simplicity: how simple everything is.*

Ramesh: Yes.

John: *I think I began to understand some of the things you said last time. But then, also, doubt would come in, and then I would lose what I had understood.*

Ramesh: Before you came to visit me, where did you go? You went to other gurus, didn't you? Jean Klein, did you say?

John: *I saw Jean Klein a bit.*

Ramesh: I see.

John: *Do you know Mrs. Irena Tweedy? I saw her a few years ago. She is a sufi teacher. I also told you that I have been with Muktananda for quite a while.*

Ramesh: That's right. I remember you telling me.

John: *After he died, I sort of did my own thing, I guess. So, I haven't really been with anybody lately.*

Ramesh: But you were with Muktananda for many years, you said.

John: *About seven or eight years.*

Ramesh: It was my impression that you were with him for a long time.

John: *I was with him in America. And I was running one of his centers in London. And when Muktananda died, the whole thing was a bit of a mess.*

Ramesh: Yes, it was a mess.

Jan: *Why was that? What was the mess?*

John: *It's a long story.*

Abe: *Sum it up!*

John: *Muktananda appointed two people to take over his function.*

Jan: *A brother and a sister; Gurumayee and her brother. What do you think, which of the two was more enlightened?*

John: *I don't know. They were both very young. She is about my age, thirty-nine or forty, and he is younger, about thirty-three. There was this big rivalry between them, and it got very messy. The brother left in the end. He is set up now as a guru on his own, somewhere in America.*

Abe: *Guru Junior!*

John: *It is a long story, and many articles have been written about it. I didn't feel good about it because I was there at the time, and I saw it all from the inside.*

Ramesh: Yes, yes. I see.

John: *There was a lot of hypocrisy.*

Ramesh: Yes. But as I understand the story, it was the brother whom

Muktananda first appointed as his official successor, was it not? I remember seeing a photograph of that occasion.

John: *Yes, there was a huge ceremony.*

Ramesh: Yes, and I remember the sister standing among a group of people and clapping her hands. That is a photograph I remember seeing in one of the magazines in India.

John: *They were both with Muktananda from their childhood. And for a year after he died they used to sit on a big throne together in public. But after a while it just got ridiculous, and the split happened.*

Ramesh: Did the teaching change much after Muktananda died — assuming there was a teaching, as such.

John: *There was a teaching. He was a very traditional yoga teacher, in a way. His main thing was about* kundalini. *In the so-called "intensives," he would go around and touch people, or pat them with these peacock feathers, you know. And this was supposed to awaken the* kundalini, *which I think it did in a lot of cases. He was very powerful. There were always these two fundamental sides to his teaching. He taught fundamental stuff, which was very similar to Advaita and Shaivism, that always had depth to it. He used to say, "When you really understand this and get it, you will be very cross with me for putting you through all of this* sadhana, *this pain."*

Ramesh: You mean, because it was difficult?

John: *Yes. I had a lot of faith in him. I think he was an enlightened man. And on the other hand, there was a lot of show. He liked ceremonies, festivals, chanting.*

Abe: *Krishnamurti had an interesting interpretation for something like a peacock feather. He said you can take a Coca-Cola bottle and put it on your mantelpiece, and then you bow to it every morning. And after a while, this Coca-Cola bottle will seem to have extraordinary powers.* (laughter).

John: *I had a lot of visions at that time, visions of deities like Shiva, Krishna, and that sort of stuff.*

Ramesh: Yes.

John: *I must say it was very powerful with Muktananda. After he died it became more dogmatic, in a way. I haven't been around anymore since then. Last time I came to visit you, I went to Ganeshpuri for a visit. Everything has changed. You can't really stay there anymore. You can only go to the courtyard and to his* samadhi. *The rest of the ashram is closed to passers-by.*

Ramesh: And yet they call it an ashram.

John: *You have to apply if you want to stay there.*

Dominica: *Maybe it is because of the bad press they received. There was a bad article in* The New Yorker *about the Muktananda ashram. I gave you a copy of that article, remember?*

Ramesh: Oh, that article in *The New Yorker*, yes.

John: *I thought it was a good, and quite a fair, article. It wasn't all negative.*

Ramesh: That's what I thought. And it was a reasonably objective article. I heard that the publishers of *The New Yorker* were threatened with dire consequences if they published the article.

Abe: *I am sorry to say that threat was a practice of Muktananda's. When I first met him, he asked me, "Do you have any questions for me?" And with typical modesty, I replied, "No, do you have any for me?"*

Ramesh: I see. (*laughter*)

Abe: *And Muktananda said, "Tell me about your work with hypnosis." That means he had researched my background. Why would he do that? I think he had a PR man who was researching the background...*

Ramesh: ... of people who went to see him.

Abe: *Of influential people whom he called in to meet him, so that he could make an impression on them in showing off how much he knew about them.*

Ramesh: How long ago was this?

Abe: *This was in about 1975, when Muktananda was coming to his ashram in Oakland.*

Ramesh: Oh, as far back as that. I see.

Abe: *Then, when one of his top administrators became dissatisfied with him, and started to say unfavorable things about him, he actually sent some gangster-like assistants of his* to beat this gentleman up. I imagine that, even if the beating up is spiritual, it would still hurt. (laughter) And when he held workshops, he would arrange to have his room next to the rooms of pretty young girls. He would then have a hole drilled in the wall so he could watch them. So, things like that would cause you to question his stature.

(To Ramesh) *But I have the feeling that you have the principle of not saying unfavorable things about other gurus.*

Ramesh: Well, I haven't met many gurus. (*laughter*) I am hardly in a position to say favorable or unfavorable things about other gurus.

Abe: *A little thing like that stops you from saying something about other gurus?!*

Ramesh: But I hear things about them.

Heiner and I were guests of a friend of Heiner's, Peter Robe. He is a psychotherapist. During our stay, two of his friends came to visit, unexpectedly. They were truck drivers, I think. One of them, John, was very close to Muktananda at the ashram in Bombay (Ganeshpuri — *Ed*.). But John had left him at some point. So, Peter said to John, "Why don't you tell Ramesh your story with Muktananda!" John then told his story, saying, "This is not second-hand; what I am saying happened to me. I am telling you what I saw." John was one of those administrators at his ashram who could go anywhere he liked at any time. He had free access to any room. So, John was telling us that he went into a room and found Muktananda playing with a young man. A young boy, as matter of fact. John was so startled and annoyed by what he saw that he decided to leave Muktananda. But before he left, he decided to meet Muktananda and tell him that he was leaving, and why. John went and told Muktananda that he saw what he was doing with the young boy, and that it made such a bad impression

on him that he felt he could not stay any longer. John asked me, "Do you know what Muktananda said to me? He said, 'Now, you have created a problem for yourself, and now you must solve it!'" I thought that was interesting.

Abe: *At the least!*

Ramesh: Muktananda said, "You have created a problem. You solve it!" There is a book. Have you read the book? It is a very good book, *Holy Madness*, written by Feuerstein. He was a member of the intimate group of Da Free John. In this book he deals with a lot of gurus. Again, it is written with astonishing objectivity. Muktananda features prominently in it, as does Rajneesh. And in that book it says that Rajneesh held J. Krishnamurti in high regard. And J. Krishnamurti is reported to have said, "What Rajneesh is saying and doing is criminal. Somebody should do something about it, about Rajneesh." *(laughter)*

Abe: *Perhaps you remember how Vivekananda summed up the situation? He said, "Of all the people who set out on the spiritual path, eighty-five per cent are liars, about twelve per cent go crazy, and just three per cent get something out of it."*

Ramesh: Yes, three per cent. That is what I told you the other day. That is what the *Bhagavad Gita* says: "Out of a thousand people, I hardly find one seeker. And out of a thousand seekers, hardly one knows Me in principle."

Abe: *Well, I am glad that you managed to gather around you those people who fit into this three per cent!* (laughter)

Ramesh: Hundreds of people don't come here. That is just as well. I wouldn't have any room for them.
 So, you were saying, John?

John: *What was I saying?* (laughter)

Ramesh: Apart from Muktananda; you left Muktananda. Then what did you do?

John: *Well, I got married.*

Ramesh: Then you got rid of the madness — temporarily, anyway.

John: *I had a lot of love for Muktananda. I learned a lot from him. He was very charismatic.*

Ramesh: So I believe.

John: *Then I went to various teachers. As I said, one of them was Mrs. Tweedy. She was a very genuine teacher. She used to have a* sufi *master in India. I forgot his name. I saw her four or five years ago. She does dream work as well, the psychological aspect of it.*

Ramesh: You said she is a *sufi* teacher. Dream work is not really part of the *sufi* teaching, or is it?

John: *No, I think it was her own interest that led her to this.*

Ramesh: Talking about the *sufi* teaching, did Mrs. Tweedy say what the core of the *sufi* teaching was? What is the core of the *sufi* teaching? I am interested in it, that's why I am asking the question.

John: *Hmm... I don't know actually what it is.* (laughter) *It was quite a mysterious thing with her. She was very much into this thing of the lineage of the guru. She used to say that she didn't do anything, everything was done by her guru. And that most things happened during the night, in dreams. And she used to talk a lot about the Beloved, and His love. The core of it I don't know. It was very emotional.*

Dominica: *She wrote a book called* Chasm of Fire. *Something she says in that book puzzles me. She makes her teacher say, "You can't really get rid of pride. There is still pride in me."*

Ramesh: Oh, her teacher says that?

Dominica: *I thought that after enlightenment has happened, there cannot be any pride left, or can there?*

Ramesh: It is interesting what the different teachers believe enlightenment is. I wish all the other teachers would have been asked this question. I wonder if their answers would correspond with what I call enlightenment? My idea of enlightenment is extremely simple. Enlightenment is the total annihilation of the "me" as an individual doer, as an individual entity with free will. So, that means any "body," any "person," being enlightened is a contradiction in terms. No "body," no "person" can become enlightened. Enlightenment is an event that happens when the sense of personal doership totally disappears. When that sense has disappeared, where does the question of pride come in?

Abe: *The body-mind mechanism might still be subject to pride, but there is no acceptance of delivery, or, as you say, no sense of doership when this pride arises.*

Ramesh: But pride is not something which arises like anger, a thought, a feeling. By definition, pride would mean taking delivery of some action which has happened as "my" action. Because it is felt to be my action, "I" feel proud.

And in fact, I often ask: what is Rajneesh's, or Krishnamurti's, basic teaching? People find it very difficult to tell me. If somebody asks, "What is Ramesh's teaching?", the answer, to me, is very simple. All that Ramesh says is that everything that happens is part of the functioning of Totality or, in other words, God's Will. And if that is accepted, then there is no individual doer. Lord

Buddha said the same thing: "Deeds are done, events happen, but there is no individual doer thereof." That is my basic teaching.

So, there is no question of "me" doing anything. My whole point is: how can a feeling of guilt or sin or frustration arise? How can a feeling of pride arise?

Abe: *One could also ask how any feeling could arise after enlightenment? At the same time, you point out that Maharaj had a very fiery nature. He was given to anger. But he didn't feel the anger was his doing. I think that is what you want to say.*

Ramesh: But in the case of the aforementioned book, the person says he is proud. Pride didn't leave him. Anger arises in Maharaj, but the anger doesn't get hold of him. A sense of pleasure may arise, but that sense of pleasure doesn't get hold of me. So, a sense of pleasure may arise, but that sense of pleasure can never be associated with pride. Pride is essentially based on the individual sense of doership.

Abe: *Oh, I see your distinction. So, there is an essential internal contradiction between the understanding of your teaching and pride.*

Ramesh: Yes.

Shiva: *But doesn't anger arise when something happens other than what is wanted or expected? When something goes against my personal preferences?*

Ramesh: Anger is a thought, a feeling that arises, over which you have no control.

Shiva: *Anger doesn't just arise. It arises in relation to something. It arises as a reaction.*

Ramesh: No. How does a thought arise?

Shiva: *But anger is a feeling.*

Ramesh: No. Anger is a reaction of the brain to an outside event. Anger doesn't arise. Anger is the reaction of the brain to an outside impulse — to something you see, or hear, or to a thought. And the reaction of the brain to that outside event is anger. And that reaction is strictly according to the programming of the particular body-mind organism.

Abe: *I happen to like the point Shiva is making. Anger, as a reaction of the brain to a thought, arises because of the sense that what is happening should not be happening, according to my preferences. Because there are preferences programmed in a body-mind organism, and because external events are not corresponding to these preferences, something arises in this body-mind organism which is called anger.*

Ramesh: Quite right. So, these preferences are not the preferences of an individual being. They exist because of the programming of the body-mind organism. Over that programming the organism had no control. The body-mind organism was conceived and created with certain natural characteristics — called programming — which include preferences.

Abe: *Does this explanation satisfy your question, Shiva?*

Shiva: *Oh yes.*

Ramesh: The preferences are not "his" preferences, they are preferences of the body-mind organism. So, having preferences means a totally different thing from judging somebody else's actions according to your preferences. In that case, an individual judges the action of some other person. That is judging. But when the actions of somebody else are merely witnessed, then there is no judging. And the actions of this body-mind organism are also witnessed. So, you don't judge actions which happen through somebody else, nor do you judge your own. Because the basic understanding is that they are not "my" actions, they are not "your" actions.

25.2 "Lineage" Means: "My Lineage is the Best Lineage"

Ynes: *I read the book* Master Key To Self-Realization, *by Siddharameshwar Maharaj, which contains some of his talks given to seekers in the early part of the century. The book was compiled and published by Ranjit Maharaj, who is still alive and who lives in Bombay. Ranjit Maharaj and Nisargadatta Maharaj were co-disciples of Siddharameshwar Maharaj. Reading it changed my idea of* sampradaya, *because there seems to be not much common ground between Nisargadatta Maharaj's teaching and the teaching of his guru. I can't actually make out much of what Siddharameshwar Maharaj has to say.*

Ramesh: *Sampradaya* means lineage. In my opinion, some gurus give an undue importance to lineage. There is a lineage, but who sends you into that lineage? It is God or Totality. Attaching too much importance to the lineage is a problem. You will then say all other lineages are not as good as your lineage. The moment you say "lineage," it means "my lineage. My religion is better than your religion. My guru is better than your guru. My lineage is better than your lineage."

Ynes: *Yes, I understand what you are saying.*

Ramesh: And, to the best of my knowledge, Maharaj did not attach too much importance to lineage. In my opinion, that is because there was full realization in his case, and he knew "he" didn't choose his lineage.

Ynes: *It must be destined as to who your guru is, isn't it?*

Ramesh: That is correct. It is your destiny at a particular moment to be at a certain place with a certain guru, who has a certain lineage. But it can be destined that the seeker is taken from one guru to the next. If that happens to a seeker, the guru who attaches too much importance to the lineage will tell him that he was disloyal to the lineage. My question is, who has been disloyal to what lineage? A body-mind organism has merely been sent by the same Power to that place where it had to be at that particular time.

Ynes: *I found some books by Wei Wu Wei which are much closer to my likings.*

Ramesh: *Sampradaya* is essentially a Hindu doctrine of lineage, to which too much importance has been given: "My religion is better than yours, and my guru is better than your guru." And that is what causes these religious wars.

Ynes: *I believe you don't have a religion.*

Ramesh: "Patriotism" is wonderful word. But basically it means that my country is better than your country. Patriotism leads to international wars.

Abe: *What seems essentially to happen in a religious war is that a person says, "In the interest of the all-merciful God, it is necessary that I kill you!"*

Ramesh: Yes. Literally and accurately, that is so. The murderer of the Israeli Prime Minister Rabin has said, "I killed him under God's orders." Strictly and literally, what he said is correct. If everything happens by God's Will, you could interpret it that anything that happens is by God's orders.

Abe: *Nobody, really, would like God's job! In a war between Germany and France, the German and the French soldiers would pray to God at the same moment, "Dear God, please kill the enemy and save our soldiers." So, God has a tough job!* (laughter)

Ramesh: So, who wants to be God?!

Abe: *Well, there is still the temptation...* (laughter)

Ramesh: It's like having the ambition to be the CEO of your company. So, in phenomenality, the boss is God. So, you want to be God, you see. *(laughter)* And that is what the thinking mind says.

Dominica: *Ramesh, is the feeling that you are the best guru an obstacle to enlightenment?*

Ramesh: Indeed, yes. It is an obstacle to enlightenment to consider your guru as superior to any other guru.

Dominica: *Is it also an obstacle to consider the teaching of the guru as superior to other gurus' teachings?*

Ramesh: The teaching is something which happens. The basic teaching in all religions has always been the same thing. The Universality, the Unicity, the One Supreme Power, is the basis of every religion. But look what the interpreters have done to the basic teaching!

Abe: *I think where Dominica gets confused is that she thinks that Ramesh is teaching, but the teaching is actually happening impersonally.*

Ramesh: Curiously, it is interesting what J. Krishnamurti has to say about this. His very close associate, one Mrs. Pupul Jaikkar, has written a biography on him. She writes that she asked Krishnamurti on his deathbed, in one of his last moments, if he had a final wish, or something final to say. His answer was, "Don't let my teaching perish!" When I read that, I thought, "Whose teaching? What teaching? And where is the question of any teaching perishing? If it is to perish, why not let it perish?" That was my reaction to reading it, you see. If it is God's Will, it will perish; otherwise, not. But that is what she said he said.

Abe: *Well, if J. Krishnamurti were listening to you now, he might say, "I take back what I said."* (laughter)

Ramesh: Or, Krishnamurti would probably say, "What I am reported to have said is not what I meant." *(laughter)*

Abe: *He actually didn't seem to be a happy man.*

Ramesh: He was not! Did you ever participate in the talks in Santa Barbara?

Abe: *I heard some of his talks in San Francisco and in Ojai. If anybody asked him a question, he would get angry.*

Ramesh: Yes, he would get particularly angry if asked questions about particular subjects. Krishnamurti had some ticks. During my very first seminar in Hollywood, forty per cent of the participants were psychotherapists. One of them asked me what I thought of psychotherapy. I replied that for a physical illness there is the physician, and for a mental illness there is psychotherapy. When I said this, a sigh of relief went through the room. They told me that Krishnamurti would fly into a rage every time psychotherapy was mentioned. Consciously or unconsciously, Krishnamurti didn't like psychotherapists, because he himself had a psychotherapist for twenty years. He underwent psychotherapy for twenty years.

Abe: *Annie Besant?*

Ramesh: No. It was a man called... — in Santa Barbara, he was my host — Ben...?

Abe: *Ben Weininger?*

Ramesh: Yes, Ben Weininger.

Abe: *Ben Weininger was J. Krishnamurti's psychotherapist?*

Ramesh: Yes, he told me the story himself. Ben told me that he was Krishnamurti's psychotherapist for twenty years. Ben said that Krishnamurti would go into a state of absolute terror before the talks. And for that reason, he went to Ben Weininger.

Abe: *He had stage fright. Did he get over it?*

Ramesh: Ben Weininger's words were, "I think I helped him. I treated Krishnamurti for twenty years."

Abe: *This is the funniest gossip I have heard in years!*

Ramesh: Ben Weininger was our host in Santa Barbara. He was very ill. He was dying, and he knew it. He made his wife write to me, calling me to his home. I asked her, "Why did you invite me to come to your house when Ben is so ill?" She said, "Ben wanted you to be here." And he died in the hospital during the time I was staying in his house. Before he died, he said, "I am glad you are here. It has done me a world of good."

Abe: *But the notion that Krishnamurti was in psychotherapy for twenty years will carry me through for a long time!*

Ramesh: You old gossip! *(laughter)*

Abe: *You're not doing so badly either, I would say!* (Abe laughs really hard)

Ramesh: Gossip is the very breath of life! *(laughter)* But this is not hearsay. Krishnamurti underwent psychotherapy. He was frightened to the point of terror before every single talk. That's what Ben told me. But once Krishnamurti started talking, he would be remarkable!

Abe: *This is the first time I have experienced* satsang *in the form of gossip. I am wondering how it is experienced by people who perhaps expected something different here this morning? I don't know.*

CHAPTER 26

26.1 "I Am Sorry to Say You are not Enlightened"

Ramesh: Are you coming as a group?

Dorothy: *Yes, we are a group coming from Satya Sai Baba's ashram in Puttaparthi. One of us rang you on the phone. The group visits India's holy places, ashrams, and gurus. In the past six weeks, we have been to the Ramanashramam, Aurobindo's ashram in Pondicherry, and many other places. The last place we visited was Satya Sai Baba's ashram. And Bombay is the end of our tour, so the journey ends with you. Tomorrow we will fly back to the West.*

Ramesh: Is the whole group from Scotland?

Dorothy: *No, we are from all over the world. But it is the Findhorn community which organizes this tour every year. The person who originally rang you was unable to come today.*

Ramesh: You see, that is curious. So, even being here is not in your hands.

Dorothy: *That is true. That was not planned.*

Ramesh: That was planned, but the one who planned it is not here! Now, how long were you in Puttaparthi, Dorothy?

Dorothy: *Six days.*

Ramesh: What did you do during those six days?

Dorothy: *A lot of meditation, a lot of* darshan.

Ramesh: What do you mean by a lot of *darshan*?

Dorothy: *What do I mean by* darshan? (laughter)

Ramesh: Well, you see something and when you have seen it, you have had *darshan*. What did you go to Puttaparthi for? What is the group of fourteen people interested in? Does the group have a common interest, or does it want just to tour India?

Dorothy: *The Findhorn Foundation is a spiritual community which runs different educational programs. The six-week trip to India is one of those programs. We are visiting sacred sights in India. The two group leaders are Sai Baba devotees. Both know the book* I Am That, *and they heard that you were living in Bombay. One of them, Angela, rang you up. And here we are — without her.*

Ramesh: *Darshan* takes only a few seconds. Now you have had your *darshan* with me. What else can I do for you? I mean, is the group really seeking something? What is the group basically supposed to do or achieve? For what purpose was the group formed, other than for visiting holy places? That can be done by tourists.

Dorothy: *The group forms the context in which each individual mirrors itself. Each individual has presumably come to a stage in their life where they are faced with many questions regarding the meaning and purpose of their life.*

Ramesh: Let's start from there. Do you have any questions?

Bruno: *Since I am a newcomer in matters of spirituality, could you explain the meaning of* darshan *a bit more, please?*

Ramesh: *Darshan* means visiting. You visit somebody and you see him. Seeing somebody is *darshan*.

Bruno: *Then I had* darshan *with the taxi driver this morning.* (laughter)

Ramesh: Indeed, that is quite correct. And the taxi driver had *darshan* with you. *Darshan* simply means seeing somebody's body-mind organism. That's all that *darshan* means. But in the spiritual world, it is turned into a big thing.

Sarah: *Could you elaborate a bit more on this topic, because some of the people we were travelling with on this journey believe that, having had* darshan *with Sai Baba, their body-mind organisms were affected for the better. They also seem to believe that, by being in the presence of Sai Baba, their chances for enlightenment have drastically improved.*

Ramesh: Enlightenment could happen or could not happen through Sai Baba's presence. I will tell you about an incident which happened during Ramana Maharshi's life. A woman brought her sick child to Ramana Maharshi. She sat there in front of him and prayed silently for the recovery of the child's health. The child did get well, and the woman thanked Ramana for curing her child. To this, Ramana Maharshi replied, "I didn't cure your child. There was no thought or intention of curing your child. It was the destiny of the child to be cured in my presence. If my presence did something, it had nothing to do with me."

Darshan might or might not produce a change. It will depend on the destiny of the body-mind organism who goes to have a *darshan*. If a thousand people have *darshan* with Sai Baba, the *darshan* will not have the same effect on all the thousand people.

Sarah: *In that case, it might be easy for those people to whom nothing happened to get caught in the illusion that they did something wrong, or that they were not as blessed as the ones who had special experiences.*

Ramesh: Do you mean to say that someone who didn't get the benefit of the *darshan* could easily be trapped in thinking, "My intention, my sincerity, or my integrity was not intense enough for blessings to be bestowed on me?"

Sarah: *For me, the dilemma is that I am not a devotee of Sai Baba. My own understanding has got me to a point where I believe that I am enlightened, because I don't want to search anymore. I no longer think there is anything to search for. I am trying to live moment by moment. And still there are times when the mind gets caught in the illusion that one can somehow get something through devotion, because of what Sai Baba appears to give to some people.*

Ramesh: If enlightenment has happened, then there will be no one who thinks he or she is living his or her life.

Sarah: *These moments are moments, right?*

Ramesh: Yes.

Sarah: *Sometimes this is so, and sometimes it is not.*

Ramesh: As long as that flip-flop — that experience of coming and going — occurs, the total understanding hasn't happened yet. There are just moments.

You see, different people may have different ideas about enlightenment. My idea of enlightenment is the total annihilation of the individual entity with a sense of personal doership. Enlightenment means the total acceptance and understanding that I do not exist as an independent doer, that everything happens by God's Will. If there is no entity with a sense of doership, how can one say: "I live my life this way or that way?" If you think you live your life this way or that way, then I am afraid to say that enlightenment has not happened yet, because there is still an entity which considers herself to be living her life a certain way.

"You" cannot be enlightened

CHAPTER 27

27.1 Thought is Connected with Consciousness and not with the Body-Mind Organism

John: *You said that what we consider our action is actually the reaction of the brain of a body-mind entity to an outside impulse, like a thought or a sense object; and that this reaction is according to the entity's programmed characteristics, which consist of genes and environmental conditioning.*

Ramesh: Yes, that's correct.

John: *I can understand the brain responding to a sense which perceives an object. That would amount to some sort of a physical process. But you say a thought comes from "outside." What do you mean by "outside"?*

Ramesh: Wait a minute. Say, you are sitting there on your chair and you have no thought. Then you suddenly get up and have a drink of water. What made that action possible?

John: *I would say it is the response of the organism to the sense of thirst which arose in it.*

Ramesh: It is the response of the brain to a thought which appeared, saying, "I am feeling thirsty."

John: *Well, why couldn't it be awareness, instead of the thought, which becomes aware that the organism is thirsty?*

Ramesh: The thought is the awareness. That's why the thought comes from the awareness which is outside the body-mind organism. By "outside" I mean to say that the brain cannot create a thought. The brain can only react to a thought.

John: *Would it not be true to say that the thought is part of the inner process, but that it is unconscious; that consciousness is needed in order to realize a thought?*

Ramesh: That is precisely what I am denying, John. I am saying that the thought is not part of an inner process of the body-mind organism. The thought comes from outside and the brain reacts to that thought, or to something which is sensed, and sets the thinking — which is involvement — in motion.

John: *But the brain could respond to the state of thirst in the organism and go and get a glass of water. It wouldn't even need a thought.*

Ramesh: No. The brain responds to a state in the body-mind organism. And that response is the thought that there is thirst. Look, the brain of a man in a coma cannot react to hunger or thirst. Why? Because there is no consciousness present in it. This example demonstrates that it is consciousness which makes the brain react to an impulse. Mind you, the thought comes from Consciousness. Thought is connected and associated with consciousness, and not with the inner body. I repeat, thought is connected with consciousness and not with the body. Thought is not part of the body-mind mechanism, because under sedation or in a state of coma the brain doesn't work.

John: *Couldn't it be that the brain is working, and that the awareness of the brain working is thought?*

Ramesh: Awareness by whom? The brain itself is the starting point for all your sensations. For instance, what is pain? It is the brain which reacts to an impulse and registers pain. If the brain doesn't exist, or is not functioning, then there is no question of any pain whatsoever. It is through the brain that the pain is made evident. The experience of pain arises only because the brain exists to register it.

John: *But there has to be consciousness for having the experience of pain.*

Ramesh: That is correct. The basis of all thought is Consciousness.

John: *Looking at this as a scientist, I can feel that it is the brain that is working, but the awareness of the brain must come from Consciousness. The feeling of being conscious, of being aware, gives us the feeling that awareness is coming from outside. The scientist can establish the existence of the working of the mind, but he has not yet been able to discover where the awareness is coming from.*

Ramesh: That is correct. Consciousness does not get into the body. The body is part of the manifestation, created by Consciousness. The scientist has been wondering all these years about how consciousness gets into the body. Goswami is the first scientist to declare — in his book, *The Self-Aware Universe* — that the ground of everything is Consciousness, and not matter. The orthodox scientists are not happy about what he says.

John: *Even if it is true that the whole manifestation, including thoughts, is a product of Consciousness — including the phenomenal process of billions of years — a thought which I have at any one time in the phenomenal world is the result of something which*

How thinking gets created *(According to R. S. Balsekar)*

happened in phenomenality before that thought came up. A thought is not coming from something outside which is going to happen ten years from now.

Ramesh: Wait a minute. The reaction of the brain to that thought is based on the conditioning of the body-mind organism. If the same thought occurs to five different people, the reaction of each brain to the thought will be different, depending on the conditioning of each programmed body-mind organism.

Madhukar: *A thought of a "car" could not have occurred to a person a hundred years ago, because the car did not exist at that time yet. What John is pointing out is that the thought "car" can only occur once the object "car" has appeared in phenomenality.*

Ramesh: Any thought which occurs is bound to be a thought about phenomenality, about something in the universe. And what is more, a thought which comes to a particular body-mind organism depends on the organism's programming. Because Totality wanted the theory of relativity be given to human-

kind — for better or worse — it created a body-mind organism called Albert Einstein, who has gone on record to say that the equation came to him from the outside. In his humility, he said that he did not discover the equation. The equation was there all the time, but the body-mind organism with the receptivity to receive it was only created with Albert Einstein. His body-mind organism was created exactly for that purpose.

John: *And the brain of Albert Einstein had to be in a particular state at the very second that the thought of relativity came to him.*

Ramesh: Sure. How do such discussions help you, John? I would like to know that. Having received an answer to this question, John's thinking mind will create another problem and ask the next question.

John: *I am slowly chipping away.*

Ramesh: No, no, no, you are adding to the bundle of problems. Chipping away would happen if you could accept the simple truth that whatever happens is God's Will. The more problems the thinking mind creates, the stronger it becomes.

John: *I have only one more question to ask, but I will save it for later. In the meantime, I'll work on the answers you have given me just now.*

Ramesh: You may ask your questions. These questions made John come to visit me. The mind is not capable of getting all the answers to the questions it creates. The source of everything is Consciousness. And Consciousness, therefore, is the source of the mind. And the mind cannot know its source. It is the thinking mind which is asking questions, but the thinking mind cannot be prevented from doing so, either. Thoughts and thinking are two different things. The thinking mind will continue to operate as long as it is supposed to. It will cause misery so long as the acceptance is not there. "I think this and I think that" — that's what John thinks. What I am saying is that John's thinking, and whatever happens, is part of the functioning of Totality, or God's Will. The thinking mind will gradually disappear only if it is God's Will. Being miserable for a certain length of time is the destiny of that organism, which no power on earth can change.

CHAPTER 28

28.1 "I Love Food, so I Strive to Be a Mahabhogi"

Bruno: *What is a* jnani? *What does the word mean?*

Ramesh: It means "the one who knows." That means he is a sage. *Jnana* means understanding or knowledge.

Bruno: *I was impressed when I heard that a* jnani *enjoys a meal much more intensely than an ordinary person. Do you know what I mean?*

Ramesh: Yes. That impressed you?

Bruno: *Very much, because I like to have good food. You can see it just by looking at my size!* (laughter)

Ramesh: If you enjoy your food now, you will enjoy it even more when you are enlightened!

Bruno: *That's what I want! Is that possible?*

Ramesh: Certainly it is possible. I will explain to you why.

Bruno: *I am looking forward to enlightenment.* (laughter)

Ramesh: The *jnani* enjoying his food much more than the ordinary person can be explained by the fact that the *jnani's* thinking mind doesn't come in. If you are enjoying your food, the thinking mind will come in and say, "Think about the food that you are eating."

Bruno: *But I don't think that while eating.*

Ramesh: Then you are a *jnani*!

Bruno: *I have no idea about that. I just enjoy the food while I am eating.*

Ramesh: I know. But when you eat, don't you have any thoughts? You just concentrate on eating so much that you don't have any thoughts?

Bruno: *Yes.*

Ramesh: Yes, what? Yes, you have thoughts?

Bruno: *Yes, I just eat.*

Ramesh: You don't have any thoughts while eating?

Bruno: *Almost no thoughts. I just eat. I never thought about it. I enjoy it so much. It tastes so good. It is so well prepared. Why should I think?*

Ramesh: When you are eating, you don't close your eyes and eat, or do you?

Bruno: *Why should I close my eyes when I eat? If I do, I will miss my mouth with the spoon.*

Ramesh: During eating, you must be seeing something, you must be hearing something.

Bruno: *Yes.*

Ramesh: And if you hear something or see something, isn't there any reaction to that happening?

Bruno: *Generally, I don't think so.*

Ramesh: Then you are a very, very special case, Bruno. I am not wearing a hat, otherwise I would take it off to you. (*laughter*)

You see, a sage is described in traditional *Advaita* language as a *mahabhogi*, a super-enjoyer. Two people are having a dinner. The dinner is very good. So, the sage really enjoys the dinner and says, "This is a wonderful dinner." Contrary to the sage, the ordinary person may say, "This is a wonderful dinner. I wonder when I will have one like it again? I may not have one like it again for a whole year!" The ordinary person's enjoyment has become less because of the thinking mind. On the other hand — for the sage — the thinking mind is not there. That's why he really enjoys the dinner much more. That's why the sage is called the super-enjoyer. Enlightenment doesn't turn the body-mind organism into a vegetable. The sage still enjoys. But if the sage is sick, he will also feel pain in his body. So, enlightenment is nothing but a change in attitude.

George: *In the act of sex, a person usually disappears for a moment. Is that the same kind of disappearance that you talk about?*

Ramesh: It is the same kind of disappearance. Because in the sex experience,

*super-enjoyer, the sage

The life of a mahabhogi*—minus the experiencer

there is no... your name is?

George: *George.*

Ramesh: There is no George. George comes back later when he says, "That was a wonderful experience." So, George is not present. And when George is not present, the "I-Am" is present. In deep sleep, George is not present, the "I-Am" is present. Frankly, it doesn't need to be a sex experience. It can be any experience. It can be sheer terror.

George: *Or getting engrossed in a job, or eating.*

Ramesh: Certainly.

George: *I think you could lose yourself in eating for a moment. Could you do that, and then come back?*

Ramesh: Not for just a moment. When you are deeply engrossed, you are there for long moments. That is what I call the working mind. In *Consciousness Speaks* I make a distinction between the working mind and the thinking mind. When you are working, and the total attention is on what you are doing, at that time the working mind is there.

George: *Also in playing a game of pool or golf.*

Ramesh: In any game you are playing. Whether it is a game you are playing, or it is work you are doing, when you totally concentrate on what you are doing, the working mind is in operation.

28.2 When All Questioning Stops: The Most Powerful Understanding

India

Wendel: *I have a question about the understanding. When we come to visit you, we hopefully increase our intellectual understanding. But in meeting you, the teacher, one-to-one, is there an increase in intuitive understanding?*

Ramesh: It will be so if that is the destiny of this body-mind organism, Wendel. Are you asking about the effect of listening to my teaching? In somebody, the listening might hit right through to the bottom of the pit in a sudden flash. The deepest possible understanding has happened, which can have a tremendous physical reaction, like laughter or tears.

Wendel: *OK, I follow this. Please comment on Ramana Maharshi, who often said that his most powerful teaching happens through silence.*

Ramesh: His teachings are most powerful when all questioning stops. Ramana Maharshi would sit down quietly, or lay down. That is the moment when the understanding is the deepest. That is what he meant. All questions asked and answered are only on an intellectual level. The deepest understanding comes or exists when there are no questions. And what he meant by silence is not physical silence, but mental silence. And the physical silence leads to mental silence.

While others ask questions, someone like you might be quiet. Then, Wendel will be quiet and in silence, and no attention will be paid by the thinking mind to the questions and answers. Ramana Maharshi speaks about that mental silence. When the thinking mind is not absorbed by the conversation which is going on here, the real understanding is taking place.

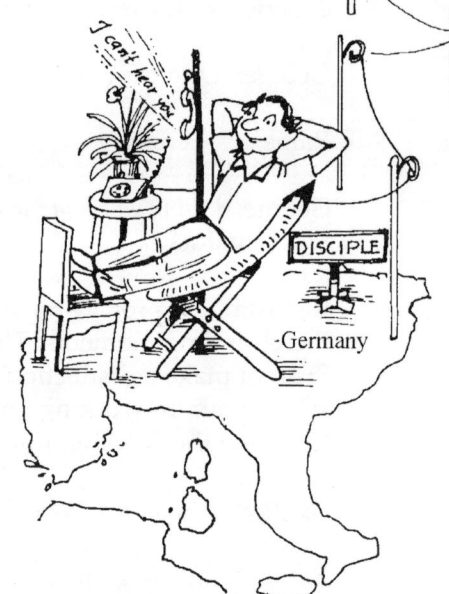

The most powerful teaching

28.3 Initiation of the Thinking Process — an External Impulse; Cutting Short The Thinking Process — Understanding

Albert: *I would like to clarify something we were talking about earlier. Can the thought, "I am thirsty," be related to an outside impulse?*

Ramesh: If a thought comes not as part of the thinking mind — meaning that you are quiet, doing nothing, nothing is happening and the thought comes, "I am thirsty" — then it is a thought from outside.

Albert: *Were you not indicating this morning that if the mind is blank and a thought comes, then it is a thought from outside? What happens if the mind is not blank?*

Ramesh: No. I didn't say when the mind is blank and a thought appears...

Albert: *...not blank; but say, doing nothing...*

Ramesh: No, I didn't say that. Wait a minute! When you are not doing anything, in that state of non-doing the first thought that occurs is not your creation — that's what I said. That past thought comes from outside.

Albert: *But a thought can also appear while you are doing something.*

Ramesh: If you are busy doing something and a thought interrupts, it comes from the thinking mind.

Glenn: *If I am running for the bus and my thinking mind is totally occupied with worry about catching it, and all of a sudden a totally different thought enters my mind, then...*

Ramesh: ... that thought comes from the "outside."

Glenn: *While the thinking mind is operating, every thought is somehow associated with a previous thought. Is that right?*

Ramesh: The thinking mind is nothing but one thought leading to another. But the thinking begins with the reaction of the brain to an outside impulse.

Madhukar: *A thought has no past and no future. On the other hand, thinking happens within the frame of time.*

Ramesh: Quite right. Thinking is horizontal.

Albert: *At the very moment in which there is no duration, we can call it a thought from outside. It can be that I am running for the bus, and while doing so I can receive the thought, "I am thirsty," right?*

Ramesh: No. It is the other way around. I don't care if you call it an outside impulse or a thought. Is it from outside or not? That's the question.

Albert: *We are examining whether it is the brain, the entity, which is creating the thought, or whether the thought is coming from outside.*

Ramesh: The entity or the brain in that entity — in that individual body-mind organism — cannot create a thought.

Glenn: *But the body-mind organism can create thinking, right?*

Ramesh: The reaction of the brain to that outside thought will lead to thinking. A thought occurs, the brain reacts to that thought, and that reaction leads to horizontal thinking.

Madhukar: *We could say that it is an outside thought that starts the thinking process, and it is the understanding which cuts off the thinking process.*

The beginning and the end of the thinking process

Ramesh: That's what I said earlier. Horizontal thinking is involvement by a personal "me"-entity. Involvement cannot be cut off by your watching the involvement. It can only be cut off by an outside agency. You can call it God's Will or Totality or understanding or destiny. During involvement in thinking there is the sudden realization that "I am unnecessarily involved," and it gets cut off at that point. At what point this sudden realization occurs is not in your hands. And the sudden realization is not John's creation. To understand this is important. The sudden realization just arises.

That's why I say, "Consciousness in action is understanding, and understanding in action produces the sudden realization that you are involved." John's involvement cannot produce something which can cut it off. The cutting off is outside of John's control.

28.4 "Fish or Chicken, Sir?" Are they in your Mind, or on the Menu, or on the Plate in Front of you Now? Working Mind — Thinking Mind

John: *If the thought comes, "I want to drink water, I am thirsty..."*

Ramesh: Quite right. Proceed! Wait a minute, no, no. You are on the right line. A thought comes, "I am thirsty, I want to drink water." Then two things can happen. One, the thought gets converted into action and you go and drink a glass of water. But instead of doing that, the thinking mind can say, "Yes, I am thirsty. Shall I have a beer or a lemonade, or just plain water?" That is the thinking mind.

John: *But it would be the working mind if you needed to make the decision, "Am I going to work this afternoon or not?", because that decision-making is just part of the functioning of the body-mind organism. If I needed to go to work this afternoon, it would be better to drink water than beer.*

Ramesh: How is your needing to go to work concerned with your thirst, John? We are talking about the thought coming to you that you are thirsty.

John: *You said it was the thinking mind, and I am saying it could be the working mind.*

Ramesh: Yes, it is the thinking mind which says, "Shall I do this? Shall I do that? Shall I drink wine? Shall I drink beer?"

John: *But isn't it the working mind which makes the choice?*

Ramesh: The working mind will make the choice. You are right, when I have the beer, the wine, the lemonade, and the water in front of me. Then it will be the working mind. But what is the point of this question? It can be either the working mind or the thinking mind. And I told you exactly where the working mind comes in: when I have before me these four drinks. When I have the menu before me and I have to decide what I shall have, it is the working mind which makes the decision; because of which, I will go through the menu. And I go a step further. The decision I come to regarding what I have will depend on the programming of the body-mind organism. I can choose between vegetables, chicken, fish, etc. If the conditioning is that I am a vegetarian, I will not go through the non-veg. section of the menu. I have the choice to go through that part of the menu, but will I go through it? I won't go through it. Even that depends on the programming of the body-mind organism. But if the programming says, "I don't like fish. Fish gives me acidity," then the decision is already made. You will take chicken. But it is the working mind which has the choice. And the choice is being made by the working mind.

An executive in a firm has to make a decision between alternatives. So, the

The choices are conditioned by the programming of the body-mind organism and by the time of the day

Enlightenment—in the mind, on the menu, or right in front of you now

working mind will weigh the consequences of each alternative and then make a choice. But it is understood that the choice might not be converted into action, because that is not in my hands. The consequences of my choice are not in my hands. With that understanding, I make my choices.

Alain: *The choice is not in my hands, either.*

Ramesh: No. The choice is in your hands to the extent that you can only weigh the consequences and then make your decision. Weighing the consequences and making a decision is done by the working mind. And even making the choice may not happen. Suppose you are the chief executive of a big company, who has six assistants. You have to make an important decision. You call together your six assistants, and three of them will tell you to do this, while the other three will tell you to do that.
   You are right, the final decision is not in your hands. So, whether you toss a coin, or whatever decision you make, depends on the destiny of the person making the choice, and on the people who will be affected by your decision.

Alain: *So, there is no choice at all. There merely seems to be a choice.*

Ramesh: Ultimately, therefore, what is to happen will happen. In between — the process of making a choice or not — is merely the mechanics of it.

Antonia: Isn't it true that if there is acceptance that I have no free will then nothing else matters anymore? It doesn't matter if it is the thinking mind, the working mind, or whatever. For me, all these discussions make no sense anymore.

Ramesh: You are absolutely right, Antonia.

Antonia: *And even that doesn't matter anymore.*

Ramesh: You are quite right, because when you truly accept that everything that happens is God's Will, then the rest of it is just conceptualizing. It is just conceptualizing. But that conceptualizing, and the resulting useless discussion, is still part of God's Will. That's why I am not blaming John for his insistence in asking questions, because that's God's Will. And, therefore, it is happening. Otherwise, it wouldn't happen.

Diana: *I admire your patience.*

Ramesh: If I know that the discussion which is taking place here is not John's problem, but part of God's Will, how can I be impatient with John?

Dominica: *Unless it were your nature to be impatient.*

Ramesh: Even if my nature were to be impatient I wouldn't be impatient, because my talking here is concerned with the working mind. You are quite right, a thought of impatience might arise if that is in the nature of the person. You are quite right. And yet, as far as the teaching goes, as far as this body-mind organism's function as a teacher is concerned, the impatience very rarely comes up.

Jan: *When there are no questions, there is witnessing going on. When someone asks a question and you react to it and answer it, where does witnessing come in?*

Ramesh: It is a fair question, and the answer is very simple. When there is something to witness, witnessing happens. When there is nothing to witness, the state is non-witnessing. So, from non-witnessing to witnessing is like the automatic changing of gears.

Jan: *But when somebody asks a question, the working mind is working and you are answering the question.*

Ramesh: Quite right.

John: *Where is the sense of "me" then? I am sure there isn't a sense of "me."*

Ramesh: No, there isn't. If the working mind is functioning, it is the working mind which is functioning. There is no question of "I," or of anybody.

John: *So, where then does the witnessing come in, in that situation?*

Ramesh: When there is one individual answering another individual's question, there will be separation. But when questions being asked and answers being provided are totally accepted as being one movement, one event, then that movement is witnessed. If there is an individual who says, "I must answer that question; it is up to me to satisfy that person," then the "me" is involved. Then, the questioning and answering are seen as two parts of one movement, the conversation that is going on.

John: *I really don't understand yet where the witnessing comes in. Just as an artist is totally involved in his work, so you are totally involved in answering questions. Isn't that correct?*

Ramesh: What you are asking concerns the working mind. The only comparative concept to the working mind is the thinking mind. The witnessing and working mind are different concepts altogether. The two are not related.

John: *What I am asking is, "Where is there room for witnessing in the event of your talking?"*

Ramesh: There is room for witnessing if there is something to be witnessed.

Wendel: *Are you saying, Ramesh, that there is no witnessing when the working mind is working.*

Ramesh: What I am saying, Wendel, is that the concept of witnessing is irrelevant.

Wendel: *During the time the working mind is in operation?*

Ramesh: So, the concepts which are relevant are the working mind and the thinking mind. The concept of witnessing is concerned only with the concept of involvement.

John: *So, witnessing is really just the opposition to the thinking mind?*

Ramesh: Yes, sure. Thinking mind is involvement. When there is no involvement and there is something to witness, then that is witnessed.

John: *Now you are talking to us here, and the working mind is functioning. The question of witnessing does not arise while you are talking to us.*

Ramesh: Witnessing will arise only to the extent I have just explained, you see. The thinking mind and the involvement will come in if I consider that one individual is discussing with another individual. The questions and the answers are one movement, one event, for me. So, that one movement — the discussion — is being witnessed. In any case, your question is purely theoretical.

John: *I see.*

Ramesh: The problem is that if you truly understood the teaching, there would be no need to ask, "Is it like this or is it like that?"

CHAPTER 29

29.1 My Mission Or Poonjaji's Mission? — Gangaji

Barbara: *I know a lady teacher. Her name is Gangaji. She is a teacher in the lineage of Ramana Maharshi. She says one can do something, that one is responsible.*

Ramesh: Where is the lineage? That is not what Ramana Maharshi said.

Barbara: *We watched a video of Gangaji last night. In that video she says, "Stop what you are doing!" With that, she is saying that you have volition.*

Claire: *Gangaji talks to the individual.*

Barbara (to Claire): *Did you get that from her?*

Claire: *Yes, a lot.*

Barbara: *So, there is a conflict here. Ramana Maharshi didn't teach that — that the individual has free will and responsibility — or did he?*

Ramesh: No, Ramana Maharshi didn't teach free will as far as I have understood him. His whole teaching was that everything is God's Will.

Barbara: *And your guru was Nisargadatta Maharaj.*

Ramesh: My original inspiration was Ramana Maharshi.

Barbara: *Oh, Ramana Maharshi!*

Ramesh: But it was not the destiny of this body-mind organism to sit at Ramana Maharshi's feet, but instead at Nisargadatta Maharaj's feet.

Barbara: *Whom will you pass this on to? Will there be someone in line when you pass out of your body? Or, are you going to pass this on?*

Ramesh: You see, Maharaj didn't believe in any lineage. He started that lineage. Therefore, he didn't have any lineage.

Barbara: *Oh, it was the Shiva mountain, Arunachala.*

Ramesh: Yes, and he didn't say so-and-so is my disciple and so-and-so is not. So, he had no disciples to whom he could hand over the lineage.

Barbara: *Where did all this talk of lineage come from, then?*

Ramesh: You decide where the lineage is. Where is the lineage?

Barbara: *Where is the lineage?*

Ramesh: Usually, where there is a lineage, a guru appoints somebody as his spiritual successor. That's how a lineage is created. Then there is a lineage.

Barbara: *Did Maharaj appoint a successor?*

Ramesh: No, Maharaj didn't. That's why there is no lineage. To the best of my knowledge, Maharaj did not pay much attention to a lineage. In fact, what Maharaj told me personally is that many of his co-disciples didn't like what he was teaching because he was not parroting his guru's words.

Barbara: *Was he expanding on his guru's teaching?*

Ramesh: No. He wasn't expanding on anything. His point was that whatever came out of his lips was spontaneous and according to the needs of his listeners. And he went a step further in saying to me, "When you talk, you will not be parroting my words." I laughed silently because there was no question of my talking at that time.

Barbara: *Do you think somebody will follow you and become a teacher once you pass away?*

Ramesh: Why not?

Barbara: *Is there anyone of your disciples who could...*

Ramesh: Yes. Why not!? You could do that.

Barbara: *Not me!* (laughter)

Ramesh: How should I know? But more important, Barbara, is that I don't care.

Barbara: *We're having a funny conversation. OK, that's great!* (laughter)

Ramesh: I don't think that Ramana Maharshi was concerned about who would continue his teaching.

Claire: *Gangaji has a very strong conviction that she has a mission.*

Barbara: *I know.*

Claire: *Poonjaji told her, "Talk, go and teach, go from door to door." She has a very strong belief in being a messenger. That is my opinion.*

Barbara: *She has a sense of doership.*

Susan: *Maharaj told Ramesh to talk, but that didn't cause him to have a sense of mission.*

Ramesh: No, no. Sense of mission has nothing to do with it. There is a World Hunger Project. The people who work in it have a tremendous sense of mission. They are totally committed to their work. Nobody gave them the sense of mission. The sense of mission was part of the destiny of those body-mind organisms.

Susan: *I see that we are back to judging again, aren't we?*

Ramesh: That is true.

Susan: *Who cares what Gangaji is doing?*

Barbara: *Whatever Gangaji is doing is absolutely perfect, because the Totality, or God, is functioning through her.*

Ramesh: Quite correct.

Barbara: *Oh, this teaching really does get rid of judgments and criticism!*

Susan: *You can't criticize anything or anybody anymore.*

Ramesh: How could you? That's my whole point.

Susan: *Just smile.*

Ramesh: If you truly accept that everything that's happening is not anybody's mission in life, how can you judge anybody? And if there is a mission, then that is part of the functioning of Totality. She doesn't have a mission in life. A mission happens through that body-mind organism. If this teaching is truly understood, there is no one who can say, "This is *my* mission in life." I have no

The mission—whose is it?

mission in life, I can have no mission in life.

Susan: *You are not the doer.*

Ramesh: That is 100% correct. I can have a sense of mission in life only if I am the doer, isn't that right? If I am not the doer, how can I have a mission in life?

Barbara: *Sai Baba talks on qualified duality and Advaita all mixed up together: "Do good, be good, see good." Is he just talking to those people at that stage of consciousness?*

Ramesh: That talking is taking place. And if that talking is to produce confusion in certain body-mind organisms, then it is those organisms' destinies for that confusion to happen.

Barbara: *It was our destiny to come to see you, and to get unconfused.*

Ramesh: I say, if any questions arise for you, go back to the basics. Then, either the questions will disappear, or they will produce their own answers. The basics are: there is no "me" to do anything; all that happens through this body-mind organism is its destiny, and the Will of God.

CHAPTER 30

30.1 Enlightenment can be Bought with Money — And the Fake Guru Takes it!

Ramesh: The urge to give to the guru has nothing to do with the need of the guru. Quite frankly, I don't have a pension. I am doing OK with my family; I am quite comfortable. And though Maharaj had only two rooms for his entire family, he also was comfortable. He was not in need. But my urge to give him money did not depend on his need to receive.

George: *I understand that completely.*

Ramesh: And yet, quite often it happens that a particular disciple goes to a particular guru and is able to help him in time of need. There is really no hard-and-fast rule about it. Earlier, I had a guru for about twenty years. He was a bachelor, but I don't think he ever officially took *sannyas*. I'm not sure whether or not he was enlightened. He still thought he had to do what his guru told him. He felt "he" was doing it. His guru was still alive and directed him in what to do.

George: *I believe it.*

Ramesh: His guru wanted him to build an ashram in Pune, so he did. It was a regular cement and concrete building, fairly big. The large plot was donated to him. Forty years ago it already cost an enormous sum. He got ten of us devotees together and asked us to form a trust, because he didn't want the ashram in his own name. We all gave donations for the construction of it according to our capacities. But in addition to the donations, much more money was needed, which he then borrowed from the disciples. It was understood that the loans would be paid back in the near future.

The problem was that my guru had many fake disciples. Just as fake gurus exist, so do fake disciples. He had some supposed disciples who encouraged him to go into this risky venture of building the ashram by promising him the support of their connections with the government, businesses, the community, and banks. "Don't worry about the finances, we will get you donations," they said. The big ashram was built, and large sums of money were spent. But the fake disciples couldn't keep their promise of getting donations. The guru was in a terrible mess.

George: *Really?*

Ramesh: He used to say, "All I need is a room to sleep in — I can even beg for food. So how did I end up like this? The house is not even for myself." He got caught in worldly matters like any other ordinary person.

George: *The mortgage.*

Ramesh: The disciples wanted their loans back. I doubt if he could have gotten a loan from a regular bank. To the banker you have to prove your income, which must be large enough to pay back the loan in twenty or thirty years. My guru had no income. He was a *sannyasin*. As you can see, even a *sannyasin* can become entangled in life through the thinking mind. As I see it today, my guru's building an ashram on behalf of the wishes of his guru was actually his own fantasy and desire.

Claire: *Didn't Maharaj do* pujas *because his guru wanted him to do so? Isn't that what Maharaj said? Or could it be that doing* pujas *was his own fantasy?*

Ramesh: When asked why he was doing *pujas*, Maharaj would say that his guru asked him to, that his guru wanted him to. That's why he did them. Doing *puja* was just a routine for him.

Claire: *Are you saying there is a difference between what your earlier guru did, and what Maharaj did, on behalf of their gurus?*

Ramesh: I believe Maharaj would not have given a damn if his routine had stopped for some reason or other. He was doing *puja* three times a day because his guru wanted him to do it. "He" was not doing the *puja*. The *puja* was being done.

Claire: *Do you mean to say Maharaj did the* puja *without personal doership?*

Ramesh: The *puja* was being done because God wanted the *puja* to be done. If Maharaj had stopped doing the *puja*, it simply would have meant that God didn't care any longer that they be done by him, irrespective of what his guru had told him. To do the *puja* on behalf of his guru means that "he" is not doing the *puja* for his own reasons. There was no personal doership in doing so.

 Let us go back to the story I was telling about my former guru. After having built the ashram, the guru was really in a tough financial situation. Luckily I, as a banker, was able to help him out of it. Even though, as a banker, I was not supposed to press any of my clients to give donations to my guru, it so happened that I knew people who had funds and were willing to give them. I was able to make those funds available to my guru, and within five years the entire loan had been paid off. My guru told me many times that he didn't know what would have happened to him and his ashram if I hadn't helped him out.

My interpretation is that I had to be my first guru's disciple for twenty years so that his difficulties were solved. I had to be the disciple of Maharaj because Maharaj, at that time, needed an interpreter with reasonable knowledge of Marathi, a more than adequate knowledge of English, and someone who knew the Western mind. The other interpreters were more or less middle-class people and had no contact with foreigners. My additional qualification was that I knew the Western mind, because I had met many foreigners during my career.

That's why destiny sent me to Maharaj. My destiny and Maharaj's destiny caused me to go to him in order to fulfill our destined roles. Similarly, the destinies of my earlier guru and myself caused us to meet. Destiny made me become his disciple so that I could help him in his difficulties. His destiny was to find a disciple who could help him.

My first guru's teaching was *Advaita*. He was a guru for more than two thousand people from all over the countryside of Maharashtra. To his credit, he remembered the names of every disciple and their family members, and how they fared in matters of health, education, etc. He saw it as his role to guide and support his disciple's material welfare. If a wife of a disciple was sick, he would suggest which *puja* needed to be performed for her recovery. Or he would make her fast on Mondays, or read a part of the scriptures by herself. Maybe he would suggest that the scriptures needed to be read or recited by a priest. If somebody lost his job, he would give a similar prescription. Although he was teaching *Advaita*, he still gave this sort of instruction.

At one point I realized that this was not the kind of guru I had expected to have or was hoping for. Because from an early age, I had the firm conviction that the destiny of every being is predetermined and cannot be changed by any power on earth. And because of this deep intuition, I felt that I didn't need any help in my bank career. I knew it would develop according to my destiny. But my earlier guru wanted to help me in whatever I did. Deep down I knew that he was not my ultimate guru.

This feeling was confirmed in a palm-leaf reading — called *nadi* — in the year 1950. It said, "This subject was born as a Hindu *brahmin*, but he is not interested in the Hindu religion. He is interested in the *Advaita* teaching. The subject has been in a passive search for a guru for several years. He will meet a guru in six years." That became true when I met my first guru. The reading said further that the subject's association with that guru would last for twenty years, and that not much would come out of it. It said that the subject would meet his second guru, his real guru, one year after his retirement, and that the results would then be quick. I retired in 1977 and I met Maharaj in November 1978.

This palm-leaf reading proves what I teach: whatever will happen in the future is already there, it already exists today, even before it happens. It's exact occurrence is destined.

George: *I can see that a palm-leaf reading is quite something!*

Ramesh: In this game of life we are just playing our assigned roles. In the case of my first guru, my donations and help happened because they were needed. In the case of my second guru, Nisargadatta Maharaj, I gave a donation out of gratitude. In both cases there was an urge in me to give. The urge to give does not necessarily depend on the need to receive. The need to give on the part of the disciple is quite different from the need of the guru to receive. The need may be on both sides. The urge is intuitive and arises out of a sense of gratitude. Gratitude brings about the need — the wanting — to give something to the guru, be it money or service. But the thinking mind asks, "Why to give such a big amount, would half that amount not be enough?"

George: *You say that's the thinking mind?*

Ramesh: And it is also the thinking mind which asks, "Does he really need it?" But the urge comes via intuition, and the amount is formulated by the working mind. When I went to Maharaj, the rupee figure came to me just like that. "This is how much I will give." It was a large amount of money in those days. At that time the thinking mind did not intrude, did not question the amount, by doubting: "Is the amount too large, or not large enough?" This is the background of my gratitude, and the subsequent donation I made to Maharaj.

George: *I understand that to give to the guru is very important for the disciple.*

Ramesh: It is very important. That is correct. In the Hindu tradition it is clearly stated that the disciple must please the guru. As one can see in my own case, pleasing the guru obviously does something helpful for the advancement of the disciple on his path. Pleasing the guru helps the disciple to go ahead on his path.

George: *You mean to say that the Hindu tradition also says what you are saying? Pleasing the guru can further his search?*

Ramesh: Tradition has always said so. And what is more, whatever exists in the world has two sides. For one genuine thing, there can be one hundred fakes. The genuine guru is not really concerned with what the disciple does. The advice to please and to give is given not to the guru, but to the disciple. But one way or another, certain gurus take advantage of this advice, take advantage of their disciples. And one way or the other, they sort of ask or demand or indicate that they will accept money. So, there are hundreds of fake

Tradition teaches that pleasing the guru does "something" for the seeker's spiritual progress

gurus who take advantage of this traditional suggestion to give to the guru.

George: *No doubt! They take money.*

Ramesh: Most don't, but some do. Even in accepting, there is no hard-and-fast rule. There are some gurus who will not accept anything, irrespective of their needs. For such a situation in which the guru doesn't accommodate the disciple's desire to give, tradition provides one special day of the year in which the guru is compelled to take whatever is given. It is the *Guru Purnima* day, the day of the full moon in July. So, tradition has looked after the guru and the disciple.

I follow the same rule which Maharaj followed in taking presents or money. Maharaj's point was very simple. There is no "me" here (*Ramesh points to himself*) to demand anything from you as a disciple. If there is no "me" to demand anything, how can there be a "me" to refuse anything. Therefore, money just comes. And it was the same with Ramana Maharshi. Ramana prevented his people from demanding anything.

George: *He gave everything away, didn't he?*

Ramesh: No, he didn't have anything. Therefore, he could not even give anything away. "He" didn't create an ashram. The ashram grew up around him.

George: *He followed the rules just like everybody else.*

Ramesh: In fact, there was such a democratic element in him that if somebody gave him fruits, he wanted them to be distributed evenly amongst the people in the ashram. At that time the general manager of the ashram was his younger brother, Chinnaswami. Today the Ramanashramam is managed by Ramana's older brother's son. Chinnaswami is reported to have said, "It is alright for Ramana not to ask for money, but I have to run the ashram!"

George: *So, Chinnaswami could accept money.*

Ramesh: No, no. Ramana Maharshi did not refuse any donations that came in. But he didn't want a demand for money to be made, overtly or covertly, deliberately or implied. But the general manager would do so anyway. Chinnaswami would talk to the rich visitors about the needs of the ashram.

Ramana Maharshi was called *avatar* by many — God in human form. But I say he was beyond being an *avatar*. Ramana was absolutely convinced that every single need of the ashram would be provided for. He was convinced that all would happen anyway, according to destiny. And that understanding was proven by the daily experiences which many who lived with him witnessed. If something was wanted, that something would usually come from somewhere. Chinnaswami, who was very much involved in the world, held the view that: "Bhagavan abides always in the Self, but it is me who needs money for running the ashram." He couldn't help making overt suggestions for donations. For instance, he would say, "We need a dining room," and then he would go to Ramana with the request.

Annamalai Swami, a devotee of Ramana for more than sixty years, published a very beautiful book about a year ago in which he narrates his life with Bhagavan. The book's editor is David Godman. I was told that Annamalai Swami died a couple of months ago, at the age of ninety. He was the personal attendant of Ramana Maharshi for many years. Later on, Ramana made use of him as a builder, even though he was not an engineer. Ramana made him build a lot of the buildings in the Ramanashramam. During the actual construction work at that time, Ramana himself supervised the work personally. What a fortunate position Annamalai Swami was in, to be physically so closed to Ramana for so many years!

In his book, Annamalai narrates the difficult positions he found himself in. In theory, he had to listen to the commands of the general manager, Chinnaswami. But it was Ramana who secretly gave Annamalai Swami the orders, in every detail, about how — and how large — to build the ashram.

(*Annamalai Swami was told by Ramana not to reveal that it was Ramana himself who made him do what he did. Annamalai Swami was asked by Ramana to pretend that he was acting on his own, which was almost always against the will and the ideas of the general manager* — Ed.)

Every time Chinnaswami found out what was being built without his consent, he threw a tantrum; he would say they didn't have the money for such a building. You can imagine how difficult it was for Annamalai Swami to work. In any case, he would do what Bhagavan told him to do. Annamalai Swami describes in his book how astonishing it was to see money coming into the ashram regularly, whenever it was needed.

The same thing happened with the ashram of my earlier guru, who started to build without having the necessary funds. In some way, I was the instrument through which the money came to him.

A further example of how needs were met in Ramana's case is reported in Annamalai Swami's book. Ramana had a digestive problem. He was constipated if he didn't regularly eat a herb called "mirabollum." Once, the ashram ran out of stock. When somebody wanted to go to fetch a new supply, Ramana told the person not to go, but rather to wait and see what would happen. Annamalai reports that an entire sack of the herb arrived at the ashram within half-an-hour, without having been ordered.

Our needs are covered many a time "by themselves" — out of the blue. But we just don't realize this fact because we sometimes want something and it doesn't come. What happens often is that help comes when it is needed, not when it is wanted.

George: *No doubt.*

CHAPTER 31

31.1 Rajneesh's Mala and Balsekar's Sacred Thread

Madhukar: *When I look back on the life of this body-mind organism, there was a time when it wore a cross for more than 14 years. Jesus was hanging on that cross. Then a time came during which I was with Osho Rajneesh. For more than twelve years, I wore a* mala *with one hundred and eight beads. A locket with a picture of the guru was attached to it. Both episodes ended at some point. Today, I am absolutely convinced that no power on earth could bring me back to believing and doing what I did while I was under those earlier spiritual influences. Energetically and existentially, that is just not possible.*

Ramesh: You can't.

Madhukar: *It would be impossible for me to touch the feet of Jesus or Rajneesh every morning before coming to you, and then listen to what you have to say. What I have heard from you has caused this body-mind organism to transcend the fear of a punishing God or a guru's promise of eternal bliss, if only his should's and shouldn'ts are followed. I couldn't wear a cross or a* mala *anymore.*

Ramesh: What you are saying, Madhukar, is that the process of understanding is usually forward. There is no going back. That is correct.

Madhukar: *What I am getting at is that I see you bowing down to a deity every morning. At the time being, in my case, it is not possible anymore to bow down to Jesus' feet. I would like to know what makes you bow down to a deity? I cannot understand this, because in my own case such reverence to my past gurus has fallen totally out of me.*

Ramesh: Why do you say the old beliefs and the teachings of your former gurus fell out of you? Because you feel happy about the fact that they fell out, isn't that so?

Madhukar: *It is not a question of happiness or unhappiness. The clearing out has been total. All of it is just gone. The belief in, and the practice of, the teachings of the earlier gurus is just not possible anymore. I can't go back to that anymore; it is just not possible!*

Ramesh: Supposing it would be possible, why would you consider it as a going back?

Madhukar: *It wouldn't be a going back. It would just happen, and be rather something like a miracle. Today, it seems that the God I had at that time was a kind of terrible God, a God of revenge and punishment. I don't want Him anymore. I am sure today that that kind of God doesn't exist and never did. How could I bow down to such a God today?*

And with Rajneesh, I found myself believing that I could manage my life according to my own will, that I could change into anything I wanted.

So, when I see you doing what no power in the world could make me do, then I wonder what is going on with you, what is happening in your case?

Ramesh: No. You are not seeing "me" doing anything, Madhukar.

Madhukar: *Well, then I say, "I wonder what is going on with the body-mind organism called Ramesh Balsekar?"*

Ramesh: You are not seeing "me" doing anything. Something happens which is part of God's Will. What happens, happens. I don't think, "Why should it happen or not happen? I am a *jnani*, why should I bow down to a deity?"

Madhukar: *A body-mind organism bowing down to a deity means that a separation between the two exists at that moment. There is separation between a body-mind organism and a piece of paper with a picture of the deity on it.*

Ramesh: No, there isn't. Something happens because that something is supposed to happen. Maharaj used to have his *puja* three times a day. The *puja* just happened.

Madhukar: *But there must be some intention or want or fear in your case which expresses itself as the energy for doing the* pujas, *for bowing down. In my case, there is no longer any energy for bowing down to a Jesus, or for doing any of this.*

Ramesh: Fine, accept that fact.

Madhukar: *For me it is not a question of accepting this fact. I have no problem with not being able to bow down to Jesus anymore. This body-mind organism, Madhukar, is asking that body-mind organism, Ramesh, which form of energy is driving his body-mind organism to put his forehead to a piece of paper with a God on it every morning. Is bowing down something like an urge for you? Or is there a promise behind it? Maybe you promised Sharda or your mother to do this ritual every day? Please, tell me what happens on your side? Any explanation will do.*

Ramesh: No, nothing like that. The ritual just happens.

Madhukar: *Just like that? Every morning the same thing happens at the same time?*

Ramesh: It just happens and I have no quarrel with whatever happens. You have.

Madhukar: *Sure! Because I believe what you are telling me. I see you bowing down to a deity. I see a separation between you and the deity. And a couple of minutes later, I see you walking into the living room and telling us that a* jnani *is Unicity, without any separation between subject and object.*

Ramesh: Wait a minute, wait a minute, Madhukar! You are seeing an individual bowing to a deity. There is no individual here.

Madhukar: *I see a body-mind organism like any other body-mind organism.*

Ramesh: That's right. It is the body-mind organism that does the bowing down.

Madhukar: *And I ask, why?*

Ramesh: Why not? Why not!

Madhukar: *Because in my case such a thing is not possible anymore. I don't believe that something like your bowing down happens so regularly in phenomenality without a cause. I don't believe what you are saying. What is not experienced here,* (Madhukar points to himself) *in my own case, I do not believe anymore. I do not believe anything outside of myself anymore. I just wonder what your motivation is? You must have a motivation.*

Ramesh: That is not true.

Madhukar: *I can't believe it. There must be a reason for you to do this. There must be a motivating energy to do this.*

Ramesh: Who wants to know, Madhukar? Who wants to know?

Madhukar: *I want to know.*

Ramesh: That is the whole trouble.

Madhukar: *I watch my guru bow down every morning to a deity and then walk into the living room and tell us that, for the enlightened one, there is no separation between object and subject. But I see my enlightened guru contradicting his own teaching every morning by his very act.*

Ramesh: There is no separation. Some event is happening. I have no quarrel with what is happening. You have. The *jnani* may cry, but he is not concerned with his crying, thinking, "I should not cry. What will people think of me if they see me crying? People may think I am not a *jnani*." When I bow down to the deity, l am not worried about what Madhukar may think of me. Madhukar might think enlightenment has not happened to Ramesh. There is no worry about what is happening. In another *jnani's* case, the wife died and he cried. He never asked why crying occurred. The crying happened. "I" am not crying. If the question of why I cried arose, that would mean involvement. "I should not be crying" would be involvement.

In my case, there is no "me" who bows down. An old habit continues over the years, that's all. I have no quarrel with this habit. You have a quarrel with it, I don't.

Madhukar: *Sure, that's why I bring it up. That's why I am sharing my doubts with you.*

Ramesh: And that's why I am sharing this with you. I have no problem with having my bath, going to the *puja* room, and doing five minutes of meditation, or whatever I am doing there.[1] I have no quarrel with what is happening. You have a problem with it, not me.

Madhukar: *Definitely, I have. I have one more question. I see you wearing the* brahmin *string. For me, the wearing of that* brahmin *string means association and identification with certain values of a religion, or of the society. It is a religious status symbol.*

On the other hand, if someone walks into this room and carries a Rajneesh mala *or a spiritual name given by another guru, you don't accept that name.*

Ramesh: No. I don't see any reason why I should not accept and use a visitor's original name. If somebody wears a *mala*, I wouldn't ask him to remove that *mala*.

Madhukar: *That I don't know. Actually, no one has come yet wearing a* mala *since I have been here. That's true.*

Ramesh: I wouldn't tell anyone not to come here with a *mala* or a uniform. If someone comes here in ocher robes, or with a *mala*, fine. Come anyway you like. And if somebody says, "I like to be called by my spiritual name," I will accept his or her wish. A few days ago, somebody called Shiva came to visit

---

[1] Ramesh performs a regular ten minute ritual. It includes a *guru-puja* to Sri Nisargadatta Maharaj and Sri Ramana Maharshi; and the recitation of what is known as the Ramaraksha Stotra (a prayer to the Hindu god Rama, the proctector against all evil)

*initiation into Osho discipleship **initiation into Brahminship

Attachment to the sacred thread (i.e. the desire of enlightenment) by birth, by choice—or by God's Will?

me. His original name was too difficult to pronounce, so I said, "OK, I accept the name Shiva."

Madhukar: *But in the cases of many other people, I have witnessed you refusing to use their spiritual names, the ones given to them by some guru or other. You told them that you wanted to use the name the parents had given to them, and not the one given by their guru.*

For me, your wearing a brahmin *string is the same as somebody else wearing a* mala. *Your string identifies you as a* brahmin. *A* mala *with Rajneesh on it also means that kind of identity. I think it does not matter with what the identification is. A* mala *or a* brahmin *string means the same kind of identification.*

Ramesh: No, it doesn't.

Madhukar: *I don't think it matters at what time identification occurs, be it at the beginning of life or thirty years into life. Identification is identification.*

Ramesh: Wait a minute. I never asked anybody not to come here because he uses the name which was given to him by any other guru. And I have never asked anybody to leave because he was wearing a *mala*. I have never asked anybody to go away because he was wearing ocher robes. I have never asked anybody to go away because he was wearing the uniform of some other guru.

Madhukar: *Well, in any case, I see a reaction and a judgement on your side when people use names like Pujarin, Shahida, Shiva, or Gandha.*

Ramesh: Why shouldn't I have a reaction? That reaction just happens. That reaction just happens and has nothing to do with me. Why shouldn't I react? Why not?

Madhukar: *Because you tell us the* jnani *has no thinking mind and therefore he is able to refrain from judgement, he is able to accept whatever comes.*

Ramesh: That is right. That reaction happens because that reaction is something which has nothing to do with me. If the reaction happens, it happens.

Madhukar: *What you are saying about yourself is true for everybody. In the case of a* jnani, *you say that a judgement is just a reaction which happens impersonally. But in the case of an unenlightened one, you say that a judgement is the thinking mind, horizontal involvement. I see no difference between you, as a sage, and an unenlightened person, as far as judgements are concerned. It doesn't matter if somebody is "home" or not, it doesn't matter if a "me" exists or not, and it doesn't matter if somebody is enlightened or not — judgement happens as a reaction in all cases.*

Ramesh: In that case, are you saying that because you consider me to be a *jnani*, I should not go to the *puja* room? A *jnani* shouldn't do that?

Madhukar: *I am not saying that at all. You are putting words into my mouth. I am simply asking you about your motivation for doing so. In my case, to go to the* puja *room or to go to the church cannot happen, because I no longer expect anything from doing so. And that is why I wonder why you should go to the* puja *room and pray. How can that happen in your case?*

Ramesh: Why not? Why not? Wait a minute! Why not?

Madhukar: *I would like to know your motivation. My question is very simple.*

Ramesh: Why shouldn't I go? I go because whatever happens through the various gurus is not something which is identical. Some gurus get angry and some don't. Now you will ask, "Why should a guru become angry?" That is your question. If somebody is realized, he should not become angry. That's what you are saying. And I say, "Why not?" The body-mind organism of a guru is programmed to get angry as a reaction of the brain to an outside event, and that body-mind organism then expresses anger. That's all. And what you are saying is, a *jnani* should not become angry or have fear.

Madhukar: *I am not saying that. I simply want to know why you go to the* puja *room. What is the motivation behind it? I see no difference between a* jnani *and a non-*jnani.

Ramesh: Don't!

Madhukar: *We are told that a* jnani *has no involvement in horizontal thinking, while the non-*jnani *gets involved in such thinking.*

Ramesh: That is the only point.

Madhukar: *That can be the only difference between the* jnani *and the non-*jnani.

Ramesh: That is the only difference. Horizontal involvement is the only difference between the *jnani* and non-*jnani*. Horizontal involvement has to do with personal doership. And that is all that matters. In the case of the *jnani*, horizontal involvement does not exist.

Madhukar: *That can be the only difference. It looks like your actions don't differ from anybody else's. In my case, as a non-*jnani, *I would need to have a motivation for going to the* puja *room, while you, as the* jnani, *don't have such a personal motivation for going there, right? That can be the only difference.*

Ramesh: It is! I confirm for you again: horizontal involvement does not happen in the case of a *jnani*. That is the only difference between a *jnani* and an *ajnani*. The *jnani's* apparent actions have nothing to do with involvement or non-involvement. I repeat again: the absence of horizontal involvement is the only difference between a *jnani* and a non-*jnani*. I repeat again, the horizontal involvement which happens in the case of an ordinary person does not happen in the case of a *jnani*. In his case, horizontal involvement is not there. In the case of a *jnani*, grief may happen, but there is no mourning.

Kay: *Horizontal involvement or not, in either case it is God's Will, isn't it?*

Ramesh: Yes. But you see, horizontal involvement is based on the sense of personal doership. And enlightenment means the total annihilation of the "me" as an individual doer. Involvement happens only when there is the sense of personal doership. And if the sense of personal doership is not there, the horizontal involvement does not happen.

Kay: *I understand this. But I can't see any difference between an action based on personal doership, and an action based on non-personal doership.*

Madhukar: *Maybe we could say that the difference is the difference. But would that explain anything?*

Ramesh: "There is no difference" — what do you mean to say by that, Kay?

Kay: *The action of the sage and the action of the non-sage, both are God's Will; and therefore they must happen exactly as they do.*

Ramesh: Wait a minute, Kay. You are saying that it is God's Will that in the case of a *jnani* horizontal involvement does not take place, while in the case of an ordinary person horizontal involvement does takes place? Of course! Sure!

Kay: *God has given you gray hair, and He has made me bald — that's it! So, in the same way that God has given us different hair, He causes us to act differently. Therefore, I see no qualitative difference between actions based on personal doership and actions based on non-involvement. So, we can stop thinking about enlightenment right here!*

Ramesh: Even after enlightenment the body-mind organism continues to function more or less according to the way it has been programmed. Therefore, there are differences in behavior between different *jnanis*.

Shahida: *When Madhukar says that you bow down to a deity...*

Ramesh: Or I may bow down to my guru.

Shahida: *OK. Ramana says that we are the deathless spirit. As the deathless spirit we do not bow to a deathless idol, because, as the deathless spirit, even the idol is not dead. We are not dead even if we die.*

Murthy: *We are making the distinction that you are a* jnani *and we are* ajnanis, *hence the conflict.*

Ramesh: No. There is a conflict because you consider yourself to be an *ajnani*. What I know is that there is no ignorance and no knowledge.

Murthy: *By observing you as realized, and myself as not realized, I think that I have not yet become what you are; but that one day, I will become a* jnani *myself if I visit you and listen to you long enough. Is that the problem?*

Ramesh: The problem is expectation.

Murthy: *Observing you and judging you as realized is part of the expectation, isn't it?*

Ramesh: No.

Murthy: *I watch and observe you closely because one day I also want to become a jnani.*

Ramesh: As long as an observation includes an expectation, expectation continues. But if you just observe something without an expectation, then that is what is called witnessing.

Murthy: *A* jnani *and an* ajnani *are witnessed here. But in witnessing, there is neither* jnani *or* ajnani, *or is there?*

Ramesh: Witnessing is impersonal witnessing. Observing is done by the mind. The mind observing is reacting to what it observes. In witnessing there is no individual mind observing something, reacting to something.

Madhukar: *You were saying earlier that wanting, and in particular wanting enlightenment, is an obstacle to the happening of enlightenment. Isn't the desire for enlightenment also predestined, as is the duration of that desire?*

Ramesh: Sure.

Madhukar: *Then there is no way in and no way out. Everything has to be the way it is. And that's the end of it. In that way, there is no obstacle. There is no thinking mind of the seeker, and no personal or impersonal doership. It is the mind which gives names to What-is. But since everything is predestined, it has to be the way it is. And that's the end of it. Where is the question of an obstacle, then?*

Ramesh: All is God's Will, that is correct. Isn't that also what Christ said?
In the scriptures, they say you accept the *Advaita* teaching but you don't apply it to your guru. The teaching says that there is no difference between you and your guru. Even though you understand the teaching you don't apply that understanding to your guru, as long as his body-mind organism is still present in phenomenality.

Madhukar: *On the physical level? Do you mean as long as the guru is alive?*

Ramesh: On the physical level, the duality of the guru and the disciple must continue. You can read about this in my book, *Experience of Immortality*, which is a translation and a commentary of the *Advaita* teaching of Saint Jnaneshwar, in which he expounds the guru-disciple relationship with great clarity. He makes it perfectly clear that, after enlightenment, the disciple knows that there is no difference between the guru and the disciple; and yet the now-enlightened disciple continues to pay obeisance to the guru. You will ask: "Why does the disciple continue to bow down to the guru after enlightenment? He doesn't need to because now he is enlightened himself, which makes him as good as the guru."

Madhukar: *It just dawned on me that in your case the spiritual upbringing and conditioning as a Hindu* brahmin *included the concepts of gods like Krishna, who actually taught the non-dual teaching of* Advaita *some thousand years ago. To follow this teaching, this religious tradition, carried the possibility of a reward in this very life time. And you were actually rewarded with enlightenment.*

In my own case, the Catholic religion and tradition taught man's free will, his responsibility for sins and good deeds, God's rewards and punishments for them, and the promise of salvation "if".... All that had to be discarded in order to become open to the teaching of Advaita.

Ramesh: The point is that nothing can be discarded. There is no one to discard anything.

Madhukar: *In my case, the process of disidentification included living according to the Catholic religion, and according to the teachings of several gurus.*

Ramesh: If I pass by the picture of Ramana Maharshi which is hanging over there, I might bow down to it. Why not!? I repeat, even after enlightenment, when the disciple has become one with the guru, the disciple is supposed to bow down and pay respect to his guru. If he refuses to bow down, he only shows that enlightenment has not yet happened. Pride is still there. "I am the same as the guru is, why should I bow down to him, or to his picture?" — that's what the unenlightened disciple says. And that is still pride.

Madhukar: *I believe that when enlightenment has happened, gratitude and devotion will arise automatically. How else could it be?*

Ramesh: That's how devotion arises.

Madhukar: *That's what I believe happened to you. But I have to share my doubts with you, and I want them to be dispelled by you. What I am saying here is only for the clarification of my doubts.*

Ramesh: I know. So, in my case devotion arises, and there is no obstruction by anybody here (*Ramesh points to himself*) to the arising of that devotion. The devotion to the deity in the *puja* room continues. The devotion to the guru continues to arise, and every time the devotion arises, the devotion turns itself into bowing.

Madhukar: *In my own case, if I now look at a picture of my former guru — Poonjaji, for example — I feel no devotion whatsoever. That is because I feel betrayed, lied to, by him.*

Ramesh: That means enlightenment has not yet happened in the case of Madhukar. If enlightenment had happened in your case, you wouldn't care whether you bowed down or not.

Madhukar: *If I had become enlightened with Poonjaji, I might bow down to his picture in devotion every time I passed it.*

Ramesh: Even if enlightenment had happened in your case with Poonjaji, it wouldn't be in your hands to bow down to him or not. Either it would happen or it wouldn't. It is not in your hands. Devotion may arise, and it may not. If it arises, there is no individual to object or obstruct that devotion. I don't think, "What will Madhukar think if he sees me bowing down to the deity?" That thought doesn't arise. If devotion arises, it takes its own course. I don't give a damn what other people think about my reaction to that arising of devotion.

Madhukar: *At the moment of devotion there is no "I," no "me." There is just devotion. That is my own experience. That is clear.*

Ramesh: If that were clear, your question about my bowing down to the deity would not have arisen. You would have understood that devotion arises spontaneously and takes its own course. It may be bowing before my God, or before my guru. "I" am not doing the bowing down.

Madhukar: *Let me make it clear one more time, Ramesh. My question regarding your bowing down to the deity in the* puja *room every morning at the same time comes out of a doubting mind. But the base of this doubt is my own experience. I can bow down only when devotion is actually happening spontaneously. In my experience, that doesn't happen to me every morning at the same time. And because my experience seems to be different from yours, this question came up for me this morning in a very strong way.*

Ramesh: And therefore, as I said, the answer to your question is: devotion arises, and there is no one to object to the devotion, to the act of bowing before my guru or my God.

Madhukar: *And maybe here* (Madhukar points to himself) *there is someone who is objecting to his guru's action.*

Ramesh: It may be that enlightenment may happen in this body-mind organism called Madhukar. And perhaps this body-mind organism won't bow down before Ramesh's picture, ten or twenty years from now.

Madhukar: *Nobody knows.*

Ramesh: That's right. Nobody knows. But if that body-mind organism doesn't bow down to his guru, most probably...

Madhukar: *...enlightenment has not yet happened.* (laughter)

Ramesh: Because if enlightenment had happened, devotion would arise.

Madhukar: *Most probably. I think so. Let's see.*

Ramesh: Devotion would arise. You see?

Madhukar: *I have had the experience of devotion, even without being enlightened.*

Ramesh: So, the devotion of the disciple to the *guru* continues even after enlightenment.

Madhukar: *Intuitively, I can feel what you are saying. Thank you very much, Ramesh.*

Ramesh: The devotion to the guru arises, and there is no individual who is proud of the arising of the devotion, or to obstruct that devotion.

Murthy: *Isn't devotion what arises for a seeker on the* bhakti *path, while for a seeker on the* jnana *path devotion may not arise; though he might still become enlightened?*

Ramesh: You see, some people are programmed in such a way that they cannot accept the abstract idea of Totality or Consciousness, which is used on the *jnana* path. For those people, it is easier to accept the word or concept of God which is used on the *bhakti* path. But there is no best path. In reality, no individual can choose his path, because an individual has no volition whatsoever. Seekers are programmed for *bhakti* or *Advaita*, and are sent accordingly to a guru — sent by that Power which created and programmed them in the first place. The teaching of *Advaita* leads to the acceptance of whatever happens as part of the impersonal functioning of Totality. *Bhakti* leads to surrender to God. But both lead to the same thing, namely, to the absolute annihilation of the sense of personal doership. A *jnani* has no sense of personal doership in whatever he does. He does not become involved in horizontal thinking, which is based on the sense of personal doership. After enlightenment, nobody remains to judge anything. In one *jnani* devotion may arise, while in another one devotion may not arise.

Murthy: *Are enlightenment and devotion the same thing?*

Ramesh: Enlightenment is not the same as devotion. Devotion may lead to enlightenment. Devotion is one of the paths which can lead to enlightenment. Another path is *Advaita*.

Murthy: *A* jnani *wants always to act devotedly, doesn't he?*

Ramesh: He wants nothing. He just witnesses whatever happens without considering it to be right or wrong. He accepts whatever happens to himself and to others. If devotion arises in him or in others, he accepts that devotion. And if such devotion does not arise, it also does not matter to him, because there is nobody to think that devotion should have arisen.

Murthy: *The basic quality of a* jnani's *actions is earnestness. That's what I notice.*

Ramesh: Whose earnestness? There is no individual in the *jnani* which could be earnest or not.

Murthy: *But he is definitely always sincere in what he is doing, isn't he?*

Ramesh: No. There is no question of sincerity for the *jnani*. The qualities of sincerity and earnestness belong to an individual. The *jnani* is not an individual anymore. He is not concerned with such qualities anymore.

Murthy: *I can see in you an enormous amount of goodness.*

Ramesh: Why are you pursuing these words, earnestness and sincerity? Why bother about them? All these words refer to an individual sense of doership, which has been annihilated in the case of the *jnani*. He accepts everything that happens as part of God's Will. The sense of personal will is transcended.
    Shall we stop here?

CHAPTER 32

32.1 Enlightenment: the End of Wanting

Ramesh: Enlightenment is freedom from wanting anything. Whether you want money or enlightenment, as long as wanting exists, enlightenment cannot happen. Enlightenment is the end of wanting.

Herbert: *Because, in seeking, the seeker still exists, right? Because the seeker is in between?*

Ramesh: That is correct. The main obstruction is the seeker. Enlightenment means the total annihilation of the seeker, who thinks he can get something by his own efforts. This is what I say enlightenment is. Quite frankly, I don't know what others mean by enlightenment. Unless the seeker gets annihilated, the seeking cannot stop. And until the seeking stops, the wanting will continue. The seeking only stops when it is totally understood that "I" cannot get anything through my own efforts. Whatever happens does so only because it is the Will of God. The total acceptance of this fact leads to the annihilation of the "me," the seeker. What is more, the ability to accept this fact is not in your hands.

"Do I really want it?"

Herbert: *Do you mean to say that even such acceptance is God's Will?*

Ramesh: Absolutely correct. That is the basis of what I have to say. Having heard what I just said, one may ask the question, "How do I live my life from now on? Should I continue to make money, make a living, or should I go to the forest and live on fruits and nuts?" In the present, the body-mind organism called Herbert has to make money in order to live. That activity is part of life. I assure you, making money is not an obstruction to enlightenment. The basis of my teaching is that whatever happens is God's Will. That means that enlightenment can happen in the body-mind organism called Herbert only if it is God's Will — no matter what Herbert does or does not do about it. God has not laid down any restrictions regarding enlightenment. Enlightenment can happen to a beggar or to a millionaire, to a saint or a sinner. That's why you find enlightenment in a wide variety of people, in a wide variety of circumstances. The only common factor for all of them is that their seeking has stopped. And that seeking stopped when the seeker understood that he, the seeker, could not get anything.

That is the basis of what I teach. Therefore, if I truly accept that everything that happens is according to God's Will, how can I ask you to do any *sadhana*?

Herbert: *Such a demand would be an interference with God's Will, I guess.*

Ramesh: Yes. On the other hand, I know that *sadhana* helps to calm the mind. That I can say. But whether or not you are really going to meditate will depend on God's Will.

32.2 Poonjaji said: "You are Enlightened!" — And Then He Went Away

Jaimie: *While I was listening to an audio recording of your morning talks, everything fell into place for me.*

Ramesh: Do you remember what it was I was saying which made everything fall into place for you?

Jaimie: *I understood that the living dream is of the same order as our nightly dream. I understood what many teachers — including you — keep repeating, namely: all there is, is Consciousness. And yet some of them say that the living dream is an illusion, that only the Source is real. Listening to your tape, I understood that all is Consciousness, that life is made of the same stuff — it is just the movement of Consciousness.*

Ramesh: That is correct.

Jaimie: *You confirmed for me that all is Consciousness, including life and the Source.*

Ramesh: That is correct.

Jaimie: *That's what made everything fall into place, and that made me very happy. Additionally, I have fallen in love with this country, India, and with her people. I see so much beauty and love here. I have never felt my heart so open as it is in this country.*

Ramesh: That is true.

Jaimie: *Then I bought a bunch of your books and gobbled them up. And I felt so blissed out that I thought that I was enlightened, because I didn't know anymore where I was.*

Ramesh: Did listening to my audio-cassette bring about the feeling that you didn't know anymore where you were?

Jaimie: *To be with Poonjaji, reading your book, and listening to your cassette — all of it did it, I think. I asked Poonjaji what this blissful state was about, and he told me, "You are there." Was that enlightenment? I was not sure what he meant by this. I wasn't able to arrange another conversation with him. I think he tries to avoid such queries.*

Ramesh: How long were you able to talk to him? Three minutes? Thirty minutes?

Jaimie: *What do you mean? After he had said, "You are there," he took off. It was not possible to have a real conversation with him.*

Two nights ago, I felt great joy, ecstasy, and a feeling of freedom, which again expressed itself in a lot of tears. Then that feeling of freedom turned into helplessness and hopelessness and meaninglessness.

Ramesh: Ah, there was a flip-flop from freedom to helplessness, wasn't there?

Jaimie: *Yes. Again, I don't know where I am now. I wonder if enlightenment means anything at all? Poonjaji says that the karmic cycle ends with enlightenment. Contrary to what he says, you maintain that there is no personal karma at all to come to an end. What to believe?*

Ramesh: Yes, I say there cannot be an individual karmic cycle. Why?

Jaimie: *Because there is no "me."*

Ramesh: More than that. I come back to the basics of my teaching again and again, namely, that God's Will prevails and not mine. And whatever happens are whose acts? God's acts.

Jaimie: *But we are also God.*

Ramesh: If you understand that whatever happens is God's act, where do "you" come in? There is no question of you being God. All there is, is God.

Jaimie: *Then it doesn't matter if I am enlightened or not.*

Ramesh: You are 100% right again. It doesn't matter at all whether Jaimie is enlightened or not.

Jaimie: *Enlightenment doesn't help the world, help Consciousness, or even help God — or does it?*

Ramesh: God does not need any help from you. God will produce the acts it wants through the instrument called Jaimie. For such acts to materialize, God or Consciousness has programmed this body-mind organism via genes and environmental conditioning. What Jaimie thinks she is, is nothing other than genes plus environmental conditioning. What Jaimie thinks is her action is nothing other than a reaction of the brain to an outside impulse, like a thought or a perceived sense object, which was sent by God. Your actions therefore are God's actions.

CHAPTER 33

33.1 "My" Action — God's Karma

Ramesh: Yesterday was your first day here. What you heard me saying yesterday, was it something new for you? Or, did you hear something like this before somewhere else with another guru?

Jaimie: *What I heard from you yesterday, just put me together again. I was lost.*

Ramesh: That is the effect of what I say.

Jaimie: *My questions and the choice of words that you use — or which the Source uses through you — for answering, had just to come together. What you said and how you said it was so different from what I have heard ever before. You cleared up a lot of my questions and doubts. And there was something very satisfying about it. It helped me to settle. And the three of us being friends spoke to each other after your talk. I must say I still have questions.*

Ramesh: You were here only one time so far. If you have more questions, yes, sure, go ahead and ask them.

Jaimie: *I have a question about karma. As I have understood it, Poonjaji says the event of enlightenment means the end of suffering and the end of the karmic cycle. Once enlightened, we don't need to come back and clear up the karma of our past lives.*

Do I understand correctly that your teaching says that there is no personal karma because there is no continuity of the same entity or soul which continues from life to life — and lifetimes are in time anyway. And you say all of the past and future exists and will always exist in the present moment, but we just can't see all of it. Is that correct? I am in confusion about Poonjaji's words and your words.

In fact, when we die, everything goes back in this pool of Consciousness and energy. That's what you say, isn't it? I heard you also say that certain effects and entities are formed again from that pool to live out these effects, right? But yet some people still may think they have a memory of their past life. And that memory feels personal. In my past-life work with people, I notice that my clients experience a past life which always turns out to be a metaphorical story that is parallel to their present-life story. In some cases people's unconscious needs to be more distant, and they need to realize that they are not in that form of their past life anymore. The clients seem to be too identified with their past lives. They believe, for instance, that they suffer today because of what they did or did not do in the past and in their past lives. And they believe they have to work out in the present life the conflexes of both the past lives and the present life. That is because we believe those conflexes are connected. Conflexes mean samskaras — *sense impressions — in the Indian terminology, so I was told. My past life work with people is based on this understanding. Are we giving too much importance to past lives? Are we thereby actually assisting people, unconsciously, in strengthening their identification with them?*

Ramesh: Your basic question is about *karma*, isn't it? You ask is it the individual *karma* — one's own individual deeds — that leads to the content and form of the next life, don't you? Or what is your question?

Jaimie: *I'd just like you to say more about* karma *and how it works. Regarding* karma, *is there a difference between a person for whom enlightenment has happened and a person who is not enlightened?*

Ramesh: In my understanding *karma* simply means action, an event, a deed. Something happens, action happens, some deeds are being done. To me the most relevant words in regard to *karma* are the words of Lord Buddha: "Events happen, deeds are being done but there is no individual doer thereof." My own words are, "Whatever happens is God's Will." My teaching has four words, "Thy Will be done." They imply automatically that whatever happens in this body-mind organism is not my *karma*. Whose will is it that creates the deed?

In fact, intention concerns the individual. The individual does something because he has an intention. But what he intends to get or achieve is not in his control to manifest. That intention has to happen because it is part of the destiny of that body-mind organism. Or, in other words, that intention is willed by God. If the consequences of his intention are not in his control, can we call those consequent acts his *karma*?

Jaimie: *No. I understand what you are saying.*

Ramesh: Then, whose *karma* is carried over from a previous life and whose *karma* will be carried forward to a future life? Whose *karma*? *Karma* means simply the event of an action or deed. I totally accept Lord Buddha's words because I know that I have no free will. All that happens through this body-mind organism is God's Will.

Kay: *You are enlightened. And you are on the level of total, absolute conviction — beyond the level of the intellect — that there is no free will and personal doership. For you this understanding is existential, and therefore personal* karma *doesn't exist.*

On the other hand, most people believe that they are personal entities. And that's why they are totally involved and identified with their actions and mistake them to be their own. Personal identification, of course, implies personal karma. *Maybe the event of enlightenment does actually change personal* karma *into non-karma. Isn't that what all the masters were telling us down the ages?*

Ramesh: Do you mean to say that the effects of *karma* stop when enlightenment happens?

Kay: No. *In the ancient* Advaita *book,* Tripura Rahasya, *it is said that the mere understanding of the truth as expounded by the true guru will effect the stopping of the personal karmic cycle. As long as we believe that there is a "me" and personal doership, there has to be the belief in personal* karma *and a life after life. An identified entity, "me," feels guilt and pride and believes he has done the respective action. Therefore, he feels responsible for his subsequent actions or his reactions to his earlier actions. And he feels responsible for the subsequent actions and reactions of others who became involved in his initial action. There is no* karma *without a "me."*

Ramesh: That is correct. You suffer because you are feeling guilty. And the feeling of guilt arises because you believe it was your bad action. You believe the bad action happened because of you. But, if you understand that there is no reason for you to feel guilty about your action, there is no suffering. So, the acceptance of this understanding means the end of the suffering of guilt. And it means the end of the suffering of pride.

Jaimie: *I understand what you are saying so far. I have a visual concept of you being an enlightened being and of myself being an ordinary unenlightened body-mind organism. What happens when you and me die, I mean, when our bodies expire? Our energies then go back into...*

Ramesh: ...into Totality. Correct.

Jaimie: *I have this visual image that within Consciousness or Reality a "wave," i.e. a body-mind organism, appears in manifestation which is the so-called world. After death and the return of our energies into Totality, I believe waves again arise from Totality. But they arise without a personal "me" or a soul or anything like this.*

If you put a pot of soup with all the little vegetables in it in a blender, you would still have all the vegetables there. But they are blended up now. Haven't Consciousness and our body-mind organisms become something like that blended soup? Isn't that soup representing Reality? Then a wave arises and a carrot pops out all of a sudden — I mean, a new body-mind organism is created.

Ramesh: But how can a carrot pop up if the soup is completely blended into one mixture, Jamie?

Jaimie: *That is my question. Am I a carrot?*

Ramesh: You described a simile. What you mean is that all the *karmas* of everybody come together in one mixture which I call "the pool of Consciousness." If you come out of such a mixture, how can it be your *karma*? It is a mixture, yes.

Jaimie: *So, I get blended up in all this?*

Ramesh: When the carrot and all the rest get mixed up, where is the carrot?

Jaimie: *When the wave happens again and a new body-mind organism appears again in manifestation, does the carrot or the potato . . . ?*

Ramesh: I am not talking of you as a carrot. As you have rightly said, the mixture has happened because the blender has mixed everything. How can a carrot come out of that mixture?

Jaimie: *But what comes out then?*

Ramesh: What comes out of the mixture has nothing to do with the old, dead and mixed-up carrot at all. That carrot is finished. A new carrot is created. A whole lot of new vegetables are created. The mixture is gone and finished.

Where does the manifestation come from? There are two ways to answer that question. *Advaita* says that Consciousness-not-aware-of-itself becomes, all of a sudden, aware of itself through the manifestation. The manifestation is merely a reflection of Consciousness-not-aware-of-itself. But they are both the same Consciousness. Consciousness-not-aware-of-itself is not different from Consciousness-aware-of-itself. Consciousness becomes aware of itself through the manifestation which science calls the Big Bang. There is nothing and then there is the Big Bang and the manifestation arises.

Jaimie: *What happens to an enlightened being and an unenlightened being after death? Is there a difference between the two? They both go into the pool of Consciousness out of which new body-mind organisms appear — is that correct? Does something of the enlightened energy return again from the pool of Consciousness? And how do we know what it is and where it has manifested again?*

Ramesh: Wait a minute! We are now on the level of the total manifestation and not on the stage of the individual human being. Consciousness-not-aware-of-itself becomes conscious of itself through the manifestation. According to Ramana Maharshi, the word "I-I" represents that Consciousness which is not aware of itself. The words "I-Am" represent Consciousness which becomes aware of itself through the manifestation. So, "I-I" becomes "I-Am."

Jamie: *Is this a process from non-manifestation to manifestation?*

Ramesh: Yes, it is a process of manifestation.

Jaimie: *Is one able to recognize this process if one is enlightened? Is enlightenment a similar process?*

Ramesh: Enlightenment has nothing to do with what is happening in manifestation other than it just happens. Enlightenment is just an event like an earthquake or a tempest or whatever. It is a happening in phenomenality. At the moment, we are talking about how phenomenality occurs. Phenomenality or manifestation is not a separate real thing of its own. It depends for its existence on Consciousness. Consciousness has created this manifestation as a reflection of itself. When you step in front of a mirror, you will see your image reflected in it. To the extent that the image is seen, that image in the mirror is real. But you know it is not real because the moment you step away from it your image disappears.

The manifestation is real to the extent that you can see, hear, smell, taste and touch it — but you can't do so without being conscious. But it is not real, because it has no existence of its own. Likewise, your image in the mirror has no reality of its own.

The shadow is real to the extent that it exists. But if you stand in the sun, the shadow depends on your body. The moment you come away from the sun, the shadow disappears. Therefore, the shadow is both real and unreal.

Jaimie: *But the potential of the shadow is there, isn't it?*

Ramesh: No, the potential of the shadow is not there at all. You are the potential of the shadow.

Jaimie: *And is Consciousness that potential?*

Ramesh: Yes. And the manifestation is the "shadow." Do you understand? The Potential "I-I" has become the "I-Am," the impersonal Awareness of the manifestation. And the "I-I" which has become the "I-Am" identifies itself with the body-mind organism and says, "I am Jamie."

Do you see the process?

It is a process in phenomenality: "I-I," "I-Am," "I am Jamie." And what is called enlightenment is still part of what happens in phenomenality. It is an event in phenomenality.

Jaimie: *Yes, I see.*

Ramesh: In the seeker this process is reversed. "Jaimie" gets wiped out by the mere understanding that "Jaimie" does not exist. Jaimie has no independent existence. When it is truly accepted that there is no Jaimie, that all that exists and happens is through Consciousness or God, and that all there is is Consciousness, then Jaimie disappears. Whose will prevails then? And when Jaimie is wiped out, the "I-Am" remains — the impersonal Awareness, which is enlightenment.

In reality, Jaimie cannot be enlightened because, according to my understanding, enlightenment means simply the total annihilation of Jaimie as an independent entity with a sense of personal doership.

Jaimie: *Is that why there cannot be a continuation of a personal* karma?

Ramesh: No. The reason why there cannot be a continuation of a personal *karma* is only one: whose *karma* exists?

Jaimie: *Nobody's; because the individual and the personal doer don't exist.*

Ramesh: Quite right. And, therefore, no "I" can do anything unless it is God's Will. Whatever happens through this or any other body-mind organism is whose deed? Is it my deed, is it Gary's deed, is it Herbert's deed? Or is it God's deed, through the respective body-mind organisms which are instruments at His command?

My point is that if there is no individual who can create *karma*, how could *karma* then be associated with an individual that is going to take "his" *karma* into a new life? Yes, there is definitely the *karma* of impersonal deeds. "Deeds are done, events happen" — impersonally.

The theory of *karma* is the theory of causation. Deeds and actions will have their effects in the immediate or distant future. The body-mind organism that is concerned with a deed will be affected if the consequences of that deed become effective in the near future, during the time in which that organism is still alive. Of course, there can be consequences for organisms which were not directly involved in the causative deed.

Say, somebody is promiscuous. I dare to say that such a person is not so. Rather, we should say that promiscuity has happened through a certain body-mind organism because it was so destined for it. It was God's Will for promiscuity to happen. The result of that promiscuity can be an illegitimate child or AIDS — depending on what is destined and willed by God.

A killing can only happen because it was the Will of God.

Jaimie: *I understand this.*

Ramesh: The killing was destined and willed by God, and the killer and his deed and the victim and his murder were part of the same event. And the consequences of the murder will also be the destiny of the same body-mind organism. The consequences of a deed can be in the near or in the distant future, according to God's Will — which cannot be understood. The same body-mind organism will have to bear the consequences in the near future. The consequences of a war will have short-term effects and long-term effects for the children and the children's children. For the consequences of a war to manifest, God creates new body-mind organisms — the children who have to bear the consequences that He has destined.

Jaimie: *The deeds and their consequences have nothing to do with their individual doer.*

Ramesh: Because "I" have not done anything. Jaimie cannot do anything. Whatever has happened, or happens, through a body-mind organism called Jaimie could not have happened, and will not happen, unless it is God's Will.

Jaimie: *And just understanding this stops the cycle, doesn't it? It is not a physical stopping. It just stops because of simply listening and understanding the teaching.*

Ramesh: That is 100% correct. Therefore I keep saying that all that is necessary is understanding. All that is necessary for you to do is not to do anything but to understand. And whether that understanding happens or not, depends on the destiny of the body-mind organism called Jamie. It is as simple as that.

33.2 Enlightenment:
The Eruption of a Volcano or the Blooming of a Flower?

Jaimie: *Is there any way to know if enlightenment has happened to one? Before I came to Lucknow, and to you here in Bombay, I had the idea that one would definitely know if, and when, enlightenment happened to one's being. I understood that there was a process from unenlightenment to enlightenment. When the thinking mind or the "me" — and with it the sense of personal doership — disappears, is there "anyone" left to know that it has happened?*

Ramesh: Are you asking, "Is it possible to know what is going to happen in the future?" The answer is that to know the future is a gift which God has given to certain body-mind organisms.

Jaimie: *Did you know when your enlightenment would happen to you?*

Ramesh: No. Nor do I know if it is raining in New York at this very moment. But some people, even though they are not enlightened, have the gift of knowing what will happen in the future, or at this moment elsewhere.

Jaimie: *My question actually is, "Did you know at the moment when enlightenment occurred that it was actually the occurrence of enlightenment that happened? Does one know it in the same way as one knows that an earthquake has happened?"*

Ramesh: Oh, yes, indeed you know! It is the same as with an earthquake. If you are present during an earthquake, you don't need to ask somebody if that happening was an earthquake.

I don't know what you understand by enlightenment, but let me explain to you what I understand by enlightenment. Enlightenment is the 100% acceptance that "I" have no free will, and therefore no personal doership. Enlightenment means "I" cannot do anything, and that whatever happens in the entire manifestation is God's Will.

Jaimie: *I understand what you are saying. I am totally convinced of it. But I still don't know where I am at. Doesn't all seeking stop with enlightenment? Does that mean one would never have another question?*

Ramesh: That is correct. If I understand that whatever happens is God's Will, what question can arise? Tell me! Which doubts could arise? Of course, questions about phenomenality can arise. If you work as a scientist, questions will keep arising regarding the field of your research. Such work will be executed by the working mind.

Jaimie: *I feel I have accepted, and I am 100% convinced, that there is no personal doership and that all that happens is according to God's Will. But this conviction didn't come about in a particular moment, accompanied by a great emotional release, or by an enormous blissful outbreak. I just know that it is so. This knowing is unshakable.*

On the other hand, you say that enlightenment occurs at a particular moment and is an event in time, like an earthquake.

Ramesh: When it becomes 100%, you will know it in one stroke. Now you still have doubts and questions. "Am I totally enlightened or not?" is your question, and your doubt, at this time.

Jaimie: *I have the 100% conviction that there is no personal doership. But this conviction is not something extraordinary, nor does it make me feel emotional or blissful. So, if this is enlightenment, I know it to be so only because of you; because you define enlightenment in this manner.*

I don't know where I am at. I only know that, for me, there is no seeking anymore, nor is there a sense of personal doership. What makes it different from your own experience is that the conviction didn't happen as an event — in one stroke — at a particular time.

Ramesh: When all doubts cease, you will not need any certificate from any guru, or from anybody else, that you are enlightened. Even after enlightenment, the person is still an individual, because if called by his name he will respond. That's why, after enlightenment, identification with the body and the name must continue. The working mind has to continue in a sage for his body-mind organism to live. But the personal doership totally disappears.

I am wearing the sacred thread of a *brahmin*. "I" am not wearing the sacred thread. What I have done is not to remove it. There is no individual who needed to remove it. It has been there for more than fifty years, and most probably it will remain on this body until it dies. Why should I remove it? There is nobody wanting to remove something which has been there for fifty or sixty years. Whatever happens, happens; "I" am not doing it.

If I pace up and down here in my living room for half-an-hour, "I" am not pacing up and down. It just happens. "I" am breathing, but there is no "me" who is breathing. The breathing, walking, eating, and so on, are happening, and those activities are merely witnessed as part of the functioning of Totality. It is anyway a fact that "you" cannot breathe or direct the digestive process.

Jaimie: *Do you have the sense that you are in the body?*

Ramesh: Oh, yes, indeed! Who is in the body? Consciousness. What is 100% accepted? That Consciousness is all there is. And what functions through every body-mind organism is Consciousness, just as electricity functions through innumerable gadgets which all were invented to fulfill their respective tasks. You know that the fan does not move by itself. It is the electricity which functions through it that makes it move. That is what I understand when I say I know for a fact that it is Consciousness that is functioning through every body-mind organism. And that Consciousness, or God, has created a particular body-mind organism with such programming that it will, and can, produce only certain acts.

Jaimie: *Is there a process whereby this understanding deepens in phenomenality? That deepening process depends on the Will of God, right?*

Ramesh: It is a process. Enlightenment is an event that happens in phenomenality. And for an event to happen, there needs to be a process.

Madhukar: *Could it be possible, in a special case, that enlightenment has happened but that the exact moment of that occurrence was not noticed by the enlightened body-mind organism concerned? Such a case could be compared with a flower that is opening and blooming and giving its fragrance, but not from an exact, particular instant onwards. However, one would find oneself being surprised by the fragrance of the flower in that one, sudden moment when one first notices its smell. Could the occurrence of enlightenment become known in this fashion in a particular case?*

In the same way, one could have become totally convinced — over a longer period of time — that there is no personal doership, and that whatever happens is God's Will. But one might not know at what exact day and time the full 100% conviction occurred. Your disciple Ben Pierce's enlightenment occurred in this fashion.

Ramesh: What you do mean by "knowing"?

Madhukar: *You have often repeated that there is an event in time and space — a sudden realization — in which one knows that enlightenment has happened.*

Ramesh: That is right.

Madhukar: *Is it also possible for enlightenment to occur without such a sudden realization happening as part of an actual event?*

Enlightenment Occurrences

Ramesh: No. Without a sudden realization, all doubts do not disappear. They only disappear when there is a 100% acceptance that all is God's Will, that "I" cannot be the doer, and that all that exists is the body-mind organism, programmed in such a way that God initiates an input which brings about an output in the form of an action. After enlightenment, there is absolutely not the slightest doubt about this fact. If you still have the slightest doubt about this fact, then the 100% enlightenment has not happened yet.

(a) A blooming whose fragrance is noticed one fine morning

Jaimie: *But who is there to know if the "me" is annihilated?*

Ramesh: That is the point. There is no "who" to know.

(b) A process, but its occurrence is sudden

Jaimie: *But how can you know, then?*

Ramesh: You cannot. The knowing is there. In fact, there is no one there who doubts whether enlightenment has happened or not.

Jaimie: *There is no one who doubts whether it has happened or not. But there is some sort of knowing that it has happened?*

Ramesh: Yes, there is knowing. There is a 100% acceptance. And in that 100% acceptance there is no individual accepter. There is a 100% understanding, in which there is no independent comprehender or understander.

(c) Building up unnoticed into a dramatic eruption

Jaimie: *Is it something like an impersonal recognition, like witnessing happening without a witnesser?*

Ramesh: Correct. It just happens. And for that reason, there is no one to need a certificate from someone else to say that you are enlightened. If one feels that one still needs to know whether the 100% enlightenment has happened or not, then it

(d) The end of a chain reaction which begins in nothing and ends in nothing

Possibilities, options, preferences

hasn't fully happened yet; because there is still someone who has a doubt.

Madhukar: *Don't you think that it is possible that somebody loses his doubts progressively as his understanding deepens, without the "Big Bang"-event of sudden realization at a specific time and place? And that, at some point, that person realizes that there are absolutely no doubts and questions anymore? Couldn't enlightenment happen that way as well?*

Ramesh: Then that person may think that enlightenment has happened until the next doubt or question arises. He may think he is enlightened. And there are plenty of people who think they are enlightened, make no mistake. They think they are enlightened, and that is the whole rub, that is the whole problem. They think "they" are enlightened. You see what I am getting at?

Madhukar: *A man in Pune, called Kiran, is saying that his life became absolutely questionless, doubtless, and free from personal problems, and that in his case the identification with a personal "I"-entity has ceased completely. He indicates that this disidentification has developed in an almost unnoticeable fashion, comparable to the flowering process of a wild flower which, on a fine morning, starts to share its fragrance. Yes, before the actual flowering there were indications that the flowering was near, he said. The flower was growing through the season, and the buds had opened. And at a certain moment it was noticed, "Oh, there is this wonderful fragrance!" Yes, the arrival of the fragrance was anticipated, but it was nonetheless a surprise when it was suddenly smelled. The event of the blooming and the distribution of the fragrance was irreversible. And from that moment onwards, that fragrance kept attracting bees (seekers) and other insects from all directions. That's how Kiran describes "his" blooming.*
  Don't you think it is possible for enlightenment to happen in this fashion? Kiran doesn't actually explicitly express that he is enlightened. But this and other stories which he keeps telling people, about the deepening process of his understanding, imply that enlightenment has happened in his case.

Ramesh: Those implications themselves mean that enlightenment has not happened, because Kiran says, "Kiran is enlightened."

Madhukar: *No, he doesn't say that.*

Ramesh: I don't know who this Kiran is. But as long as a person feels that he is enlightened, enlightenment cannot have happened, because enlightenment means the total annihilation of the "me," "him," "her," or "you."

Jaimie: *If somebody asked you, "Are you enlightened?", what would you answer?*

Ramesh: I would say that no "me" can be enlightened.

Jaimie: *Yet, you know. There is a knowing that enlightenment has happened.*

Ramesh: There is a knowing. There is a knowing that all there is, is Consciousness. There is a 100% knowing that all that happens is the Will of Consciousness, or God. And there is a 100% knowing that there is no individual doer. And therefore, there is a 100% knowing that there is nobody to feel guilty or proud.

Jaimie: *And in phenomenality, the very second after this realization happened, was there a knowing of that "something very different"?*

Ramesh: It can be. I will tell you a simile, a metaphor, which illustrates these moments. You are lost in a labyrinth, a completely dark cave, and you don't know where the exit is. You are stumbling around in the darkness searching for the exit until your intuition somehow leads you towards it. You begin to sense some light, or less darkness, in the direction you are heading. You are not sure, but you definitely keep moving towards what you believe to be some light, some hope. Soon you are certain that there is light. And as you keep moving towards it, you find the exit.

Similarly, one will notice signs of the approach of enlightenment, certainly. But, in fact, those signs mean danger. Because those signs may turn out to be the very obstructions for enlightenment to occur. "Oh, I am enlightened," can be the very obstruction.

Jaimie: *That's why I had my doubts with Poonjaji in Lucknow, when he told me, "Accept that you are already there, you are already enlightened." I replied, "I can't accept that I am enlightened. I do not want to presume that I 'know.'"*

Ramesh: Because there is still a "me" wanting to know. There is still a desire to know. With enlightenment, even that wanting disappears.

Jaimie: *And there is nothing I can do about it.*

Ramesh: That is, as the Americans say, the bottom line.

Jaimie: *We can only let it happen. Not even that. It is just happening.*

Ramesh: If it is to happen it will happen in spite of you, not because of you.

Jaimie: *Is there something like a last state prior to enlightenment happening?*

Ramesh: Yes. That last state is the total acceptance that there is nothing I can do to bring about enlightenment. In the context of *bhakti*, or devotion, that acceptance means, "Alright, God, if You don't want to bring about enlightenment in this body-mind organism, don't! I don't care. Your Will be done, not mine." That is the final surrender in which there is no individual "me" to surrender. In any case, what does the "me" have to surrender? What capital does it have to surrender to God? Everything you have has come from God anyway, hasn't it?

Jaimie: *The individual has nothing to surrender.*

Ramesh: Except the feeling of the sense of personal doership, the sense of individuality as the "me."

Jaimie: *And that surrender means the end of desire.*

Ramesh: Correct! That is the end of desire. That is even the end of desire for enlightenment.

Jaimie: *Poonjaji says, "Don't even let one desire, don't even let one single thought, arise."*

Ramesh: I don't agree. What he says cannot be done.

Jaimie: *I know you don't. I know it can't be done. And I can see why. I am aware that, when I go into silence, the desires stop on their own, without me doing anything to make them stop.*

Ramesh: That is correct, Jaimie. Therefore, I say the brain is inert matter. It cannot create a thought or a desire. A thought, a desire, a feeling may arise even in the sage who is enlightened, because his programmed body-mind organism continues to exist. His brain will keep reacting to outside events, like thoughts, according to the program of the body-mind instrument. That's why anger may arise in a sage as a reaction of the brain to a perceived outside event, but he will not get horizontally involved with the anger. The anger will drop immediately. On the other hand, an average person will carry the anger along for a long time. He may say, "I am angry. I should do something about it, it is not good to be angry." The false guru may say, "I am enlightened and I should not become angry. What will people say?" In both cases, there is horizontal involvement.

33.3 Sex, the Sage and the Working Mind

Herbert: *I don't understand what you mean with "thoughts coming from outside." I witness the thought arising within myself. I am sure that thoughts arise in a man which cannot arise in a woman and the other way around. Thoughts about pregnancy and childbirth may only arise in a woman. In this way, thoughts are very personal and they are related to a specific body-mind organism. How can you say that thoughts come from outside?*

Ramesh: There is really no outside and inside. For me, "outside" means that thoughts are not your creation.

Herbert: *What about thoughts which arise from memory?*

Ramesh: There are millions of sense impressions collected and stored in the memory. Surely, a thought can arise from memory and can be made available to consciousness. A particular thought does not need to arise fresh from this present moment. Why should one particular thought arise out of the millions of stored thoughts in the memory? Because of destiny, one could say. Even a thought that arises in a particular body-mind organism is part of that body-mind organism's destiny. That thought leads to some action.

Jaimie: *That particular thought is destined to arise, as is the reaction to that thought. Is that correct?*

Ramesh: Correct.

Jaimie: *The thoughts which come to my boyfriend are destined to arise, as well as his reaction to those thoughts. And these thoughts can only come to him because he is programmed for them.*

Ramesh: Then what is the difference between an ordinary person and the sage? A thought about something which was said yesterday can arise to both the sage and the ordinary person. In the case of the sage that thought will pass away because it will not be taken delivery of. A sage will not get horizontally involved in thinking something like: "I will tell that person this or that in response to what he said to me yesterday."

Jaimie: *The thought doesn't hold on.*

Ramesh: Yes. An average person will hold on to that thought and get horizontally involved in it.

Jaimie: *Since I have been in India, I have had very few desires. I almost eat nothing. I have no desire for sex with my boyfriend. I feel this desirelessness has to do with enlightenment coming through. Does a sage not desire sex anymore?*

Ramesh: A sage doesn't desire sex. But if sex happens he doesn't prevent it. Who is there to prevent anything?

Jaimie: *But it can happen?*

Ramesh: Yes, certainly sex can happen. For the sage, sex is something which just happens when it happens. For the ordinary person sex begins in the mind with a thought.

Here is a little story. A young married man from Kerala came, some 80 years ago, to Ramana Maharshi with a deep concern. He told the Maharshi that he was deeply in love with his wife. But he was attracted by the breasts of the lady neighbor and he was afraid to commit adultery. The Maharshi is reported to have answered, "Adultery may happen or not. It may not happen because the girl may go elsewhere or you may be transferred and you may never come together. Why worry about adultery which may not even happen? But if it happens, why would you think 'you' have committed adultery?"

The Maharshi didn't condone adultery. He simply pointed out that all that happens is part of the impersonal functioning of Totality. Adultery would be part of the destiny of that organism, irrespective of the consequences.

Jaimie: *You just said that sex starts in the mind. If, in the case of a sage, the thoughts are witnessed and get cut off immediately without any involvement, how could sex ever happen in the life of a sage?*

Ramesh: Sex may begin in the mind but it doesn't end there. Where does it ultimately happen?

Jaimie: *In the case of a sage, does sex get cut off at the level of the mind, and then just happen?*

Ramesh: Sex can also be started by the partner. If your boyfriend starts making love to you, your body responds naturally. There is no question of mind or thinking or horizontal involvement. Sex may have been in his mind. The thought then led him to make love to you. Sex was not in your mind. The sex act was initiated by someone else and the body-mind organism responded to it. And sex happened.

Jaimie: *I see what you mean.*

Ramesh: But if you think, "I had sex. I should not have sex because I am supposed to be enlightened," you are not enlightened.

Jaimie: *What happens if the sex act is initiated by the partner and the sage keeps witnessing? Is sex going to happen at all?*

Ramesh: In that case sex may happen or not. If there is no response of the body-mind organism of the sage, sex will not happen. If the body of the sage responds, sex will happen. In both cases, the sage will not get horizontally involved in thinking, rather, whatever happens is being witnessed.

Jaimie: *If the body of the sage doesn't respond to the sexual advances of the partner and the sage is being challenged to respond, what will the sage do? Will he get involved horizontally in thinking?*

Ramesh: The sage will react spontaneously. He may explain to the partner what is going on. But his explanation will be done by the working mind and not by the thinking mind.

Parso: *You were talking earlier of the young man who came to Ramana Maharshi. Can that man try to overcome his thoughts of having sex with his lady neighbor?*

Ramesh: He can think of overcoming his desire. But it is not in his hands to succeed or not to succeed. Where does the thought of overcoming the desire come in, Parso? This thought is a reaction of the brain to the thought of that desire. The brain reacts to the thought of adultery and creates a resistance. Whether that re-

Reactions to an erection

Sage and non-sage

sistance remains or disappears, is part of the destiny. A thought comes and the brain reacts. And that reaction is what you call your action. If the reaction of your brain is resistance and the resistance happens, you say, "I have resisted a bad thought." And you feel proud. I would say that a bad thought being resisted is part of the destiny of that organism. That is the difference.

Parso: *We should not take credit. Is that what you mean?*

Ramesh: Or blame. If you accept that whatever happens is God's action, there is no question of credit or blame. If that is understood there can be no feeling of guilt if your action turns out to be a failure, and there can be no sense of pride if your action turns out to be successful.

Jaimie: *I have another question. I just want to get all of them out, all of them.*

Ramesh: Good. But before you do that, let me formulate for you the question which you had earlier. Let me answer that question for you first. It is a natural question which demands an answer.

As long as enlightenment has not happened, the individual still exists. And it is quite normal for the individual to wonder, "Am I progressing or not in the process of enlightenment?" Isn't that your question? That question is bothering you. You may say: "I understand when Ramesh is saying, 'All that happens is God's Will,' and I accept it whole-heartedly and still I feel enlightenment has not happened yet." The answer to your question is fairly simple. If you find yourself in daily life more tolerant towards other people's weaknesses; if you find yourself not having as many desires as you used to have and if you find yourself being more generous to others than you used to be, then you can take it that the understanding of the teaching is in the process of going deeper, and the process of enlightenment has progressed.

When seekers posed this question to Ramana Maharshi, he used to answer that to be a seeker after Truth — or God, or Reality — is, in itself, God's Grace. Out of millions of people, only a few are spiritual seekers and you are one of them. God's Grace has already descended on you. He would say, "Your head is already in the tiger's mouth." God has created this body-mind organism with such programming that spiritual seeking is happening, instead of seeking for money or fame. I tell you that you are already on your way. Why be in a hurry? The tiger will definitely snap his jaws. He may take his time. So what! There is no need to worry when that will happen. In the meantime, enjoy your life, the food, the sex, whatever comes along.

33.4 Why Does God Create Misery? — Why Not!

Jaimie: My grandmother died recently. She was my last relative to pass on. She wasn't really interested in spirituality. She often said, "When I die all is over and nothing will come after life." I had visited her a couple of times before she died. On those occasions I told her that I knew her belief. But I asked her anyway if she would let me know if, on her way out, she found something different from what she believed. She agreed. I had a dream one night in which a beautiful bird landed on my hand. It had long eyelashes. It tried to communicate with me. And I knew in the dream that the bird was a spirit which wanted to communicate with me. After I woke up, I found out that my grandmother had died that afternoon.

Ramesh: Sure.

Jaimie: I really sensed that she was trying to let me know...

Ramesh: ... that she was dying or whatever.

Jaimie: You said earlier that there is no personal carrying over of personal deeds into Reality at the moment of death because there is no personal doership. My question is: how could this have happened? How could she have communicated with me?

Jaimie's boyfriend: We found out later that she had died before you had the dream.

Ramesh: Maybe there was a time difference between your place and her place. And your dream occurred at the time when your grandmother was in the process of dying. I would say she must have been dying at the time when you had your dream.

Jaimie: Yes, yes. Maybe you are right.

Ramesh: So, it must have been the same moment when you dreamed and she died. I am sure that's what you would find out if you calculated once more the time difference between the two locations.

Jaimie: So, time has nothing to do with that?

Ramesh: You see, the present moment is the present moment anywhere in the universe. The clock may show different times. Here it is 11:00 a.m. now which in the United States is maybe three o'clock in the morning.

Jaimie: So, then I also had an experience with my grandfather. He came to me in a dream some time after he was dead.

Ramesh: Yes.

Jaimie: *He told me that I was going to know the secrets of the universe. That was 15 years ago when I was not even...*

Ramesh: ...concerned with spirituality.

Jaimie: *This was long after he had died, a month later.*

Ramesh: That he came to you is something which happened. Anything can happen in the world.

Jaimie: *At that time, I imagined that it had been him. But it wasn't "him." It was, rather, something like a thought or a dream — just as a dream is happening at this very moment here in this living room with you.*

Ramesh: It is just a thought.

Jaimie: *A thought form coming through as an image.*

Ramesh: Some time ago, I was asked if I believed in spirits. I said that I see no reason why God should not be able to create beings without bodies, since he is able to create ones with bodies.

Jaimie: *Just as the sleeping dream and the waking dream are of the same kind, spirits must be of the same kind. Is that what you mean?*

Ramesh: Yes. The moment you ask, "Why does God do this and not do that?", you are limiting the supremacy of the Supreme Power, God. It is so simple. Why does God create misery? Why not! God never promised to anyone that he would not create misery. In fact, life means a combination of opposites.

Why does God create misery?—Because He does!

33.5 Is Gratitude a Precondition for Enlightenment to Happen?

Ramesh: When you really understand that everything is Consciousness, that everything happens in Consciousness — and part of it happens through you, who are functioning as an instrument — then where is the question of anyone seeking anything? If someone is seeking a million dollars, it is Consciousness that wants him to play that role and to seek a million dollars, along with whatever else may happen in that search — maybe a lot of frustration and unhappiness. After having gotten his million dollars, but no happiness, the mind of that person may turn inward and the search for enlightenment may begin. Qualitatively, there is no difference between the two kinds of seeking. No matter what you seek, any seeking means frustration, until there is the realization that there is truly no "one" who can seek anything, and that the process of seeking is merely part of the fundamental functioning of Totality.

This process is witnessed, but not by an individual. What is witnessed is the process of the individual trying to get something and being frustrated, until gradually the individual fades out, while witnessing keeps on happening. At a certain moment, there is the true realization that there is no individual. The one who has been witnessing turns out not to exist. The witnessing has been impersonal. The body and the mind seem to belong to someone else. And you see, gradually, the individual disappears, and finally gets annihilated.

What appears to be your action — including your search — is truly God's action and according to His Will. He turned you into a seeker, and it is Him who will decide if you will do *sadhana* or not, and if and when enlightenment will happen to this body-mind organism. There is no "you" who can become enlightened. When you understand that all that happens is part of the functioning of Totality — willed and destined by God — you may come to the conclusion that enlightenment may or may not happen. And you may say, "OK, God, if You want enlightenment to happen in this body-mind organism, let it happen, if not, don't." Ultimately, this final firm conviction arises: "I don't care if enlightenment happens or not," or, "I don't care if I care." (*laughter*) This is the penultimate stage before enlightenment can happen. Who is there to care? You see, you can seek something because you want to enjoy it, but enlightenment is a state in which there is no one to enjoy the state — so why should you bother?

Michael: *So I don't care, because I realize there's no "I" really. There's no "I" in any of this, and I guess there's no "you" either.*

Ramesh: That's right. "Come to me and I will give you some experience or enlightenment." Such promises are made by some gurus. But there is no "I" to give "you" any experience. Experience happens. Only when it is understood that any experience is an impersonal experience can something happen. What happens through the body will have its repercussions and effects on the body. That understanding will cause you to stop judging other people and yourself. There will be no room for guilt and judgment, or for considering someone else your enemy.

Any teaching which says "You must give up this or that" should not be accepted. I have never been able to accept do's and dont's as part of a teaching. The teaching is part of What-is, and you, as you are, are also part of What-is — and the What-is has to be accepted. "This (which is part of What-is), I accept, and that (which is also part of What-is), I don't accept" — how can this be? Who is to make this distinction and choice?

This is what I teach. The teaching is so simple.

Jaimie: *Earlier you were quoting Ramana Maharshi. Does his saying "Your head is already in the tiger's mouth" mean that enlightenment can happen at any moment?*

Ramesh: Yes, absolutely. Enlightenment can happen at any moment, without any precondition. Ramana's statement is a great encouragement for the seeker.

When I say enlightenment is a process, it doesn't mean that every seeker has to go through each and every step of the process. During the process quantum jumps are possible, over which one has no control.

Jaimie: *It can happen slowly, or in stages, or in an instant.*

Madhukar: *You said to me the other day that first a certain gratitude needs to arise, without which enlightenment cannot happen. How can enlightenment happen at any time, if gratitude has to happen first? Is there, or is there not, an "only if"? Yesterday's statement contradicts what you were saying now.*

Ramesh: So, the necessary gratitude will happen.

Madhukar: *So, gratitude is a precondition for enlightenment to happen, and therefore enlightenment cannot happen at any time. If there is no gratitude, there will be no enlightenment. Are you speaking about cause and effect here?*

Ramesh: This gratitude can happen at the moment of enlightenment. I have forgotten in which context I was speaking of gratitude and enlightenment yesterday.

Madhukar: *You were saying the other day that only within a state of gratitude can enlightenment happen.*

GAMBLING FOR ENLIGHTENMENT

(1) Welcome to the seeker's world—advance 1 square
(2) Stop the rock and roll! Meditate! No lazy man's enlightenment here!—recede 2 squares
(3) Give all, get all! The only sure way to enlightenment —advance 3 squares
(4) Meeting the guru! The first leg of the journey accomplished—advance 5 squares
(5) You are an earnest and sincere meditator —advance 2 squares
(6) From sex to super-consciousness: Go for it! —advance 4 squares
(7) You are avoiding disciplehood!—recede 2 squares
(8) The guru's presence and pleasing him are the only short cuts—advance 4 squares
(9) Gratitude: the highest and last condition for enlightenment to happen. You made it! Congratulations!—advance to enlightenment
(10) Enlightenment

Ramesh: No. What I am saying is that a feeling of intense gratitude, a feeling of intense devotion, can arise, which leads to the immediate occurrence of enlightenment. There is no limitation in time for enlightenment to happen.

Let me tell you an instance in the life of my own brother-in-law — my wife's sister's husband. He had always been interested in spirituality. But he used to say, quite frankly, that he wasn't interested at all in my *Advaita* because it went over his head. He was deeply devotional, and even though he enjoyed my talks, he could never accept the concept of the impersonal functioning of Totality. And he was not supposed to, because his body-mind organism was programmed to be a *bhakta*, a really devotional seeker. He would cry every time he sang a *bhajan*. This man was an extremely wise and good man, by all standards.

He was also an extremely good and helpful doctor, who was loved by all his patients and by his fellow co-doctors. During the last years of his life, he had a couple of heart attacks. One day he felt a pain in his neck. As a doctor, he knew what medicine to take. But the medicine didn't work; rather, the pain moved from the neck to the heart. This was when he called for medical assistance, which was made available to him within half-an-hour. An ECG was taken immediately, and, shockingly, it showed almost no movement. He was dying. He knew it. When his wife wanted to take him to the hospital, as she had been advised by the attending doctor, he said, "Let us wait and see what will happen." Now, he began to describe what was happening to his body. He said, "My feet are becoming numb, and the numbness is now creeping up to my calves, now to my knees." He kept describing the movement of the numbness in his body, until it had crept to his heart. He died with a smile on his face.

I would say that enlightenment happened to this relative of mine at the moment of his death. Pure witnessing had happened. He was not worried about his death. This event proves that enlightenment can happen at any moment, even up to the moment of death. There is no point in anticipating or worrying about the occurrence of one's enlightenment. It will happen at its predestined time.

Parso: *I don't understand. How do you relate his death with enlightenment? How did this incident create enlightenment?*

Ramesh: Because enlightenment means the total absence of an individual with a sense of personal doership. Impersonal witnessing then happens. In this case, the doctor was witnessing the process of his own death without involvement. How many people would be able to do that? Most get involved and cry for help: "I am dying, I am dying, do something!" He was merely witnessing, and that's why I can say that enlightenment happened, in his case, at the moment of death. But, mind you, what I say is merely a concept, a belief. There is no question of knowing it.

Jamie: *Is enlightenment only for living people? I thought that enlightenment would change one's life and one's death. You say enlightenment doesn't necessarily change anything in practical life. What you say goes against what everybody else — including all religions — is saying, especially what you say about death.*

Ramesh: Even seekers who are on the path for several decades say that what I have to say is totally revolutionary. I say, "On the contrary! What I say is very basic. All there is, is Consciousness or God, and all that happens is God's Will." That's the basis of what I say. But on this basis, all the religions have built an enormous structure of beliefs and dogmas and myths.

Jaimie: *Those religions always propagate a continuation of life, of a soul, after death. And that makes us insecure on the path, because we don't know if what they say is true.*

Ramesh: That's correct. Is there really a rebirth or not? I am really not interested in whether there is rebirth or not. Rebirth or not, it is part of the mechanics of phenomenality. I am not concerned with phenomenality at all. I don't care what mechanics God uses to bring about phenomenality.

In any case, Jaimie is now in this birth, and she is not concerned at this moment with what she was in the previous births. And why should Jaimie be concerned with her future lives? Why to be interested in the mechanics of phenomenality if what you really want is to transcend phenomenality?

Jaimie: *The concept of rebirth can only exist with the concept of time. But the sages say time doesn't exist at all. What-is is.*

Ramesh: That is correct. And what is at the present moment anywhere in the universe is the What-is of this present moment. It is all there — here and now. The rest of it is all conceptual. Why bother with it?

Parso: *Having understood the "Here and Now," is that the end of the spiritual search?*

Ramesh: The "Here and Now" is the beginning and the end. There is no beginning and no end. It is this now/here, always, without beginning or end, without past and future.

Murthy: *All the time we create a beginning and then we want an end.*

Ramesh: That's right. You create a beginning. The mind creates a beginning and wants to know the end.

33.6 Enlightenment Happened in My Case

Jaimie: *Do you differentiate between mind and knowing?*

Ramesh: Sure. Knowing is in duality. You know something. You understand something. "You" that understands is the subject and that which is known and understood is an object.

Jaimie: *When enlightenment happens, there is a knowing of enlightenment but no "one" who knows it. Isn't that what you had said?*

Ramesh: Yes, there is a knowing in which there is no individual knower, an understanding in which there is no individual comprehender.

Jaimie: *Is that knowing like the intuitive knowing? Like a flash?*

Ramesh: Yes, it is intuitive knowing. In this kind of knowing there isn't that somebody who could say, "Now 'I' know." What does every seeker want to know? "'I' want to know God or Reality." Just understand the basics of it! The seeker as the subject "I" wants to know God, the object. That means the subject has usurped the Subjectivity of God, of Reality. And worse still, it has converted the Subjectivity — God or Reality — into an object. How could an object know Subjectivity? The object can only *be* Subjectivity.

By the same token, "you" cannot know enlightenment. Enlightenment can only be there. And when enlightenment happens, there will be no Jaimie who knows that she is enlightened.

Jaimie: *It seems to me that intuition happens to me, when opposites meet. Then there is a knowing. And my thinking mind cannot conceive that both opposites can operate at the same time.*

Ramesh: That is correct. In that knowing there is no thinking mind nor the working mind.

Fairly recently, the British astronomer and physicist Fred Hoyle was attending a physicist's conference in Paris. He reports how he was working on a problem for several days without finding the solution. Crossing a busy street in Paris, the solution occurred to him. He didn't need to write down the discovery because it was absolutely clear and obvious. And the answer stayed with him. He wrote it down after his daily routine, after dinner.

Once enlightenment happens, it remains there. There is no flip-flop anymore. No doubts, no questions; absolute conviction and clarity, because the individual "me" has been totally annihilated.

Jaimie: *Before enlightenment happens, would you call it intuitive knowledge versus mind?*

Ramesh: Indeed. If enlightenment has not happened yet you will say, "I must ask somebody if enlightenment has happened or not. I must get a certificate from my guru."

Murthy: *Our role after enlightenment is just to write down what occurred. Or, is there something else to do?*

Ramesh: Your role is to write down whatever is necessary to write down for

The anointment

you. Otherwise, it is not necessary to write it down. If enlightenment has happened, there is no need for you to write down the account of the experience.

Murthy: *When your enlightenment happened, it was you who did announce that you were enlightened. The world wasn't told about this event by your guru or by your wife or anyone else except by yourself. I don't announce my enlightenment.*

Ramesh: You see, that is the problem. Because you are not enlightened, you can't announce it and that's why you don't announce it.

Murthy: *I hear the news from you that you are enlightened. If you hadn't announced it, nobody would ever know that you are enlightened. And if nobody had ever announced it or written about it, nobody would ever know about the existence and the possibility of enlightenment, isn't it so? Because I heard it from you and I read about it in your book, I know now that you are enlightened. And now I also want enlightenment because I hear from you how great that state is.*

Ramesh: You see, if you go to Ramana Maharshi and ask him, "Has enlightenment happened in your case?" he will reply, "Yes," because there is still a body-mind organism called Ramana Maharshi which has to answer a question with his working mind. Even after enlightenment, the body-mind organism continues to function in the role which has been assigned to it by God or Totality.

Murthy: *But I can come to know about enlightenment only through a person who knows about it, isn't it? It will make no sense to ask an unenlightened person about enlightenment. After your enlightenment, you sat down and wrote about your experience.*

Ramesh: But Ramana Maharshi did not sit down and write an account of his enlightenment. For whom would he write down such an account? For whom?

33.7 Grace Or Practice?

Hans: *In my meditations, I suddenly realize that I have been horizontally involved in thinking, maybe for quite some time. That realization puts me back into the present moment. These two states alternate, being lost in horizontal thinking and being jolted back into the phenomenal present moment. What is the factor that makes one remember the present moment again and again? Is it entirely grace?*

Ramesh: Yes, you could say that. Anyway, it is God's Will that it happened. We could explain it in two ways: it was God's Will, or it was the destiny of the body-mind organism called Hans, that that event happened again and again in his meditation.

Hans: *I meditated for many years in the Buddhist tradition. For more then 2000 years a dispute is going on in Buddhism regarding self-effort and grace. The Buddhists train the mind to return to the present moment by constant witnessing.*

Ramesh: Who is to train the mind, Hans? You are the mind, you are the thinking mind! Who are you to do any *sadhana* and to train what and whose mind? You are the mind! And if something has to change the mind, it can only come from "outside." That you can call God's Grace if you like. The mind can only change through understanding.

Hans: *And yet it is my practical experience of many years, and therefore a fact for me, that the intervals of being engaged in horizontal thinking became shorter and the periods of pure awareness of the What-is became longer.*

Ramesh: That is correct.

Hans: *It seems like it doesn't matter if such progress is caused by grace or if it is a result of practice.*

Ramesh: Quite correct.

Hans: *But you stress that no "me"-entity exists whatsoever that could "do" something by "my" own efforts to favor progress in stilling "my" mind — which is the "me." Only surrender will effect anything. That's what you say, isn't it?*

Ramesh: That's why I suggest you go back to the basics whenever doubts or questions arise. The basics are: All there is, is Consciousness or God. This body-mind organism in which thoughts arise is merely an instrument through which God functions.

Practice or grace?

Hans: *This instrument has the tendency to practice various disciplines that actually bring about noticeable results.*

Ramesh: But it is still an instrument.

Hans: *But it is part of Totality and destined by Totality to practice. In this light, what is wrong with practice?*

Parso: *You say, "All there is, is Consciousness." The body-mind organisms are just available, present. From which place do thoughts start?*

Ramesh: All thoughts begin from Consciousness which is all there is. You are merely a programmed instrument, a computer created by God or Consciousness in order that certain actions can be produced by God through it — not according to your plans but according to God's plans. To produce a desired output, i.e. an action, God sends an input in the form of a thought or a sense-object which is perceived, and the brain makes the body-mind organism react to it. And that reaction you call "your" action.

Kay: *In many cases the body-mind organisms are programmed to want to be special. The more special one wants to be, the deeper is the personal identification of "I am Kay," and the stronger is the separation from the impersonal "I-Am" state.*

Ramesh: The same Energy or Consciousness produces both processes — the identification from the impersonal state "I-Am" to the personal state "I am Kay," and the reverse process of disidentification. Kay has nothing to do in both the processes. They are part of the impersonal functioning of Totality or God in phenomenality or manifestation. All that Kay can do is watch what happens.

Kay: *Or, instead of watching, I can get involved.*

Ramesh: Yes. If involvement is destined for this body-mind organism, involvement will happen for as long as it is destined to happen.

Kay: *I really can't believe that there is any difference between the state of enlightenment and the state of what you call the ordinary person.*

Ramesh: That is correct. Why bother? Let things happen as they happen. That means witnessing whatever happens without being involved in it. Involvement is always personal. Witnessing is always impersonal.

Kay: *According to my own experience, involvement happens on its own. The thought to do something comes to me. I then start doing. I get into the action. Involvement and absorption happen. That you call the working mind. Then I find myself judging what I am doing and I start thinking how I could do it better. That is the thinking mind. The working and the thinking mind alternate back and forth, on and on.*

Ramesh: No, it doesn't. The moment you realize that you are horizontally involved thinking stops.

Kay: *Of course, horizontal involvement stops at that moment.*

Ramesh: The involvement continues until that stopping happens at the moment of realizing, "I was unnecessarily involved." That realization is not your doing. It is God's doing. That sudden realization of the unnecessary involvement and the cutting off because of it, is the understanding in action. The sudden realization cannot happen unless there is some understanding. The understanding produces the sudden realization that I have been unnecessarily involved, and the involvement gets cut off. And as the understanding deepens, the sudden understanding, and the consequential cutting off, happens quicker and quicker and more frequently and the involvement lasts less and less long.

Hans: *The Buddhist approach attempts the same goal by training the mind. The goal is to stay aware in every moment. And the more you train the mind the more you stay aware. As I said, that is my personal experience. So, I see no difference, except in the approach.*

Ramesh: What mind? And who is to train the mind? Hans, you are the mind!

You are not different from the mind. Who is this "you" to be asked to do *sadhana* in order to stop the mind that you are?

Hans: *And yet, meditation practice definitely brings about results regarding cutting off horizontal involvement. This I know for sure.*

Ramesh: Of course, if you go to a gymnasium and work with weights, muscles will develop. Your results are of the same order. The scientists experimented and the result was the nuclear bomb. Every action has its result or consequences. You think you are doing *sadhana* in order to quiet the mind in order to stay aware without getting involved in thinking. That will happen, just as you will get psychic powers if you train for them. But they will make you more proud. The problem with *sadhana* is that it produces pride in the person who is doing it, and it makes his ego stronger.

Jaimie: *But if that is meant to happen, it will happen.*

Ramesh: Absolutely correct.

Herbert: *Does every* sadhana *make the ego stronger? Or does it depend on how we do* sadhana?

Ramesh: If there is a person who says, "I am doing *sadhana* in order to get something," the ego will get stronger. If that *sadhana* produces results, the ego will be strengthened even more.

Herbert: *Is it OK to exercise my body and keep it fit? Does exercise strengthen my ego?*

Ramesh: No, exercises will make your health alright. The ego only gets stronger if you think "you" are doing something. On the other hand, if something is happening on its own, there is no "you." That is fine. That is exactly what happens in the case of the sage. He doesn't sit idle either. Everything happens to him. He walks, talks, sleeps, reads the newspaper etc., but there is never any feeling of "he" himself doing anything. Whatever happens is merely witnessed.

In your case, Hans, *sadhana* may happen. If you like to meditate, meditate. Fine. The Buddhists call it *sadhana*. But if you also call it *sadhana* and if Hans thinks "he" is doing *vipassana*, then the ego will become stronger. But if you merely witness meditation happening, and you feel happy with the meditation, there is no ego.

Jaimie: *And if it is meant for me to keep trying and trying to quiet the mind and therefore to keep doing sadhana, I'll do so till that trying is exhausted and it stops. And all of it is God's Grace.*

Ramesh: Absolutely correct.

Hans: *After putting in so much effort into Buddhist meditations all these years, I actually came to the point of exhaustion. But still, I am not yet able to drop meditation all together.*

Ramesh: Your Buddhist years are part of the destiny of your body-mind organism. These years didn't happen to some other person.

Murthy: *In all actions that happen through you, you don't have the feeling that a "you" is doing those actions because you don't have any expectations. Did I understand you right?*

Ramesh: When whatever is happening is merely witnessed as something in which "you" have nothing to do, then there is no ego involved.

Parso: *You distinguish between working mind and thinking mind. When you said to Hans, "You are the mind," do you mean he is both minds?*

Ramesh: The masters have been saying mind is the thinking mind. Ramana Maharshi says very clearly in one of his verses, "You are nothing but the mind, and the mind is nothing but a collection of thoughts." I say for the same thing "horizontal thinking and involvement."

Parso: *If there is a horizontal thinking and involvement, there must be a vertical thinking and involvement as well. What is that?*

Ramesh: What do you mean by vertical thinking?

Parso: *That's what I am asking you.*

Ramesh: What happens, happens vertically. What you think you are doing, happens horizontally. You are involved, and there is sudden realization that you are involved. And that cuts off the involvement. That sudden realization is vertical.

Jaimie: *That's why the feeling of "dropping in" happens.*

Ramesh: Yes.

Parso: *I didn't understand what she said.*

Ramesh: That is the feeling of dropping in.

Parso: *I see.*

Ramesh: I repeat, Parso, your involvement is horizontal. That which cuts it off — the sudden realization — is vertical. As far as the mind is concerned, there is nothing like vertical or horizontal. The mind is always horizontal.

Parso: *Guru Nanak says that the mind is to be trained to understand that it is the final obstacle. Once we realize this fact, we are capable of realizing our own Self. Then it is easy to attain salvation.*

Ramesh: What the *bhajan* says is wonderful as a *bhajan*. My question still is: "'Who' is to do what the *bhajan* says? Is there a 'you' who can do something? Or, if something is to happen, can anything happen without God's Grace?" This is the whole problem. You are told to do something. Whom are you asking to do what? Why doesn't anybody ask that question? Is it possible for me to ask something which is not God's Will? Nobody asks this question either. So everybody should like this *bhajan*. All these masters tell an individual to do something because that's what they have to do at that level. *Sadhana* happens at a certain level, *bhajans* on another level. They are being performed on that level until it is realized that they didn't produce anything. But that has to happen, because it is so ordained by God. So, this statement of Guru Nanak is addressed to those who need to do *bhajans* at that time. That is the stage at which those seekers find themselves spiritually.

Hans: *It seems that many seekers have gone through a lot of practice and* sadhana *in one form or other with other teachers — oftentimes more then one — before they find their way to your living room. It seems that your teaching demands a certain maturity. Is that correct?*

Ramesh: Yes, many come after having gone everywhere else, doing lots of things and many years of *sadhana* and being frustrated. And yet, some seeker comes with the age of 20 or 21 from the USA. What *sadhana* can he have done? Still that Power sends him to me. The only interpretation of such a case is that the necessary *sadhana* was done in a previous life — "a" previous life, not "his" previous life. Ramana Maharshi didn't have a physical guru. He didn't do any *sadhana* and in spite of that, enlightenment happened to him. When asked, he answered that the necessary *sadhana* must have been done in a previous life.

Jaimie: *I haven't done any* sadhana *in my life.*

Herbert: *What is the difference between "a" previous life and "his" previous life?*

Ramesh: Let me explain it to you. You see, a certain action of a body-mind organism today has consequences which appear in the future in another person or other persons whose new body-mind organisms are created in that future.

Herbert: *Are you saying that the merits of* sadhana *done by a specific entity in a past life are not bound consequentially to the same entity in the present or in a future life?*

Ramesh: No body-mind organism can do anything. That is my whole point. If a body-mind organism has been created by God or Consciousness with a receptivity that allows the spiritual process to proceed only up to step number 25 out of the total of 31, it is destined to reach only that level. There is no other way. That body-mind organism will die with the attainment of the 25th step. A new body-mind organism will then be created which takes up the spiritual process on the level of the 25th step again.

Herbert: *What is the connection between these two body-mind organisms?*

Ramesh: None!

Jaimie: *Didn't you say earlier that Ramana Maharshi must have done his* sadhana *in a past life? Did you mean to say* sadhana *wasn't done by him, but enough* sadhana *was done to produce a body-mind organism such as Ramana.*

Ramesh: That is correct.

Jaimie: *I didn't do any* sadhana. *But I am here in your presence.* Sadhana *must have been done in my case in past lives as well. Is that right?*

Ramesh: That is correct. But you see, Hans has done it for years in this life. And you haven't done any.

Jaimie: *My* sadhana *was to learn dream-work, and to look into and study the unconscious of the human being.*

Ramesh: That is not *sadhana*.
    Some years ago, a 21 year old American came to visit me. He had graduated from school with only A's and A-Plus's. He applied for admission at the four top universities of America. All four accepted him. And two of them even offered him a scholarship which he didn't need because his parents were wealthy enough to provide education for him. Then, one day, it struck him that all of

what was to come in his life wouldn't mean anything to him: to graduate from college with a degree or even honors, to have a successful career and to be a successful man. And then what? That thought, which stunned him so much, just occurred to him. When he told a friend about it, he suggested that he go to India. And another friend told him to go to Bombay and see Ramesh. He came to me totally open. No *sadhana*, you see.

Herbert: *In this case, somebody else has done the* sadhana *for him in an earlier life — is that what you are implying?*

Ramesh: Not somebody else. If *sadhana* was necessary to produce a body-mind organism at the receptive level of intuitive understanding which I encountered in the young American, then an organism must have been created to do such *sadhana* in a previous life. He did no *sadhana* in this life.

Herbert: *But a great amount of* sadhana *must have been done at some point. And that* sadhana *enabled the spiritual high state to manifest in this young American man, without him having done any* sadhana.

Ramesh: That's right. There is no "who," Herbert. That's where you are mistaken.

Herbert: *But there must be a connection between the past and the present life.*

Ramesh: Sure, there is a connection. Enlightenment is a process stretching through many different subsequent lives. A part of the process of enlightenment is done through one body-mind organism. Further progress is done through another organism. And finally in one of the body-mind organisms enlightenment happens. But no "body" has become enlightened. No "one" has become enlightened.

Herbert: *I heard the story of an ape on an island. He started to use a tool to open nuts. His fellow apes very quickly learned the new technique from him. One day, the apes on a neighboring island followed suit without having been in direct contact with the inventor ape.*
Does the spiritual level of a body-mind jump from a past life into a present life?

Ramesh: Sure. You can use your simile as a good concept. There is no direct connection between the apes of the two islands.

Herbert: *There is no connection between them on the physical level. But on God's level there may be a connection between them.*

Ramesh: Of course, it is at God's level. Everything I speak about is at God's level, not the individual level.

Jaimie: *I haven't seen many gurus. I am not very educated in spirituality really. But what comes from you as a spiritual teacher brings about an understanding in me which actually continues to deepen. This understanding and its deepening happens by just listening to you. With you I don't need to do something to become silent or surrendered. It is the meeting with you which brings the understanding, and everything else follows.*

Ramesh: Quite correct, Jamie. That's why I say Consciousness is everything. Consciousness-in-action is understanding. Understanding-in-action is witnessing, or the sudden realization of involvement. All of it is happening outside the body-mind organism's wanting anything.

Kay: *I am convinced that there is really no difference between involvement and witnessing. Both are God's Will. Who am I to judge that witnessing is better than involvement? That means there is also no need for enlightenment.*

Ramesh: So, involvement may happen through a succession of ten thousand body-mind organisms until, later, a body-mind organism will be created without the events of involvement. Then there is no "one" who is involved. There is no "one" who is witnessing, there is no "one" who is enlightened. Do you understand what I am saying?

Kay: *There is only Consciousness, and Consciousness is one.*

Ramesh: Yes. Sure. The whole problem arises when you say, "'I' am involved. 'I' am not involved. 'I' am witnessing," which is all nonsense. Therefore, "I" cannot be enlightened. Enlightenment is an event which happens because God wants it to happen, and for that He creates a body-mind organism to receive it. Who is ready to receive enlightenment? There is no "body" to be enlightened. Enlightenment is just one event in phenomenality.

Shall we stop for today?

CHAPTER 34

34.1 God has a Problem

Madhukar: *Ramesh, the other day I was talking to you about how I see you put your forehead to that Krishna picture every morning. For me, this means that there must be a "you"-entity, a subject, bowing to an object, a God outside of yourself. Using your own words, I asked you, "Who is bowing to whom? If you understand your own teaching, how could this happen?"*

I asked you further how you can possibly demand that your visitors use only the name which was given to them by their parents, and not their spiritual name. You sometimes refuse to address them by the name they are using at present, the name which was given to them by another guru.

I also asked you how you can behave like this if, according to your teaching, the sage accepts "What-is" and merely witnesses it. Furthermore, you judge the seekers for their identification with their new name, while you yourself still carry the identifying brahmin *string today.*

You responded to me by saying that there was no "I" to judge and to bow down to the God. All of it just happens, without personal doership. You said the problem lies solely with me, the disciple, who takes the guru for a person. You told me, "You have a problem." What you have said causes me to ask you, "'Who' has a problem?" According to your teaching, isn't it God or Consciousness who has the problem — through the instrument called Madhukar?

Ramesh: There is a problem, yes. What did you say about my problem?

Madhukar: *I didn't say you have a problem, I said that I noticed that your action is not according to your teaching. Instead of saying that the "you"-entity has a problem, wouldn't it be more correct to say, "There is a problem?"*

Ramesh: So, the problem is created by God through that body-mind organism.

Madhukar: *So, "I" cannot have a problem.*

Ramesh: "You" cannot have a problem. But when I talk, do I have to say every time that a problem has been created by this body-mind organism? Do I have to say every time that God moves through this body-mind? I just use the words "I" and "you" to indicate that God acts through this and that body-mind organism. I say, "I walk into this room, I sit down in this chair." Do you want me to say, "God is making this body-mind organism sit in this chair?" Are you saying I should not use the words "I" and "mine," but instead to say each time that whatever happens is God's action?

Madhukar: *I was confronting you on the personal level regarding your personal behavior, which, in my judgement, is not according to your teaching. If you don't live your teaching, what is it worth? You reacted to the confrontation in a very personal way. You spoke to the Madhukar-personality here as if it existed, and as if this personality were wrong. How could that be? How could God be wrong? You as the sage should know that both of us are mere instruments of God, and therefore neither of us can be wrong. As a sage, you could have responded on the impersonal level of Totality instead of reacting to a seeker's personal accusation with a personal condemnation. In my eyes, that's what happened here yesterday.*

No doubt, there is still a feeling of a personality, a feeling of a "me"-entity, in my case. I have no problem with having a problem. As a seeker, I wonder what is wrong with having a problem? The seeker is a problem. The problem is the seeker. But isn't the seeker an instrument created by God exactly for the purpose of being a seeker and having a problem?

Ramesh: Who is saying that there is anything wrong, Madhukar? On the contrary, Madhukar...

Madhukar: *Well, I felt that there was a condemnation of the seeker by the sage.*

Ramesh: Your mind has created the feeling that there was a condemnation. If a problem has to be there, it has to be there. It is part of the functioning of Totality.

Madhukar: *Ah, that's the purity of the teaching! That's what and how I understand it.*

Ramesh: If Madhukar has a problem, Madhukar is supposed to have a problem — according to God's Will. Is that clear?

Madhukar: *Absolutely clear.*

Ramesh: If that is clear, where is the problem?

Madhukar: *On my side, there is not even a problem with having a problem.*

Ramesh: If there is a problem which Madhukar considers a problem, then that is destined to be a problem for Madhukar, according to God's Will.

Madhukar: *This is clear for me.*

Ramesh: Is it clear?

Madhukar: *Absolutely.*

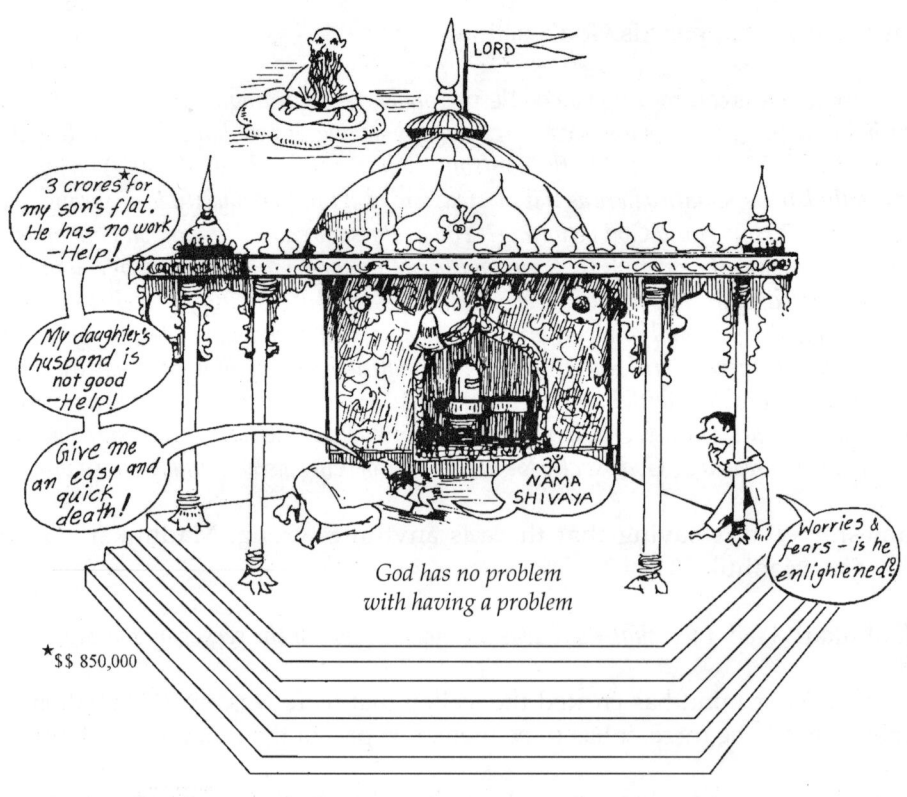

CHAPTER 35

35.1 "I Hate Your Teaching!" — Sadhana is both Necessary and Not Necessary for Enlightenment to Happen

Murthy: *I think life would be much easier for me if I could always remember that whatever happens is God's Will. Wouldn't that help?*

Ramesh: But is that remembering in your hands? Wanting to remember is still a desire. If you remember, there is no need to feel proud and happy about it. And there is no reason that "you" have remembered.

Murthy: *If the remembering makes me feel happy, I wouldn't reject that feeling.*

Ramesh: There is no question of rejecting, either.

Murthy: *I will say, "Oh, I remembered."*

Ramesh: That's the point. If you remember, you feel proud; and if you don't, you **feel** guilty.

Murthy: *Yes, I feel bad then, and that will make me remember next time. I will try.*

Ramesh: Having missed this time, you definitely want to remember next time.

Murthy: *I must remember next time, otherwise there will be involvement.*

Ramesh: It is not in your hands whether or not you remember next time. Your desire to remember next time is only a reaction of the brain to what has happened. If you don't remember next time, you will get frustrated.

Murthy: *Are you saying the understanding will cause one to remember that all is God's Will?*

Ramesh: Let the understanding work on its own. Your wanting something one way or the other, is an obstruction to the working of the understanding. If you are destined to remember, that understanding will produce the remembering. But to say "I must remember" is an obstruction to the understanding producing the remembering.

Murthy: *So, the understanding automatically provides the remembrance that all is God's Will.*

Ramesh: The understanding does not provide "you" with anything. There is no "you" to take the understanding as an instrument and make use of it for your own benefit. That's what you want. "I understand this teaching; it is a good thing," you say.

Murthy: *Yes, I want some benefit from the understanding.*

Madhukar: *If you speak of obstruction, it would be an obstruction for the "you."*

Ramesh: It is.

Madhukar: *But how can there be an obstruction for a "you" which doesn't exist in the first place? Whatever happens is according to God's Will, and is therefore destined. In that way, the obstruction is destined to happen, it only looks like an obstruction. That's why there cannot be any obstruction for anybody — anywhere or anytime.*

Ramesh: I say it will be an obstruction if you try to use the understanding as an instrument. And if there is an obstruction, it was your destiny to produce an obstruction.

Madhukar: *In the context of destiny — all that happens is God's Will and action — there cannot be a personally-created obstruction.*

Ramesh: There is an obstruction.

Madhukar: *Any obstruction is God's Will; therefore, how could there be an obstruction?*

Ramesh: Why? If it is God's Will it is not an obstruction?

Madhukar: *It is not an obstruction within the plan of God. He has determined what is going to happen and uses His instruments to produce His actions. The seeker is God, or rather, God's instrument. How could there be an obstruction for God, Who is the One Who willed that a certain instrument — His instrument — should not have an understanding at this point in time? The obstruction you speak about is on the level of a personal entity with free will. For an obstruction, there must be a "you" with free will. But an obstruction cannot be avoided. Speaking of obstruction, you speak to the "you."*

Ramesh: Wait a minute, Madhukar. What is your problem? The obstruction happens because it is God's Will that it happens.

Madhukar: *Definitely.*

Ramesh: Then it is not an obstruction?

Madhukar: *It is not. From God's point of view there are no obstructions.*

Ramesh: Then that is your understanding.

Madhukar: *There is no obstruction. How can God have an obstruction?*

Ramesh: It is an obstruction. (To the others) Can you understand what he means?

Madhukar: *The whole picture is already created and finished, as destined by God — including what you call the obstruction. God wants a certain body-mind organism not to have an understanding yet, and that is according to His plan. From this point of view there cannot be an obstruction for some "one" just as there cannot be enlightenment for some "one." To understand this is the end of all talking. And that's the end of it.*

The same confusion arises in the seeker when you say to Hans that no method and no practice will help "you" to attain enlightenment, because enlightenment is an impersonal event in the functioning of Totality. On the other hand, you tell us almost every day about how Ramana Maharshi became enlightened in a single stroke — out of the blue — as a sixteen-year old boy. He had no training and practiced no sadhana. *OK, but then you tell us in the next sentence, that his homework, his sa-dhana was done in some past lives. In other words, you are contradicting yourself by telling us that there is actually benefit in practice, at least in the long run. In other words, you are actually saying that* sadhana *is necessary in order for enlightenment to happen.*

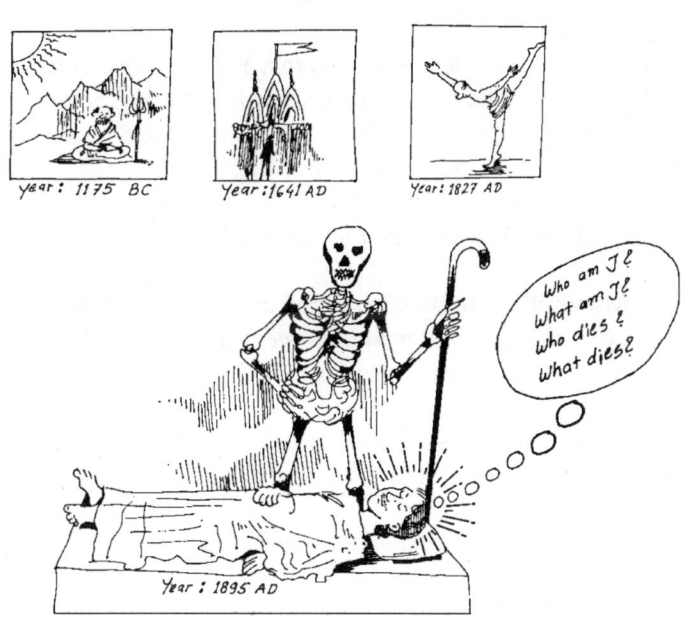

Enlightenment caused by sadhana in past lives

(OK, if you want to believe in reincarnation)

So, what is it? Are there benefits in sadhana, *or are there none? It cannot be both,* sadhana *and no* sadhana, *obstacles and no obstacles. How can you say there are both? That's the worst teaching for the seeker. I hate this kind of "both"-teaching. I hate this!*

Ramesh: All right, if you hate my teaching, why are you here?

Madhukar: *Because I cannot help but to be here.*

Ramesh: Aha! That's precisely what I mean, Madhukar.

Madhukar: *You are practicing double-talk. On the one hand, you address the seeker's ego-personality in telling him that he can do something for or against his enlightenment. On the other hand, you tell the seeker that nothing can be done for enlightenment because all is according to God's plan, or according to the impersonal functioning of Totality. So, to which view does the Ramana example belong? You cite his example for both views. How can you have both teachings? This is a terrible teaching!*

Jaimie: That's the paradox.

Madhukar: *There is no paradox. You must teach one or the other: either the seeker can practice and do something for his advancement, or he can't. If he can, there are obstacles on the path to his goal. If he can't do anything, there aren't. It's all the way, one way or the other. Or, what you are teaching is a lie.*

Herbert: *You can say a lemon is a lemon and an obstruction is an obstruction.*

Murthy: *I take the obstruction as a fact. When Ramesh says the "me"-entity does not exist, the teaching appeals to me; I am just inquiring, and I expect to stumble across some truth, some compassion.*

Ramesh: You see, until the understanding happens and reaches the extreme and total understanding, there will be obstruction.

Jaimie: *On the level of phenomenality.*

Ramesh: Oh, indeed.

Jaimie: *We are talking on the level of apples and oranges in a sense, on the level of phenomenality.*

Murthy: *I am at the level of phenomenality.*

Ramesh: Wait a minute. We are talking at the level of phenomenality. If we were not talking on the level of phenomenality, there would be no talking; there would be total silence.

Jaimie: *Non-obstruction is not on the level of phenomenality, right?*

Ramesh: That is right. And the obstruction is on the level of phenomenality. If you have transcended phenomenality, there would be no more questions. Then, there would only be silence.

Madhukar: *That's what I mean to say. The confusion is kept alive by speaking about both — about phenomenality, which can only be known and explained by the mind, and about the Absolute, which cannot be known at all — but which one is. Why to speak about both? I cannot understand why you are doing this.*

In the big picture — on the level of the Absolute — there is no teaching. There is nothing like that. If whatever happens is once understood to be God's Will, then it is always God's Will — including everything that you call an obstruction. Then all explanations regarding phenomenality and the spiritual search are finished.

Murthy: *But can't we accept that the present happening here is also God's Will?*

Madhukar: *Of course, that is accepted.*

Hildegard: *How can you deny God's Will?*

Ramesh: How can you deny it?

Madhukar: *I am not at all denying that all is God's Will.*

Hildegard: *What are you saying, then?*

Murthy: *Why are you then attacking the teaching?*

Ramesh: What are you saying, Madhukar?

Madhukar: *I am not attacking the teaching, I am defending it. I am saying that your teaching is contradictory. For instance, you are saying the seeker cannot do anything to bring about enlightenment. And you say Ramana didn't do any sadhana in this life, but practicing was done during many past lives, and therefore enlightenment could happen in his case. So, what you are saying? How does this fit together?*

Ramesh: Then there is no need to talk at all. Then why should people come here?

Madhukar: *I wonder. You are the guru, you should know.*

Ramesh (to the others): You see his misconceptions!?

Murthy: *Oh, my God!*

Madhukar: *I believe you must have an intention for the way you teach. Or you don't really know or care what you are saying to the seekers.*

Sushila: *I heard that Ramana Maharshi is reported to have said that he didn't need to do* tapas *or* sadhana *in this life because he must have done them in his past life. Is that correct?*

Ramesh: That is correct.

Sushila: *Even in Ramana's case, there was* sadhana*. So, why then do you say that no* sadhana *can enhance the advent of enlightenment. How can you say both? That's what Madhukar is saying.*

Ramesh: You see, nothing can be done. If it is understood that nothing can be done, then all there is is silence. Whatever we talk about is in phenomenality.

Sushila: *Do you mean that on the level of phenomenality something can be done, because the search for enlightenment is a process?*

Ramesh: The search for enlightenment is a process. "Nothing can be done" means the process can only be witnessed. Whatever is happening can only be witnessed.

Jaimie: *Is it correct to say that on the level of phenomenality, on the level of so-called reality or unreality, good and evil and obstructions exist; while on the level of the Absolute, none of it exists.*

Ramesh: That is correct.

Jaimie: *When we start talking about them, the two levels get mixed up. You, Madhukar, are seeing only the Absolute level, while Ramesh has to speak from both levels, and therefore has to mix them up.*

Madhukar: *Speaking means speaking in phenomenality. Ramesh talks to the disciple on this level. But whatever is said from this level needs to be integrated into the context of the Absolute — the place of phenomenality within the Absolute should not be lost sight of. If the Cosmic Dream-nature of phenomenality is not clearly pointed out again and again, then all talk of good, evil, obstruction, enlightenment, one's own personality, and the personality of the guru, is taken for real by the seeker.*

I think Nisargadatta Maharaj was wise because he spoke only from the level of Consciousness — or so I have heard. And he didn't go into mixing up all these confusing concepts regarding phenomenality and the Absolute. To speak in the conceptual terms which Ramesh is using is a fooling of the seekers. They hear these contradictions and try to understand them. If they have accepted one of these concepts as the Truth, they are automatically bound to accept the opposite as the untruth. But you tell us that the opposite concept is also true. How can both contradictory concepts be true at the same time? What to believe? What to do? Both cannot exist at the same time. If we continue to listen to you, we seekers will keep going round and round. But we will not be helped.

Herbert: *You don't know this.*

Madhukar: *I see it in my own case.*

Herbert: *Yes, you may see it in your own case.*

Murthy: *Yes, we are going round and round. Hence we have come to Ramesh.*

Madhukar: *The two contradictory concepts cannot exist, cannot both be true, at the same time. They cannot both be true.*

Jaimie: *Yes, they can.*

Madhukar: *They cannot.*

Jaimie: *They can, because phenomenality is both real and unreal.*

Ramesh: That is correct, Jaimie. The shadow is both real and unreal. This manifestation is both real and unreal. It cannot be one or the other. It is both.

Herbert: *And why only two levels? Buddha himself has described 87,000 ways of practicing, all of which were given by God. And if someone finds himself meditating, he is meditating according to one of them. What could be wrong? I see no contradiction.*

Ramesh: That is correct.

Madhukar: *Your teaching says that whatever happens is according to God's Will, and therefore it happens. That's it. Nothing needs to be added to that. All further talk is useless.*

Hildegard: *But there are paths!*

Ramesh: If you don't need the talks, then why do you come here? I am not forcing you to come.

Madhukar: *It seems that I needed these talks for some time. I was compelled somehow to come to your talks because some energy brought me here, and the search does not seem to be finished yet. That's why I came.*

Ramesh: Why? Why? You have just said that there is no need to talk about the teaching, that all talking is useless.

Madhukar: *It is, because according to your teaching, no method can enhance enlightenment. That means that your talk must then be useless, too.*

Herbert (to Madhukar): *But you are the one who is doing all the talking.*

35.2 Enlightenment Cannot be Enhanced in Any Way, Though Money Can Help

Jaimie: *It is not the words themselves, but their content which is Consciousness. And Consciousness cannot be grasped by the thinking mind.*

Ramesh: That is correct.

Madhukar: *I can very well grasp the meaning of your words, "The true guru doesn't ask for or imply that he wants money, overtly or covertly. Only fake gurus do that. They take advantage of their disciples and ask for money." But every seeker who comes to you finds out very quickly that you like money, that you want to be pleased by being given money. So, again you are saying both: a fake guru takes money, yet you indicate that you would like to be given money. So, what are you? How can you say both? That's why this contradiction is terrible for me, because I want you to be a true guru. I hate this contradiction! There is no problem for me in your liking money. But if you do — and you do — let's put this fact on the table. And let us not transform your personal, mundane liking for money into a mysterious spiritual practice of "giving money." You know that every seeker will happily take to heart any suggestion which promises him the hastening of the arrival of his enlightenment.*

Ramesh: Look, Maharaj accepted money.

Madhukar: *Yes, I know Maharaj was also after money.*

Ramesh: Wait a minute. Maharaj did not demand money.

Madhukar: *Of course he didn't demand money openly or directly.*

Ramesh: Maharaj did not demand money.

Madhukar: *The seekers were made to understand that he wished to be given money.*

Ramesh: Maharaj did not demand money. And in his case, there was no individual who could have demanded money. In my case, there is also no individual to demand money.

Madhukar: *Every time I have made you aware that you are acting just like any ordinary person — for example, when you are judging others — you tell me, "There is no one here. There is no 'me' here with a sense of personal doership." You say, "Yes, judgment happened, but there was no doer thereof." Can you prove what you are saying? This is a very convenient take-it-or-leave-it-answer which doesn't give space for further questions. But this answer doesn't dispel my doubts.*

According to you, only fake gurus take advantage of, and take money from, their disciples. You are my guru, and so I believe what you are telling me. But, after all, what are you? Every seeker who visits you for a couple of days comes to know that you like to be pleased with money. Why is that? Because they hear it from you.

Ramesh: I repeat...

Madhukar: *I hate it, I hate it, I hate it! I hate these double standards of yours. You are lying. It's a lie, it's a lie, it's a lie. That you don't care about money is a lie. And even if I catch you lying red-handed, you will tell me, "Well, lying happened, but there is no one here who was lying. Who was lying, Madhukar, who? Don't you understand?" You are telling me that a guru's lie is not a lie because, in his case, lying happens impersonally; a guru's lying is part of the functioning of Totality and therefore it happens without a "me"-entity, without a sense of personal doership.*

The seeker can't do anything to help bring about enlightenment because he, as an entity, just doesn't exist. All is God's Will. This is your standard teaching. But contrary to this teaching, you are also telling us that the seeker can actually buy his enlightenment. You call that pleasing the guru. In addition, you say that the physical presence of the guru does something for the advancement of the seeker's search for enlightenment. So, pleasing the guru with money, and being in the guru's presence, both are nothing but a kind of sadhana, then. So, what is it? Sadhana helps to bring about enlightenment, or not? Again, you are saying both and therefore contradicting yourself. Something can be done and nothing can be done for enlightenment. I hate these double standards of yours. I hate them, I hate them, I hate them. Your teaching is so confusing. I hate your teaching.

Why are you doing this? Why?

Ramesh: Alright, if you hate it...

Madhukar: *Why can't the teaching be pure? I can only presume that you must be motivated by some personal interest. Money and guru-ship. You want money and you want to be the highest guru with the Final Truth. It must be this motivation that makes you say what you are saying. This is the only explanation I can find for what you are doing. And what you are teaching is absolutely not helpful, it is totally confusing, for me. What you teach is not final. I hate it! I feel lied to, insulted, abused, and cheated by you. It is just terrible.*

And the worst of it all is that you are the only one of my gurus who was after money. But you are not only not honest enough to admit your hunger for money, you even have the audacity to condemn all other money-taking gurus as fake, even though they are behaving exactly the way you do. As a witness to your daily morning talks for about six months, I can give testimony to the fact that you are the only one in your living room who talks about money almost every single morning.

Ramesh: What you are saying is that the guru should not take any money, isn't that right?

Madhukar: *No, not at all. I am not saying a guru should take or should not take money. What I am saying is that a lie is a lie. I am saying that you are telling us that the seeker can't do anything to hasten the process of enlightenment; and at the same time, you are saying that the seeker's pleasing the guru with money, and his being in the guru's presence, are actually hastening the seeker's process. You are actually begging the seekers for money every day, and you are pretending at the same time that you are not. You are accusing your fellow gurus of what you yourself are doing, namely, of taking financial advantage of the agony most disciples feel during their search. The worst of it all is that you cover up your greed by making "pleasing" a spiritual discipline for the seeker. And when all this is pointed out to you, you have your magic formula ready: "In the case of the sage (yourself), there is no personal doership; whatever happens with him is part of the impersonal functioning of Totality."*

That's what I am saying.

Murthy: *According to you, a guru should not like money, right?*

Madhukar: *That is not what I am saying. Ramesh says a true guru does not ask — overtly or covertly — for money.*

Murthy: *I still think that a guru can take money. Why not?*

Reaching higher and higher — and the means for it

Madhukar: *I have no objection to a guru taking money. It actually makes it easy for the disciple to give if he knows that the guru takes money. He doesn't need to figure out with what else he could make the guru happy. I have told you my objections.*

Jaimie: *If the guru doesn't care whether money comes or not, then what could be wrong if he takes it when it comes? If he were to refuse it, that would only prove that he still has the preferences of an ordinary, personal "me"-entity.*

Ramesh: That is the whole point.

Madhukar: *No, that is not at all the point that I am talking about. If you could only tell the truth and say, "I like to be given money" — full stop — then there would not need to be any discussion whatsoever. But because of your attempt to cover up your personal likings with a discipline called "pleasing the guru"...*
  In short, you are not living what you are teaching. And that is what brings up this doubt in me, and which therefore gives rise to this whole discussion.

Jaimie (to Madhukar): *I don't know if it is true what you are saying. I haven't been here long enough, I've been here only two days. Has anyone of you heard Ramesh asking for money? Madhukar?* (Madhukar keeps silent)

Jaimie: *Madhukar, have you heard Ramesh ask for money?* (Madhukar remains silent)

Murthy: *If I were in need of some money, I would ask for five bucks.*

Jaimie: *Yes, you wouldn't ask all the time.*

Murthy: *But that asking wouldn't prove anything. Even this discussion we are having here doesn't prove what you are saying, Madhukar.*

Jaimie: *I just would like Madhukar to tell us why this discussion is happening.*

Murthy: *For Ramesh's work to go on, some money is necessary. That's all.*

Hildegard: *Why should he not like money? Why not? But if we have much money, we get attached to it. I don't think Ramesh has much money, and I think he is not attached to money.*

Jaimie's boyfriend: *I think Ramesh accepts whatever is given. Does that need to be associated with liking it or being attached to it or desiring it? If somebody gives flowers, they are accepted.*

Murthy: *As God's Will.*

Jaimie: *Certain gurus accept a donation when you come to their* satsang. *You are expected to tip. At Papaji's, no money was asked for* satsang. *But when they were short of money and couldn't pay the bills, we were asked to donate money. Is there something wrong with this? I am curious. There is nothing wrong with you, Madhukar. It is just what is happening inside of you right now.*

Murthy: *Or is it just horizontal thinking? With your permission, Madhukar, may I ask you a question? When thinking happens, we tend to take it for real. But such thoughts may just be baseless thoughts. Such thoughts go round and round, and finally I am blaming Ramesh. But maybe there is some truth in what you say, I don't know. I am new here. We have to inquire. Ramana Maharshi said just to inquire, "Who am I?" That inquiry will destroy all thoughts. What happens in inquiry is the total destruction of the ego. That's what is happening here. Some of us may resist what happens here.*

Ramesh: No, no. He is not talking of that. Madhukar says no guru should accept any money. The guru must live on thin air. No guru should accept any money.

Jaimie's boyfriend: *No, I think he says you have to take a stand and say you either like money or you don't like money. And he is saying, if I am correct, that you are not taking a stand one way or the other.*

Ramesh: Which is exactly why there is no "me" in this body-mind organism called Ramesh. There is no "me" to demand any money and there is no "me" to refuse any money.

Jaimie: *If it comes, it comes.*

Ramesh: If it comes, it comes; if it doesn't come, it doesn't come.

Murthy: *It is as simple as that.*

Ramesh: There is no "me" to demand money, and there is no me to refuse money.

Jaimie's boyfriend: *If someone gives you money, does that create a certain happiness in you at that moment? Does that create a feeling in you at that moment?*

Ramesh: You see, the point is that I also give donations sometimes. That means money comes to me, but it also goes from me. I am given a donation, which means money comes to me. But it also goes. Many donations have been given by me, you see? Money comes and money goes. If I give some donations, there is no happiness. If the money comes in, there is no happiness. The money going out as a donation is witnessed. That money went because of an inspiration to give a donation to an ashram, or to an association, or whatever.

Jaimie: *I think what is happening is that Madhukar's thinking mind wants it one way or the other, because that is logical. That's part of the conditioning.*

Chuck: *No, what's happening with Madhukar is that he sees at least a covert asking for money on Ramesh's part. For Ramesh often, in the presence of a gathering of people, says to a person, "Thank you for your generous cash donation."*

Ramesh: Yes. That is a social act, a social courtesy.

Chuck: *But this seems to be at least a covert asking for money. I think that's what Madhukar means.*

Jaimie: *You think that to say "Thank you for your money" in the presence of a group of people means asking for money?*
    (six people are now speaking at the same time, discussing the issue)

Ramesh: If somebody gives a cash gift to me, I say thank you very much for your generous donation.

Sushila: *Ramesh, a few days ago you said in your talks here that only fake gurus — those who take advantage of their disciples — ask for or expect money, either covertly or overtly. You said that such fake gurus are taking advantage of their disciples. Madhukar seems to have a problem with this statement because he believes that you are doing just that yourself.*

Ramesh: I never used the words "overtly" or "covertly." I repeat, I have never used the words "overtly" or "covertly." The only thing I said was that there is no "me" here. And there was no "me" when Maharaj did not demand any money. There was no "me" here to demand money. And there was no "me" to refuse money. And I am following exactly what my guru did. He never demanded any money, and he never refused any money.

Jaimie: *And why not to say thank you? Wouldn't you say thank you if somebody gave you some money?*

Ramesh: You say thank you as a social courtesy. One says "thank you" and one says "sorry." If I hurt you, I say "sorry."

Jaimie: *Then you don't need to feel guilty.*
(*At this time a visitor arrives with a bouquet of flowers, which he presents to Ramesh.*)

Ramesh: Now, I don't know if I should accept the flowers or not.

Soren: *What?*

Jaimie: *This is the dream-happening in action.*

Ramesh: Soren comes from Switzerland. This is the third time he is visiting me. I remember.

Herbert: *Madhukar, can you tell me how a guru should be? I think you have a very strong opinion about how a guru should be, how he should behave. I believe that, in your eyes, he should not be an ordinary man.*

Madhukar: *In short, I want only for the guru to be and do what he says. I want only for him to follow his own teaching.*

Herbert: *I believe that the guru is more, that there is more behind what he is saying. He is on a higher level. And he speaks from the level where he abides, and points to that higher level. Of course, at the same time the guru is an ordinary human being, too.*

Madhukar: *I expect that my guru actually lives what he is teaching. That is the minimum that I expect from him.*

Herbert: *How do you know what is the maximum? He has a maximum, also.*

Madhukar: *I don't care about the maximum if not even his daily life is according to his own teaching. For me his maximum is then worth nothing.*

Jaimie: *Have you ever known a guru like you describe? A guru who is totally consistent?*

Madhukar: *No, I haven't. I have had several gurus, and I stayed with and served them altogether for sixteen years. In each case, I thought I had found the highest guru. So far, all of them have turned out as not being able to live according to their own teachings.*

Jaimie: *I have been searching for a long time for a consistent guru, the perfect guru.*

Madhukar: *Let me know when you find him. I wonder if such a guru exists.*

Jaimie: *I have come to the conclusion that there is no such thing as a consistent guru.*

Madhukar: *By now, I have come to believe that, ultimately, such a thing as a true guru doesn't exist at all. True guru, consistent guru — they seem to be just words.*

Herbert: *Ramesh, if I hate something, I must be full of hate myself. Otherwise, I couldn't hate something. If I love something I am full of love, and I share it.*

Ramesh: No. There is either love or hate. There is hate, and at that moment hate is part of What-is. If hate has arisen, it is God's Will that hate should arise there (*indicating Madhukar*). And because of this hate, we encounter things like in Bosnia and Chechnya, you see. There is tremendous hate, which is part of life.

Jaimie: *And it is only relative to love.*

Ramesh: That is correct. Love is relative of hate. Opposites are the very basis of life.

Herbert: *My question was something else. Madhukar exclaimed, "I hate this, I hate this!" When I hate, I experience hate for myself. I hate myself.*

Ramesh: Yes.

Herbert: *If I didn't hate myself, I couldn't hate something or somebody.*

Ramesh: Yes. That's right. I think that's very true.

Lauran: *But isn't the depth of my hate not also the result of the depth of my love? If one says, "I hate you so much," it usually means that hate happens because "I love you so much."*

Ramesh: It could be like that. Yes, sure.

Lauran: *All my life, it has always seemed that what I took to be words of wisdom wound up having come out of the mouths of people who turned out to be fools. This is the first time I feel I am with someone who is not a fool. And yet, everything you say is problematic in the English language, because it is contradictory. Trying to follow what is said is sometimes like walking across a mine-field and trying to step around the mines before they go off. I almost get dragged in thinking, "Oh, wow, that's a contradiction," and I go on being busy thinking about it until the thought goes off. So, it is very frustrating. But I think I am not listening to a fool.*

Ramesh: Hmm.

35.3 The Seeker's Earnestness for Enlightenment, Or Free Entertainment

Ramesh: So, how has the teaching been treating you, Soren?

Soren: *When I saw you last time, the impact of the teaching was strong.*

Ramesh: Yes, your friends told me that you were taking to the teaching. They said that the impression it made on you was deep.

Soren: *For a week after I had met you, I constantly cried. But, in relation to what you have been saying about hate, it seems much more difficult to feel love than to feel hate. Hate comes very easily. During my last visit to you, I experienced — through the teaching — that it is much more difficult to open oneself up to love, especially to love of the guru. I wonder why it is so difficult?*

Ramesh: "It is difficult to be open" means it is difficult for Soren. My point is that whatever happens is supposed to happen. If the love for the teaching or for the guru is not to happen, it will not happen. It is as simple as that. The occurrence of love for the guru is taken by some seekers emotionally, while for others it happens almost without emotion. The reaction to what the guru says can be anything. In some cases, there might be no receptivity at all. Some seekers are totally closed to me. They have resistance. There is such resistance that there is no openness. That also happens.

Soren: *I wonder why I have this fear of opening?*

Ramesh: Because the "me" deeply understands that the ultimate that can happen is enlightenment, which the "me" is seeking without really knowing what enlightenment is. The "me" is subconsciously seeking enlightenment. In the beginning of the search, it is the individual who wants enlightenment. At the same time the "me" knows intuitively that the ultimate understanding means the annihilation of the "me." It is afraid to be annihilated. The "me" wants enlightenment, and at the same time is afraid of it.

Soren: *I experienced this fear and desire very strongly after I met you last time. Though I feel the desire for enlightenment very strongly, I likewise feel the fear very strongly.*

Ramesh: I told you.

Soren: *I like to give gifts to people. But each time I visited you, I resisted giving you anything.*

Ramesh: Fine. No problem.

Soren: *And last time I met you, you suddenly spoke about giving to the guru in gratitude. You told me that nobody in India would visit the guru without a gift. They would bring at least...*

Ramesh: A flower. Yes, that is the tradition in India.

Soren: *Since then I have been thinking a lot about what to give to you.*

Ramesh: So you brought these flowers today.

Soren: *You cannot imagine how much fear I had in bringing them. And then, on my arrival, everybody began laughing. And I didn't know why.*

Ramesh: Why everybody was laughing? Before you arrived we were discussing the subject of whether the guru should accept money or not. And the point that was made was that in the case of the sage or guru, there is no "me" to demand money. Usually, how does a transaction take place? There is a demand, which is supplied by the money being given. But as far as the guru is concerned, there is no "me" who demands any money or refuses any money. There is neither any demand or any refusal. If money comes, it is accepted. If it doesn't come, it is not demanded.

Soren: *To offer something to the guru it is absolutely different from giving to somebody else. I have the feeling it needs a kind of opening. I was afraid of this opening. It was difficult.*

Ramesh: Ah! The fear is generated by the "me" who does not want to be influenced by the guru. The fear is that listening to the guru might annihilate the "me." Therefore, I often say that if you have the choice — and you don't have the choice — between seeking enlightenment or seeking a million dollars, I would suggest that you choose the million dollars, because then there will be a "me," a Soren, to enjoy it. On the other hand, if enlightenment happens there will be no "me," no individual Soren-entity, to enjoy that enlightenment. That's why if the ego, the "me," is strong, it is afraid to go to the guru and become enlightened. If the ego, the "me," is strong, the ego is frightened to be annihilated. That's why there is fear.

Soren: *I wonder what is the relationship between the "me" and the heart? I have the impression that something is opening for me, not on the level of the "me," but on the level of the heart.*

Ramesh: That is correct. The opening of the heart happens in spite of the "me" and its fear. The "me" resists. But if it is in the destiny of the organism, the opening of the heart will happen in spite of the resistance.

Jaimie: *But do you think that the gift itself, or the bowing to the guru's feet, is the only way to express openness and gratitude.*

Ramesh: Sure. Certainly. That is why when I met Maharaj, the very first day, there was such a tremendous feeling of relief. I knew that I had finally arrived at the final destination. And I felt such a deep feeling of gratitude when I heard what he had to say. At that moment, I decided that I wanted to give a large sum of money to Maharaj. This desire had nothing to do with his need for it. The need to give did not depend on the guru's need to receive. Maharaj was financially quite comfortable.

Jaimie: *I noticed that Poonjaji's disciples touched his feet out of traditional formalities. Myself, I did this only when such a desire arose in me out of genuine reverence and gratitude.*

Ramesh: That is absolutely correct.

Jaimie: *I didn't want to feel at any given point that I had to bow down to Poonjaji.*

Ramesh: Quite correct.

Jaimie: *My gratitude and openness may come in a different form.*

Ramesh: Bowing down to the guru is an Eastern tradition. In the West, the guru-disciple relationship is unknown. It cannot be compared with the teacher-pupil relationship of the West. In India, a guru — even for music, dance, or painting — is a venerable person. And there are gurus who refuse money or any other gifts. But on a special day, on the *Guru Purnima* day — which is on the full moon in July — the guru must accept what is given.

I have seen Westerners resisting the practice of bowing down to the guru. Some do not even bow down to him when they take leave. Other Westerners do bow down when they leave. For me it makes no difference if somebody bows down or not because I, as the guru, know that there is no difference between the disciple and the guru. The disciple doesn't know it, but the guru knows it. The disciple bows down and the guru folds his hands. The guru does not demand devotion, because he knows that devotion may or may not arise.

Jaimie: *Devotion shouldn't be an empty gesture, which most traditions become.*

Ramesh: I entirely agree. "Such-and-such devotee didn't bow down to me" is not something a guru should think. A genuine guru knows that there is no such thing as enlightenment. The genuine guru knows that there is enlightenment in every sentient and insentient being, and that there is no difference between the disciple and the guru. The disciple doesn't know it yet. But at a certain point, the disciple knows that there is no difference between him and the guru. Yet, in phenomenality, the disciple will continue to bow down to and revere the guru as long as the body-mind organism stays alive. That's how it should be. And that's what is said in the scriptures. And what Ramana Maharshi says is that, with enlightenment, the duality between the guru and the disciple disappears. But the resulting Unicity is not applied to the guru-disciple relationship as long as the guru is alive. Therefore, the disciple will continue to bow down to the guru out of gratitude, even after he is enlightened.

You are quite right, Jaimie, the expression of devotion should not be forced. But if devotion arises naturally, it is felt very deeply. And then the bowing down is not done by the disciple, but it happens as a matter of compulsion arising out of gratitude.

But many people who come to me don't come to me as a guru. They come to me for free entertainment. Fine, they are entitled to. Others have an enormous feeling of gratitude. In any case, the teaching is happening through this body-

For enlightenment or free entertainment?

mind organism. What happens to the people who come to visit me, immediately or later on, is according to their destiny. I am truly not concerned in converting anybody. I am not concerned if the teaching reaches somebody or not.

CHAPTER 36

36.1 "Poor Fool, You Don't Understand the Teaching!"

Herbert: *Is love a concept? Where does love come in? Does love happen on the phenomenal level or on God's level? Can an enlightened master kill somebody?*

Ramesh: What I am saying is that no unenlightened or enlightened person can kill anybody. There is no person. If the average person kills somebody he thinks *he* killed somebody, and thinks, "I have killed him." Killing may happen through an enlightened master if that is the destiny of both the body-mind organisms concerned. The enlightened master does not kill. In fact, he knows that not even the ordinary person can kill. A killing just happens. Often killers say that they didn't mean to kill. A killer sometimes says, "The victim tried to molest a women. I saw this and I hit the man, and he died. I am sorry."

Herbert: *So, we can't attribute any special quality to an enlightened being. Not even love, right?*

Ramesh: That is correct. The whole problem arises because the unenlightened person considers the enlightened being to be a person, and thus criticizes him and judges him: "The sage should not do this, he should be like that."

Herbert: *But why is it then that, from the enlightened master, a certain amount of love emanates, and not hate?*

Ramesh: Certainly.

Herbert: *It is love, not hate, that emanates from him.*

Ramesh: That is correct.

Herbert: *So, the love of the sage is a specific attribute which is specific for the sage?*

Ramesh: No. What happens to the sage is that a feeling arises in him as a reaction of the brain to an event. Somebody says or does something, and then a feeling of anger may arise in the enlightened person who witnesses it. But that anger is temporary. From a deeper place, then, a feeling of compassion arises in him. If somebody says something bad about me, the feeling of compassion is stronger than that of anger. I feel compassion for the person who doesn't understand the teaching, and therefore is judging me. That person may have said all kinds of things to me, and about me, assuming that the master is an individual being. (*Madhukar is not present during this part of the conversation, but Ramesh keeps pointing to the chair in which Madhukar usually sits during the talks*) Therefore, what arises is not so much anger as compassion. But compassion or love or anger are feelings which arise as a reaction of the brain to an outside event. The enlightened master is not always full of love. Anger can arise in him, too. And compassion can arise. And both can arise at the same time.

Claire: *Both can arise at the same time?*

Ramesh: Yes. Of course.

Claire: *Isn't it that the feeling and state of anger had to end first, and then compassion may follow as a feeling afterwards, in clock-time?*

Ramesh: No, both can arise at the same time. If somebody insults me the feeling of anger arises and immediately, along with the anger, the compassion arises in me in the form of the thought, "The poor fool! He doesn't understand." (*Ramesh continues to point at Madhukar's chair*) And because he doesn't understand the teaching, he is suffering. Whatever that fool says — this, that, and the other — the fact remains that he is suffering. If somebody tells me I have done something and asks me why I have done it, and — even though I told him why — he still says I am inconsistent, then more than a feeling of anger arises. A feeling of compassion also arises, because I know that he hasn't understood the teaching. You see, Claire? You understand?

Claire: Yes.
   (*At this moment Madhukar enters the room*)

Speaking God's Mind

36.2 The Seeker Leaves the Guru and Tells him Why

Madhukar (kneeling on the floor in front of Ramesh): *Ramesh, I came to take leave of you.*

Ramesh: Oh, yes, you are going somewhere?

Madhukar: *I don't know where I am going. But I believe that my days with you are numbered.*

Ramesh: OK.

Madhukar: *I feel that your enlightenment is a hoax, and made-up. And that you are just making money by pretending to be enlightened.*

Ramesh: I see.

Madhukar: *And even some disciples of yours, whom you declared enlightened, don't accept the enlightenment certificate you gave them. They themselves believe they are actually not enlightened. One of the cases I am talking about is that of Ben Pierce. He says he is not enlightened. And your enlightened and unenlightened disciples are only busy with discussing how enlightened or un-enlightened the "enlightened" co-devotees of yours are.*
In the case of Marc, he acknowledges that he was enlightened. But he himself told me last summer, one-and-a-half years after his enlightenment, that he still has a mind which gets involved in horizontal thinking, where the psyche is concerned. He says he just doesn't know what you are talking about when you mention again and again that the sage has no thinking mind.
I see the same game going on here with you as a guru, as happened earlier in my seeking career with Poonjaji, in Lucknow. I see you declaring disciples enlightened because you want to become famous as a guru. These enlightened disciples then give talks and satsangs and bring more people to you, which, in turn, brings more money into your pockets. I think this whole thing is just a hoax.

Ramesh: Alright. Fine!

Madhukar: *It took quite some time to see all this. And I know that most of the stories which you are telling us about you and Nisargadatta Maharaj are half-truths, falsifications, fabricated. You want to make us believe that Maharaj gave you an enlightenment certificate and made you his successor. In your stories you make it look as if you were a special disciple of Maharaj, and that there was some mysterious spiritual connection between you two. "At last you have come!", "Why don't you talk!?", "You will not parrot my*

words," are words made up by you. You even went so far as to hold yourself up as Nisargadatta'a successor. This pure lie you even got printed up in pamphlets and advertisements for your seminars. My doubts about you have grown in the days I have spent with you. Instead of decreasing, they increased. That's what happened.

Ramesh: Sure.

36.3 The Seeker's Last Question

Madhukar: *I have one last question before I leave. How much money was that large sum you gave to Nisargadatta Maharaj? You brag about this sum every day in your talks. So, let's put the mystery on the table. I would like to know the amount.*

Ramesh: To Nisargadatta Maharaj?

Madhukar: *Yes, you always talk about this large sum of money. How large was it?*

Ramesh: The first time I gave money to Maharaj it was considered a large sum by me, in the circumstances I was in at that time. And it was a large sum for Maharaj as well, considering his circumstances.

Madhukar: *In rupees?*

Ramesh: Why should I give you the number?

"I assure you that's what did it in my case"

Madhukar: *It is a very simple question. The answer to it is just as simple, a simple word. And the secret will finally be out.*

Ramesh: No, I will not give you the answer to that simple question. I will not tell you the amount. The answer is: what I gave Maharaj at that time was considered by me, in my circumstances, and for his standard and circumstances, a large sum of money.

Madhukar: *Two thousand or five thousand rupees?*

Ramesh: Maybe. Whatever the amount was, it was large for me and for him, in the circumstances of that time. What the seekers and devotees give to me now is much larger. And I do not advertise for people to come to visit me.

Madhukar: *I am not saying you do.*

Ramesh: Alright. I do not advertise for people to come here. And once they are here, I do not demand any money from them.

Madhukar: *I am not talking about a direct demand for money on your part. I am not saying you demand money from them.*

Ramesh: Oh yes, you are, you are! You say that I demand money from the people. I am not asking people to come here.

Madhukar: *The truth is...*

Ramesh: Wait a minute! What I am saying is that I am not asking people to come here, and I do not demand money from them.

Madhukar: *The truth is that every person who comes here for longer than three days knows that some money should be given to you. There is very frequent and repeated implication of this. And money means gratitude — in cash. To make your point, you retell every second day your "large amount" story with Nisargadatta Maharaj.*

Ramesh: Look...

Madhukar: *This is what I understand.*

Herbert: *This is not true, Madhukar.*

Shalini: *That's not true.*

Jaimie: *I don't feel this at all.*

Shalini: *That's not true. That's not true.*

Madhukar: *Maybe you have not yet been here long enough to know.*

Herbert: *What you say...*

Madhukar (to Herbert): *I am speaking to Ramesh and not to you! You shut up! It is my turn to speak. You shut up! You can talk to him when it is your turn.*

Herbert: *You don't tell anybody to shut up!*

Madhukar: *Shut up!*

Herbert: *No, I won't shut up! I won't shut up! I won't shut up!*
(Madhukar jumps up, takes a glass of water, and throws it in Herbert's face)

Ramesh: Wait a minute. Please, let him talk.
    (Madhukar is silent)

Ramesh (to Madhukar): Have you finished? Carry on as long as you want to.

Carry on as long as you want to.

Madhukar: *So, you want to take this "large amount of money" figure to your grave?*

Ramesh: Yes! Yes! Yes! And, as I said, large is comparative. I repeat, what people give me here is enormously greater than what I gave Maharaj. It is enormously greater.

Madhukar: *What's the problem? Just be frank. Just speak that number out loud. You see, what happens after your talks is that your visitors think that I am a kind of administrator of yours, because they see me doing my recordings. They ask me how much money they should give to you. Often, they ask me how large was the sum which you gave to Maharaj. And I tell them, "I don't know how much should be given."*

Ramesh: Correct.

Madhukar: *I say, "I don't even know how much I myself should give to him. I only know that he doesn't like it when a seeker doesn't give him money."*

Ramesh: Quite right. Therefore, I keep repeating: nothing is demanded, whatever is given is accepted. Nothing is demanded, whatever is given is accepted. I am not advertising for people to come here. They come here of their own accord. In fact, I am truly worried that the space here might soon be too small if more people come. I don't want too many people. I don't want too many people. I was quite happy when we used to sit in the small room with two or three people. I have no room for many people. I do not want too many people!

Madhukar: *You see, if you tell us now how much money you gave to Maharaj then we will know what a seeker should give to you. It is very simple.*

Ramesh: No! Why should they know? People need not know. They can give whatever they want, or they may not give anything.

Madhukar: *That is clear. I asked you a simple question.*

Ramesh: And I gave you a simple answer.

Madhukar: *I just want to hear the amount.*

Ramesh: No answer! If you ask me how much money I spend per month, I will tell you that it is none of your business! My monthly income is none of your business, nor how much I pay in income taxes.

Madhukar: *I am not asking you about this. My question is very simple.*

Ramesh: What is my monthly income? It is none of your business!

Madhukar: *I am not asking you this question.*

Ramesh: What income tax do you pay? It is none of your business!

Madhukar: *I am not asking you this question. I am asking only about the amount of your "big cash gift" to Maharaj*

Ramesh: What does somebody give to me? It is none of your business!

Madhukar: *I am not asking this question.*

Ramesh: What did I give someone else? It is none of your business! What did I give whom? None of your business!

Madhukar: *I am not asking you about these things.*

Ramesh: What donation have I given to somebody? It is none of your business! What donation did I give to the World Hunger Project, or to the Annamalai Swami Ashram Trust? It is none of your business! What donation I gave to someone else? It is none of your business! You see?

Madhukar: *I am asking you a simple question. Still, you don't want to answer it?*

Ramesh: No.

> *During the entire conversation, Madhukar was kneeling in front of Ramesh. At this point Madhukar folds his hands in* namaste, *then he bows down and his forehead touches the ground. Madhukar touches Ramesh's feet one last time. Then Madhukar takes leave of Ramana Maharshi, Nisargadatta Maharaj, Ramesh's father, and Ramesh's house-god Krishna by* namaste-*ing to their pictures. As Madhukar is about to leave the flat, Ramesh calls after him:*

Ramesh: Oh, incidently, Madhukar, all this recording equipment — the microphones, amplifier, and speakers — is yours.

Madhukar: *Yes, but I don't want it. You need it, so keep it.*

Ramesh: All this is your stuff. If you don't take it with you today you might come tomorrow and say, "I gave all this stuff to Ramesh and I didn't get it back." Please, take it with you. I mean, this is your stuff. It was you who decided to put up the mikes, the amplifier, the recording equipment, and the speakers. It is your stuff. It is yours. It is yours.

(*After Madhukar leaves Ramesh's flat*) I feel tremendous compassion for him, you see. He went to Rajneesh, and then he left him. He has been to Poonjaji, and then he left him, too. He came to me for two or three years, and now he has gone away again. I feel compassion for him. He suffers, make no mistake.

Claire: *It seems that the same cycle has repeated itself for him with different gurus.*

Ramesh: You see, that is his destiny. What can I do?

Claire: *Nothing.*

Ramesh: It is of no use to contradict him. That's why I told Herbert to let him speak. He is hurting and suffering.

Murthy: *He cannot demand an answer. His demand creates the suffering.*

Ramesh: That's the whole point. If suffering is part of the destiny of the person, the suffering will happen.

Murthy: *Christ said, "Do not resist evil." There is no point.*

Ramesh: Quite right. Why not to resist evil? Why did Christ say that? Because evil is part of God's creation.

Lauran: *Is compassion different from pity?*

Ramesh: They only differ in the words used. The dictionary will use one in the place of the other. But maybe they are different.

Lauran: *I get involved a lot in self-pity, and then I get involved in pity for people who are suffering. It seems like compassion is not such a big, melodramatic deal as pity.*

Ramesh: Hmm.

Shalini: *In pity there is judging. In compassion there is no judgement.*

Ramesh: Compassion just arises.

Jaimie: *It seems that Madhukar represents the doubt and the fear in the world. To witness what happened here today seems almost like a test for me, to see if the energy of today's event can shake me, can shake me into doubt. It doesn't.*

Ramesh: Sorry, I didn't get what you said.

Jaimie: *It seems that the doubt and the fear and the anger of Madhukar is no different from the fear and the doubt in the world at large.*

Ramesh: That is correct.

Jaimie: *Madhukar can't help but to do what he is doing. He should understand that the world will continue with anger, doubt, and evil, and all of that.*

Ramesh: Quite right.

Murthy: *Is compassion the solution for such incidents?*

Ramesh: It will be a solution if compassion is in your hands. But the arising of compassion is not in your hands.

Murthy: *Does compassion arise only if I don't get involved?*

Ramesh: It may or may not.

Murthy: *But compassion will definitely not arise if I get involved, right?*

Ramesh: That is correct. Then it won't arise.

Murthy: *So, I better try not to get involved.*

Ramesh: Yes. But getting involved or not is not in your hands. (*after a long pause*) I am really worried about Madhukar. The other day Madhukar had a confrontation with Glenn, in this room after the talk. Were you here at that time, Claire?

Claire: *No, I wasn't here. But I came a few days later and heard about it.*

Ramesh: Madhukar hit him. And there was no reason for him to exhibit such behavior, such violence, towards Glenn. But Madhukar is violent.

Claire: *The violence is a manifestation of his suffering.*

Ramesh: Yes, that violence is part of the manifestation of his suffering. He suffers, make no mistake.

Herbert: *I felt very safe when he threw the water into my face. I felt totally safe. At that moment I just took the water as a refreshment.* (laughter by everyone)

Ramesh: Violence is part of his nature. And he was violent in another incident, also.

Jaimie: *He takes a certain enjoyment in doing violent acts. After he was violent towards Glenn, we saw him on the stairs kissing and hugging a woman. He was very happy. The violence didn't seem to bother him afterwards.*

Herbert: *You mean right after the talk? Outside, on the stairs?*

Jaimie: *Yes, it was after he had expressed his anger. There is a certain enjoyment in him that this has been happening.*

Ramesh: Sure.

Jaimie: *So, that's all he knows right now. He must have enjoyed it this time, too.*

Ramesh: Yes. (*laughs*)

Claire: *This violence could also turn against you, Ramesh. I think everything is possible for him. He could do anything.*

Ramesh: Yes, anything is possible for him.

Claire: *Anything is possible. That's right.*

Herbert: *I think that if he would accept your love he would not need to get all this attention. I think he always wants to get attention. That's what I see.*

Ramesh: Yes.

Herbert: *Because he can't see and accept your love, and the love of the others here in the room, he needs to do this.*

Ramesh: Yes. But I feel tremendous compassion for Madhukar. He is suffering and he has been suffering for years. He went to Rajneesh for twelve years.

Herbert: *To me, his behavior seems very German. I am German too, and I understand his strong German conditioning.*

Ramesh: Yes.

Claire: *What is the German conditioning?*

Herbert: *To get it the way you want, with power and with fight.*

Jaimie's boyfriend: *The mind. To have to understand with the mind.*

Ramesh: That's the point, you see. To understand something with the mind, but not being able to actually do what you have understood, brings about tremendous frustration.

Claire: *When Madhukar started speaking, did he actually say that your days are numbered?*

Ramesh: He said, "His days with me are numbered."

Herbert: *But he doesn't know that.*

Ramesh: His days with Rajneesh were numbered. Then his days with Poonjaji were numbered. Now he says his days with me are numbered. I hope he finds somebody who meets with his requirements and standards.

Jaimie: *But isn't this what happens, though? Madhukar seems to be just like the person in the movie, "Ground Hog Day." That person keeps repeating the same day over and over again until finally love wakes him up, and things don't repeat themselves anymore.*

Ramesh: Oh, yes. I see.

Jaimie: *This is what happens. I see this happening to me all the time. In my past I repeated certain patterns over and over again. It must be God's Will that we play it out fully over and over again until...*

Ramesh: ...it exhausts itself.

Jaimie: *When it is this strong, as it is with Madhukar, it must exhaust itself somehow.*

Seema: *In* vipassana *practice we learn to witness whatever we sense, feel, or do. This technique helps to condition the mind to be a witness, rather than to be judgmental and comparing. Without training, the mind is usually judging. The introductory course takes ten days. That course helped me very much.*

Ramesh: But my point is that there is still someone witnessing. In real witnessing there is no one to witness. Witnessing happens as an impersonal process. If the individual "me" comes in, we can no longer call it impersonal witnessing. But this "impersonal witnessing" is also a concept. A "me" cannot witness. The ego, the "me," the thinking mind, judges and compares. That is its very nature.

Murthy: *Let us take the incident which just happened here with Madhukar. I can't just witness it and take it as God's Will and forget about it. To do that is difficult for me.*

Ramesh: That incident is God's Will. Why should it be difficult? It is God's Will.

Murthy: *Yes, we can take it as God's Will, but we can't just accept it and forget about it.*

Ramesh: Why not?

Murthy: *Because this incident was so strong, and keeps bringing up thoughts about what happened.*

Ramesh: Yes, it is bringing up thoughts. But why can't you accept it as part of God's Will? The incident is part of God's Will, and what happened is his destiny.

Jaimie: *During this incident, when a feeling of worry arose in you from your compassion, did it get cut off as soon as you noticed it?*

Ramesh: Worry didn't arise. There was not even anger. Compassion arose. There was not even anger.

Jaimie: *I understand. It was coming from compassion.*

Ramesh: There was compassion. So?

Jaimie: *So, the worry...*

Ramesh: No, the worry wasn't there.

Jaimie: *So, the worry arises from this compassion, you said earlier. Being worried arises from compassion. That's what you said.*

Ramesh: No, compassion just arose, seeing Madhukar suffer.

Jaimie: *Yes, but you used the word "worry." You said, "I am worried about him."*

Ramesh: No, no, nothing to do with this. No, no. Murthy said yesterday that when you understand and accept that all that happens is according to God's Will, worry stops. When you accept the What-is as God's Will, worry stops.

Jaimie: *I understand that. But you said a while ago that you were worried about Madhukar.*

Ramesh: Oh, yes. Worry about him in the sense that, if you see somebody walking along and you see him about to fall, you worry about him getting hurt. This worry is part of the compassion.

Herbert: *What you said verbally you didn't mean in the verbal sense.*

Shalini: *Worry is just a word. You are not worried mentally.*

Ramesh: Yes. That worry is part of the compassion.

Jaimie: *But you have no horizontal involvement in this, right? Worry just arose.*

Ramesh: No, there is no involvement. Worry just arose.

Claire: *I think you must have meant, "I feel for him, I care for him."*

Ramesh: Certainly. Yes.

EPILOGUE

I swear it wasn't my plan to disturb or to shock you, dear reader, but what can I do? The transcripts you have just read document a series of events which occurred as part of the impersonal functioning of God or Totality. They simply record what the What-is was at that time, and how it eventually led me to openly challenge my guru's teaching and then to walk out on him.

Those readers who may be curious as to what became of "the poor fool who doesn't understand the teaching" after his stormy departure from Ramesh's *satsang*, and who might appreciate some further discussion and clarification of the contradictions, inconsistencies and confusion that the last few chapters have highlighted, will find such matters addressed in the Postscript which follows. For now, let us focus instead on your own situation, in view of what you have just read.

Maybe you have still got the "enlightenment bug" pretty bad, and find that your life is centered around your spiritual progress. Alternatively, having understood and been persuaded by Ramesh's teaching, you may find that your concern about such things has suddenly faded, or that your spiritual *angst* has softened somewhat. And yet you know that enlightenment still has not happened, and you can't help but wonder, "Where am I at in my search? Have I made any progress at all?"

Ramesh's answer to this kind of question is simple and may be of some help to you when such questions arise. He says: "If you find yourself in daily life more tolerant towards other people's weaknesses, if you find yourself not having as many desires as you used to have, and if you find yourself being more generous to others than you used to be, then you can take it that the understanding of the teaching has gone deeper and the process of enlightenment has progressed."

Another common response to Ramesh's teaching is for people to feel somewhat at a loss as to how they should proceed, once they have heard and understood it. The teaching has led them into unfamiliar territory in which the customs and convictions that previously shaped and guided their spiritual search no longer seem relevant. Hence, you may find yourself wondering: "What do I do from now on? What about my spiritual practice? Should I drop it altogether, or should I intensify it? What about my career, and making a living? Should I abandon all that and head off into the forest like a hermit, to live on just nuts and berries and Truth?"

Again Ramesh's answer is astonishingly simple: "Keep doing exactly what you have been doing so far. If you have been meditating, meditate. If you feel like stopping your practice, stop it. Or enjoy life, food and sex — whatever comes along. Or keep making money. I assure you, making money is not an obstruction to enlightenment. God has not laid down any restrictions regarding enlightenment. Enlightenment can happen to a beggar or to a millionaire, to a saint or a sinner, to a meditator or a drunkard. However, if you have the choice — and you don't have the choice — between seeking a million dollars and enlightenment, seek the million dollars, because then there will be a 'me' to enjoy it. On the other hand, when enlightenment occurs, there is no one to enjoy enlightenment. The 'me,' the enjoyer, gets annihilated in the impersonal process of the event."

What are the functions of the guru and the seeker in this process? Ramesh says, "In the knowledge of the true nature that the guru imparts, the guru and the disciple become united; or rather, both become united in the annihilation of the individual entities. Negating the entity, the guru negates the disciple as an entity and, at the same time, negates himself as the guru. Consciousness is speaking to Consciousness. This understanding annihilates the entities of the disciple and the guru. The only liberation is the liberation from the idea of bondage. However, as part of God's Will, the guru can only point to the Truth. What is it? That which is sought is that which is seeking. The seeker and that which is sought (and the guru and that which is teaching), are 'this-here-now' — that which is always present: the sense or presence, Consciousness."

So, dear reader, if you have apperceived Ramesh's teaching finally and totally in the depth of you heart, I offer you my warmest congratulations. However, before concluding, I feel it is my duty to reiterate Ramesh's warnings about the final two obstructions to enlightenment: clinging to the guru, and wanting to be a guru. With regard to the first of these, he says, "The guru, being an obstruction, remains for a long time. When the relationship starts with the guru, there is not enough the seeker can do for him. The notion that the seeker is something separate from the guru is the final obstruction that has to go."

More insidious than this fixation with the guru is the second obstruction — wanting to be a guru. This obstruction arises when the seeker — acting in ignorance or from more cynical motives — lays false claim to the complete and final understanding of enlightenment. As Ramesh puts it: "The worst obstruction occurs when the ego of the seeker says, '"I" have the complete and final understanding.' Such a person thinks that he or she is enlightened and wants the world to know it. When such an attitude prevails, real enlightenment is out of reach."

In this context, I would like to conclude with a story, inviting you to step one more time onto that bridge of humor and laughter upon which the seeker and his search find no room to stand. It tells of someone who quite clearly cared not a jot for his own enlightenment or for his progression up any spiritual hierarchy, but who... well, you'll see when you read it for yourself.

A devotee knelt to be initiated into discipleship. The guru whispered the sacred *mantra* into his ear, warning him not to reveal it to anyone. "What will happen if I do?" asked the devotee. The guru answered, "Anyone you reveal the *mantra* to will be liberated from the bondage of ignorance and suffering, but you yourself will suffer eternal damnation. You will be permanently excluded from all discipleship and doomed to remain unenlightened forever."

As soon as he heard these words, the devotee got up and rushed to the marketplace where he gathered a large crowd around him and, at the top of his voice, shouted out the sacred *mantra* thrice for all to hear: "*Om tat sat! Om tat sat! Om tat sat!*"[1] The other disciples were scandalized, and reported this outrageous behavior to the guru, demanding that the man be expelled from the monastery for his disobedience. The guru smiled and said, "He has no need of anything I can teach. His action has shown him to be a guru in his own right."

Dear reader, I sincerely hope that, while reading this book, a similar secret and liberating understanding has been revealed to you. If it has, then those of us who haven't quite got it yet will be looking out for you at the next weekend market, hoping you will come and reveal the *mantra* or teaching which worked for you by announcing it for all to hear from the clock tower in the square. Failing that, perhaps we'll bump into each other at the local bookshop as we try and hunt down a more powerful *mantra* or teaching in one of the other books in this series. But, dear reader, before you rush off to the marketplace or to your local bookshop, check out the Glossary which is given at the end of this book. There, you will find a concise but comprehensive expression of classical *Advaita* Vedanta teachings. Immerse yourself in their pristine clarity and depth — having come this far, you sure deserve a good dip.

And if you find that neither the *mantra*, nor the Glossary nor any of the other Neti Neti books work for you, do feel free to e-mail me (neti_neti@yahoo.com) with your comments or questions about the how, when, where, what and why of your own personal spiritual search, or take a peek at my website: www.neti-neti.org. I am offering these facilities because I know from my own experience that if the seeking hasn't died completely, it will keep nagging at you until it does die. In *Advaita* it is said that: "We are *made* to seek until we are *made* not to seek anymore." That is why I know you can't stop seeking. You *have* to seek — it is somehow programmed into your being. So I guess you are going to keep trying — anything! That's what I did too, until... I started to publish these books, got e-mail, opened a website, and... Good luck! Meet you (t)here!

---

[1] "All there is, is Consciousness!"

POSTSCRIPT

From Ramesh to Adi Shankara...

"What the seeker is seeking, is seeking. The one who is seeking is already what he is seeking: the sense of presence, Consciousness." Hearing these words from Ramesh's lips, a deep understanding occurred. That is how it all began. Meeting Ramesh, the guru, and recognizing the true Self in his presence, was the most mysterious, wonderful and powerful event. This was followed, three years later, by the most heart-rending experience imaginable, as I knelt before him and told him that I was leaving him and why.

Dear reader, please don't get me wrong. I am not denying the validity of Ramesh's teachings — I certainly wouldn't have gone to all the trouble of publishing a series of books on them if I thought they were worthless. But I feel it is my *dharma* to reflect briefly on the unsettling events documented in the final chapters of this book, and to clarify, once and for all, the grounds of my "quarrel" with Ramesh. What troubled me most about his teachings was the confusion as to whether there was any way in which a seeker could hasten (or retard) his spiritual progress. For anyone on the spiritual path, this is obviously going to be a crucial issue. Are there any do's and don'ts that a seeker should follow? Is pleasing the guru (for instance with money) a *sadhana* that hastens the advent of enlightenment? Ramesh, as you will have noticed, offers no clear guidelines on this matter. In fact, he contradicts himself repeatedly. On the one hand he says, "Whatever happens, is willed and destined by God — God does it all. Therefore nothing can be done by the seeker and the guru." But then he also says that the guru, and his presence, and the seeker's pleasing the guru, all do something for the seeker's progress. And also that clinging to the guru, and wanting to be a guru are obstructions to spiritual progress. As I see it, this inconsistency stems from the fact that he repeatedly switches between two distinct and mutually exclusive standpoints: one which sees things from an individual perspective, and one which is rooted in the Absolute. Let me briefly expand on each of these in turn.

The *individual standpoint* is that habitually adopted by all of us — seekers and non-seekers alike. From this standpoint, the seeker and the guru exist as individual entities in phenomenality; they have personal volition and doership; and they can influence the advent of enlightenment one way or the other. From this perspective, it is possible to list certain do's and don'ts regarding the spiritual search, or indeed any other aspect of life.

This can be contrasted with the *Absolute standpoint* — or what Ramesh refers to as the enlightened standpoint. The perception from this standpoint is that whatever happens in manifestation is God's Will. Since we are merely instruments of God through which He works His Will, there is nothing that the guru or the seeker can do to influence the occurrence of enlightenment one way or the other. Indeed, seen from this standpoint, the seeker and his search, the guru and his teaching, together with the goal of enlightenment and the concomitant issue of how to hasten (or avoid hindering) one's spiritual progress, are understood to be mere changing appearances in the Cosmic Dream of God or Consciousness, and are therefore, *in toto*, illusory.

Clearly, these two standpoints are diametrically opposed to each other, and yet they run like twin strands through Ramesh's teaching. I would suggest that, when combined in this way, they are almost bound to generate confusion in his audience. Now that we are aware of these two standpoints, however, it should be possible for us to review Ramesh's teachings with them in mind, identifying the context in which each aspect of the teaching is being presented. And since all aspects of the teaching can be related to either the individual or the Absolute standpoint, it is now up to us to choose — of course, as God's instruments — the one which best suits our particular understanding and intuition.

Believe me, it is only after much heart-searching that I have dared to include this critique. In doing so, I may perhaps be going against the Indian tradition, which governs conduct in the guru-disciple relationship. This tradition holds that, while the guru still lives, the disciple should not divulge or comment on his teachings unless explicitly authorized to do so. Should a disciple go against this tradition, he forever forfeits his chance of reaching enlightenment. Moreover, the disciple is told that he will burn eternally in the fires of the worst — the seventh — hell. Having decided to speak up without the personal permission of my guru, it will be evident that I really don't care about my own enlightenment any longer, or about an afterlife on earth, in heaven or hell. That is indeed so, but — as we have seen from the *mantra* story in the Epilogue — this lack of concern is not without precedent.

Be that as it may, I found that Ramesh's teachings triggered a whole new set of questions which eventually led me to study the teachings of Sri Adi Shankara, the eighth century master who established *Advaita* Vedanta at a central position in the Hindu tradition. In the process of doing so, all my doubts were dispelled; and all questions, all yearning and the longing which had been with me for as long as I could remember, were finally dissolved in the transcendent understanding of what "I" really am — prior to all categories of guru and disciple, Gods and fools.

Some readers may be surprised to hear that Ramesh's main tenet, "Whatever happens is willed and destined by God (the individual doer doesn't exist!)," is not the final and supreme teaching in Shankara's *Advaita*. Ramesh's understanding of total destiny is still merely an explanation of phenomenal manifestation. While he emphasizes the supremacy of Consciousness or God pervading and functioning through all the various components of this manifestation (including the guru and the seeker), Ramesh's assertion that the entire manifestation is pre-programmed and is unfolding impersonally according to God's Will is actually no more than an idea. Admittedly, this idea encompasses the biggest possible picture, but it is still just an idea. The picture it paints is nothing but speculation, on a par with all the other religious doctrines that speak of God and His manifested creation. But in Truth, what we really *are* transcends all phenomenal appearance, including the "me" and God, both of which are mere phantoms that never existed.

Furthermore, classical *Advaita* makes it quite clear that all spiritual benefits and impediments to which Ramesh keeps referring, are merely products of the illusory realm of seeming diversity where the seeker imagines that the spiritual search takes place. Even if seekers like you and me keep asking about them, classical *Advaita* will not dwell on the ways the guru and the seeker differ with regard to their spiritual understanding and their experiences of, or attitudes towards, events that occur in their respective daily lives. It may well be that, compared to other people, the guru has effortless access to a whole range of spiritual "goodies," feeling no enmity, guilt, or pride etc. But even if such descriptions and comparisons are true, they relate solely to illusory phenomenal appearances; they are therefore as useless to the seeker as a wife's attempts to accurately describe the sensation of childbirth are to her husband.

Classical *Advaita* wants the seeker to realize just who or what he really is. And that realization can only be pure (object-less) knowing, where what one knows is nothing more or less than what one is. In that knowing, all comparisons dissolve, as does any concern with the quantitative or qualitative classification of experience before and after enlightenment.

Since the seeker's questioning can only occur on the phenomenal level of appearances, classical *Advaita* must necessarily engage the seeker at this level — the level of the limited individual standpoint. However, no matter what the question is, classical *Advaita* always calls the seeker away from the illusory phenomenal appearances of objects (including the body-mind organisms of the guru and seeker) that he takes to be real. Each and every one of the seeker's questions are used as stepping stones (and nothing else) for a totally uncompromising investigation into the pure, direct experience of one's own immediate reality — *prior to all phenomenal appearances.* Through the examination of his own direct subjective experience, the seeker is made to turn around and face what he really is — pure Subjectivity.

In the instant of this recognition and understanding, all differences dissolve. All differentiation ceases. There is no separated seeker, divided from what is sought. There is no ignorant disciple, divided from an illuminating guru. Such divisions are transcended through a reflective intuition which returns back to

That which underlies all seeming thought and intellect. Thus returned, the seeker disappears, and with him vanish the guru and the entire manifestation. (Hence Ramana Maharshi's declaration that "There is no creation, no dissolution, no free will, no predestination, no path, no goal.") What remains is what the seeker really is, was and always will be — prior to the arising of all perception and the intervention of any ideas pertaining to the time/space and cause/effect qualifications of phenomenality. Without any "one" who knows or is, pure knowing and being remain. And this *being* transcends all discussion about the illusory mechanics of phenomenal appearance — worldly, spiritual or otherwise. It transcends even silence. Therefore, it surely transcends what Ramesh describes as enlightenment: the apperception that God's entire manifestation — including the guru and the seeker — unfolds (and keeps existing!) without any individual "me"-entity with its sense of personal will and doership.

But according to classical *Advaita*, where doership ends, no manifestation remains. Without a sense of personal doership to produce the illusory appearance of partial perception, there is no world of seeming names and forms and qualities. These partial appearances of limited objects which make up the world are all created by the sense of a personally acting perceiver. This perceiver sees particular forms, thinks of them through particular names, and values their particular qualities.

So, while the world still appears, the seeker has no option but to care about progress and enlightenment; and this caring is, in fact, the positive and essential heart of the spiritual search. The seeker's fundamental aim is *not* just to arrive at the point where he doesn't care about enlightenment any longer, and to halt there, waiting to see what is going to happen. And so it is that, at that point of the spiritual search (as at all others), *Advaita* constantly prompts the seeker to keep searching beneath his superficial and frustrating desires for limited transient things until that which is truly worth caring for is "found," or rather realized as his own being.

This search drives him, to perform *sadhana* — a positive effort of striving towards Truth — and in this sense, seeking out a guru and listening attentively to him (or her) is surely *sadhana* too. Thus, anyone who follows this course of action cannot truly claim not to care whether enlightenment happens or not. If the disciple is honest, he will admit that his association with the guru is motivated by his desire for lasting peace and happiness. Although he may not know it, what he seeks is what he really is. Enlightenment or self-realization means simply returning to one's own true nature which is the unaffected Source and Center of all caring and love. All our experiences express that unaffected Center. The whole apparent world and all our desires revolve around it; all that we do, say, think and feel expresses it; but when we return to what it is, in each one of us, there all expressions of caring or not caring are superfluous.

...and Back to Ramesh Again

Since leaving Ramesh at the end of February 1996, I have visited him twice at the traditional festival of *Guru Purnima*. This is a time when disciples renew their dedication to their guru — something which, I thought, was especially necessary in my case. I also met him briefly in June 1998, while he was in Germany giving a seminar. This was shortly after the publication of the first Neti Neti book documenting his teachings — *Enlightenment: An Outbreak*. I presented copies of this book to him and to his disciples Mark and Margarete Beuret, Elke von der Osten, and Wayne Liquorman.

Then, on December 16, 1998, I went to Bombay to present Ramesh with a copy of the second Neti Neti book on his teachings, *Enlightenment May Or May Not Happen* (the prequel to this volume). Here is the story:

I arrived at Ramesh's residence at about 11.20 a.m.; *satsang* had already begun. I counted 42 pairs of shoes outside the entrance of his flat. I entered the flat, took the book out of my bag, and sat down on an empty chair outside the small but crowded *satsang* room. Through the open door, I could see and hear Ramesh, seated about 4 meters away.

I waited for what seemed an eternity while an ex-Rajneeshi in his late 50s spoke at length about his life and his experiences in the spiritual search. When he had had his say, Ramesh gestured to Murty's wife Kalandi and said, "Well, let us have the *bhajans*, now." I got up from my seat and entered the room, making my way towards Ramesh. I knelt down in front of him and namasted — greeting him in the Indian tradition with palms folded together. I laid the book on the floor before him, bowed down and touched his feet. I heard Ramesh say:

Ramesh: Oh, it is Madhukar! Where did you come from? From Pune?

Madhukar: *Yes.*

Ramesh: How are you doing? Are you keeping well?

Madhukar: *Thank you, Ramesh. Yes, I am doing very well. You too, are you keeping well?*

Ramesh: Oh, yes, quite well, indeed. (*Madhukar touches first his forehead then his heart with the book, and then offers it to Ramesh saying:*)

Madhukar: *Here is my next book on your teaching. I came today to present it to you. It has just come from the press.* (When Ramesh receives the book, Madhukar again bows down to his feet in silence.)

Ramesh: Thank you very much, Madhukar. Congratulations! This is your second book, isn't it? How many more will come?

Madhukar: *Yes, it's the second book. I don't know how many more will come. Quite a few, I guess.*

Ramesh: Nobody knows. (*Now Ramesh looks at the title page, then at the back cover and then he reads out loud:*) "Enlightenment May Or May Not Happen." (*He opens the book and reads on:*) "Talks on Enlightenment with Ramesh S. Balsekar." Madhukar, you must sign this book for me.

Madhukar: *Oh, please, no. I can't do that. I am nobody. This book is as much your book as it is mine. Perhaps, it is actually more your book. I just made it. It just came into existence. That's all.*

Ramesh: How have you been doing all this time? Are you keeping well?

Madhukar: *Thank you for asking. I am doing absolutely fine.*

Ramesh: You see, I remembered you quite often. My wife Sharda and I remember you almost every day. You see, my wife's sister's husband is also called Madhukar. Whenever we speak of him, we come to speak of you. While we call him "Madhukar," we use the name "Thompson-Madhukar" for you. This is how I remember you quite often.

(*To the others*) You see, Madhukar lives in the most spacious, most beautiful, most luxurious and most fantastic apartment. And he paid a fortune for it, didn't you, Madhukar?

Madhukar: *That's right.*

Ramesh: He lives in a pyramid. How many rooms are there in that pyramid? I heard there are only four rooms like yours.

Madhukar: *There are eighteen rooms in the pyramid I live in.*

Hilda: *Where does he live?*

Ramesh: Oh, he lives right in the middle of the Osho ashram in Pune. Yes, he has a really fantastic place there. So I was told.

Madhukar, why don't you lay out your book over there? (*Ramesh points to the table on which his books are laid out for sale.*) You can sell it here.

Madhukar: *That's great! Thank you very much for the offer — and the money that comes from the sales will go to you — all of it. That's how I can do some good for you.*

Ramesh: Thank you very much, Madhukar.

Madhukar: *Thank you for all, Ramesh.*

Ramesh: Well, shall we have the *bhajans*? Madhukar, please, sit right here. (*Ramesh point to an empty space beside him. Three* bhajans *are sung. When they come to an end, Ramesh asks:*) Madhukar, how much are the books?

Madhukar: *480 Rupees per copy.*

Ramesh: 420?

Madhukar: *Four, eight, zero.*

Ramesh (*laughing*): I will ask for 500. It makes it easier change-wise. Hundred Rupee bills are easier to handle.

Madhukar: *You can ask whatever price you like. Whatever comes from the sales goes to you anyway.*

Copies of *Enlightenment May Or May Not Happen* were delivered to Ramesh by Zen Publications in time for the next *satsang* on Thursday, December 17. I also sent him copies of *Enlightenment: An Outbreak*. Before returning to Pune, I asked the proprietor of Zen Publications, Yogesh Sharma, to call Ramesh and tell him that the copies were complimentary, and that he needed only to ring Zen Publications in order to get new stocks. Shortly after my arrival in Pune the next day, I received a call from Yogesh, saying, "Ramesh asked me to call you. He would like you to call him in Bombay." Wondering what it was that Ramesh wished to talk about, I gave him a ring.

Madhukar: *Hi, Ramesh! This is Madhukar. How are you?*

Ramesh: Oh, it's you, Madhukar! Good that you call.

Madhukar: *Yogesh said you wanted to speak with me, so here I am.*

Ramesh: You see, I wanted to pass this on to you since a long time. But we haven't met for such a long time and I never got around to tell you: the big cash gift I gave to Maharaj in the late 1970s was 1000 Rupees. That was one fifth of my monthly salary. It was a big amount for me, and for Maharaj too, at that time. I know in today's money this amount looks like chicken shit; it is not comparable with what some of the people are giving me today. But let me tell you: at that time it was a big amount for me.

Madhukar: *I know it must have been a lot. I was doing business with India in those years. As I remember it, the Deutsch Mark/Indian Rupee ratio was about 1 : 4 in those days.*

Ramesh: That's correct. And the US Dollar was not even 9 Rupees yet at that time. You see, I have been wanting to tell you this for a long time. But I never got round to telling you.

Madhukar: *I want to thank you for taking the trouble to let me know this. Thank you, Ramesh.*

Ramesh: I want to thank you too, Madhukar, for the books that Yogesh has delivered to me.

Madhukar: *I have advised Yogesh to deliver more books to you at any time. You just need to give him a ring. And, as I said, the books are complimentary.*

Ramesh: Thank you, Madhukar. Thank you.

Madhukar: *I want to thank you too, Ramesh. I want to thank you for the teaching. And I want to thank you for the understanding that I have received from you.*

Ramesh: Are your other books going to be ready by May (1999)? Are they in the making?

Madhukar: *Oh, yes, very much so. I hope they will be published within two or three months.*

Ramesh: Oh, really! That means the manuscripts must be already completed.

Madhukar: *Definitely. At present, I am already in the process of designing and shaping the form of the books.*

Ramesh: That's amazing! You must have been working a lot.

Madhukar: *I am working day and night. I am doing nothing else. The working mind — you know!*
Why do you ask about the specific May publishing deadline? Did you think of the coming seminar in Germany? Are you asking if they will be out in time for it?

Ramesh: No, I am not asking with a specific reason in mind. I read in *Enlightenment May Or May Not Happen* that your other books are scheduled for publication for May 1999. I just wondered if your schedule is really viable.
OK, Madhukar, stay well. I wish you all the best.

Madhukar: *Thank you for everything, Ramesh. I wish you all the best, too. Good bye.*

And now, looking back, it seems that my leaving Ramesh in 1996 was exactly what needed to happen at that time to this body-mind organism called Madhukar. My un-answered questions lead me to the doorway of Sri Shankara's final *Advaita* Vedanta teaching and understanding.
And so, after all that happened, I find myself at this present moment saying from the depth of my heart: "Thank you, Ramesh, for leading me to Shankara's door, and thank you, Sri Shankara, for leading me back to Ramesh."
The circle is complete and my journey with my masters has come to an end in an endless obeisance of reverence, gratitude, silence and transcendence.

Om Tat Sat

Glossary of Concepts —
Ramesh's Teaching According to Classical Advaita Vedanta

Advaita

Non-duality. ("*A-*" means "non-", "*dvaita*" means "duality") The philosophy of *Advaita* Vedanta comes to the conclusion that there is no duality between the subject that knows and an object that is known. No object is ever known apart from the subject that knows it. So in truth they are not two, but only one.

Somewhat paradoxically, this non-dual position is reached by first distinguishing the pure Subjectivity of Consciousness from everything objective. Body and mind are seen as objective instruments through which appearances are perceived. Consciousness is pure illumination, from which all perceptions and appearances get their light. It underlies all experience, as the illuminating basis upon which all appearances come and go. All personal faculties of body and mind are only changing appearances, illuminated by an underlying Consciousness that has no trace of physical or mental personality in it. This is the one Subject: unqualified by changing personality, and therefore the same in all experience.

Body and mind perceive objects that are different from themselves. So where there is personal ego, identified with body and mind, there is duality. But from underlying Consciousness, there is a radical change of perspective. All that is known are appearances, which have no existence apart from Consciousness. All seeming objects are nothing but Consciousness: the one Subject, each person's own true Self. In this non-duality, all differences dissolve.

aham

First person Sanskrit pronoun, equivalent to the English "I." Through the false identification of ego, it is habitually taken to mean a person, consisting of a body and a mind. But what does it really mean? That is thrown fundamentally into question, in *Advaita* philosophy. *See* ego, "I-Am," "I-I," Self.

ajnani

One who is not a fully enlightened sage (*jnani*).

Amritanubhava

A classic work of *Advaita* philosophy by the sage Jnaneshwar. It is in old

---

[1] Written by Ananda Wood, 1A Ashoka, 3 Naylor Road, Pune 411 001, India, Tel: 020-620737; E-mail: awood@vsnl.com

Marathi, combining clear philosophical analysis with moving poetry, for the ordinary people of its time (in thirteenth century Maharashtra). Translated by Ramesh in his book *Experience of Immortality*. *See* Jnaneshwar.

anubhava
Direct experience, which one undergoes oneself. All objects are indirectly experienced: through actions, perceptions, thoughts and feelings. Such experiences become direct only when they come back to the Consciousness from which they rise. And there they come to end, dissolved in the pure "I-I": the one principle that is not a concept, but one's own, immediate reality. *See* concept.

ashram
An institution of retreat where people withdraw from the distractions of worldly activity, in order to seek simplicity and peace.

avatar
An incarnation of God.

awakening
See enlightenment

belief
See concept, intellect

Bhagavad Gita
A classic philosophical and religious text: in which Krishna (who is God incarnate) tells the warrior Arjuna to do his duty without attachment to the fruits of action.

bhajans
Songs of devotion. *Bhajan* is devotional practice, in particular prayer and songs.

bhakti
Devotion. The path of love; devotion or love for a God or a guru who represents the ultimate Truth. A *bhakta* is a devotee, following a selfless love in which all trace of separate ego must dissolve.

bodhisattva
A savior on the verge of Buddhahood, postponing his own entry into *nirvana*, to help others attain enlightenment.

body-mind organism
Combination of body and mind, functioning as part of the totality of manifestation, in which the ego pretends to the role of seeming doership and personal independence.

Brahman
: Complete Reality, ultimate and absolute. Ramesh describes it as "Totality" or "all there is." *See* Totality, What-is.

brahmin
: In Hinduism, the priestly caste, or a member of this caste, having the duties of learning, teaching, and performing rites (*pujas*) and sacrifices (*yagnas*).

brain
: That body-mind mechanism which merely reacts, from past conditioning, to thoughts and sensations arising from Consciousness. The brain's reactions are not deliberated. Deliberation and worry result from the ego or thinking mind, which reacts in a secondary and complicating way to the primary reactions of the brain.

concept
: Any experience that may be believed or disbelieved: in particular a thought, idea, name, form, object, or nothing. "Nothing" is also a concept, the opposite of "something." A concept depends on how it is viewed and interpreted by the mind. So in one state of mind, it may be believed; but in another state, it may be disbelieved.

But all states of experience, all belief and disbelief depend on Consciousness. Without that, no mind, no states, no belief or disbelief could appear. It is not subject to either belief or disbelief; for it is always there, quietly present in each of them. It is plainly and simply there: illuminating each appearance that we call "something" and also each disappearance that we call "nothing."

Consciousness alone is not a concept; because it is not just an experience, but Experience itself. *See* Consciousness.

conditioning
: The cumulative effect upon body and mind of their environment: including parents, family, society, country, upbringing, education, culture and so on.

Consciousness
: The common principle of all experience. Anything known can only appear in the presence of Consciousness. So Consciousness is always there, as pure Subjectivity. All physical and mental things, all names, forms and qualities appear in Consciousness. But they also disappear, while it does not. They are only appearances, which do not exist apart from it. Consciousness is completely independent of all physical or mental things, of all names or forms or qualities. See *jnana*.

consciousness
In the illusion of personal identity, it falsely appears that Consciousness is a qualified activity of body and mind. When the word "consciousness" is used with a small "c," it refers to this illusion of a personal "consciousness": which wrongly seems fragmented from other such "consciousnesses," in other bodies and minds.

Consciousness-at-rest
When appearances are not produced, as in deep sleep, everything disappears. But even "disappearance" has no meaning without Consciousness. So even in a state like deep sleep — where all apparent things have disappeared and no activity produces any appearance — there is Consciousness. When referring to it in this context, in the absence of manifestation, it is called "Consciousness-at-rest."

Consciousness-in-action
When activity appears in experience, as in the dream and waking states, it produces a stream of changing appearances that come and go. In all this change, Consciousness is there throughout, implied in all activities and appearances, as the continuing basis on which both differences and relationships are understood. When referring to it in this context, as shown beneath manifesting activity, it is called "Consciousness-in-action."

Consciousness-not-aware-of-itself
No appearance has any existence independent of Consciousness. All appearances are thus nothing other than Consciousness. As it illuminates appearances, it just illuminates itself. Accordingly, throughout all appearances, it may be called "Consciousness-aware-of-itself."

And when appearances vanish, it may be called "Consciousness-not-aware-of-itself": for there it shines by itself, with nothing else reflecting back at it.

darshan
Seeing. In particular, the word is used for seeing or meeting with a deity or a guru. It is also used to describe a philosophical position, as a way of seeing things.

death
Only an end to that personal expression of life which appears in body and mind. At death, a particular body and mind is no longer seen to express Consciousness, in the way it did before. It is only the expression that dies. Death is a mere appearance that comes and goes in Consciousness. The word "death" does not apply to Consciousness, which is life itself.

deep sleep
　The state where waking and dream appearances are dissolved in Consciousness. *See* the three states.

destiny
　The march of events, expressing the impersonal functioning of Consciousness. Thus events progress as in a movie that appears on the screen of Consciousness; with the same Consciousness as the purely witnessing spectator who fully appreciates what happens, without the complications of any personal involvement. Despite their show of independence, all characters and happenings are just expressions of that Consciousness. So all personal involvements are only expressions, just part of the movie. They make no difference to Consciousness: the unaffected witness and background, from which the expressions rise.

dharma
　The natural order by which the phenomenal world is governed, including the conditioning of character by actions and experiences. Literally, the word *"dharma"* means "supported or well-grounded," showing that this natural order is conceived to be a grounding of the world's phenomena in the Consciousness from which they rise. To the extent that cultural codes of conduct and duty are firmly grounded in nature's underlying order (in their own times and circumstances), they too are called *"dharma."*

dhyana
　Meditation; *see* meditation.

Divine hypnosis
　The hypnosis that fools the fictitious ego into believing its own fictions. It is called "Divine" because its source is Consciousness, and it is thus the medium through which Consciousness is expressed everywhere in the world that ego perceives.

doer, doership
　The ego depends on a sense of personal doership — that one is a personal doer, involved in the world which one knows. On the one hand, this personal doer is a dependent part of the world, in which it is an involved actor. But, on the other hand, it has to be independent so as to enable the independence of judgement that is needed to know the world.

　So a personal doer is fragmented off, as an independent and separate part of the world. And the moment such a fragmentation is made for the doer, it spreads immediately to the world of objects that the doer perceives. *See* ego.

dualism
   The philosophical position that experience is divided into two, with a knowing subject on the one hand and a known object on the other. From this position, different objects can be known, and the world of multiplicity arises. But when it is realized that no object is ever known apart from the subject that knows it, then all multiplicity dissolves. There really are no different objects, nor different people perceiving them. All such different-seeming things are nothing other than the pure Subjectivity of Consciousness, the real "I." That is the non-dualist position. See *Advaita*.

duality
   The world of divided experience: starting from the division of experience into subject and object, proceeding through pairs of opposite qualities, and going on to the multiplicity of objects and people in the world.

dream
   See the three states.

ego
   The false sense of "I": as a personal doer consisting of body and mind. Through this false identification, body and mind are mistaken to be a personal "I," with a limited "consciousness" of particular objects in the world. Thus the true nature of Consciousness is obscured by personal limitations, and a fragmented world appears perceived. To correct the problem, there has to be a clear understanding of what Consciousness really is, beneath its misleading expressions in personal ego and the world that ego perceives.

enlightenment
   The end of seeking: in a final understanding of Truth that always is, and always was, immediately here.

experience
   See *anubhava*.

free will
   Misleading expression of independent Consciousness in the driven dependence of personal will. When an act of choice expresses the freedom of underlying Consciousness, it appears free; but this appearance does not change the fact that the expression is never free, while Consciousness always is.

God
   Concept used in religious worship, for the purpose of devotional surrender. Though the personal element of worship makes "God" seem a transcendent person to whose Will one must surrender, this is not what the concept

finally means. In truth, God is pure Subjectivity, unmixed with any limited personality. That is identical with Consciousness.

God's Will

What happens in the world, as distinct from what is wished to happen, in some person's mind. Both the happening and the wish are passing expressions of the same, impersonal principle of Consciousness that is found at the unchanging core of everyone's experience.

grace

Spontaneous perfection of all that takes place. When things are seen partially by the ego, what happens may seem wrong and unfair. But when everything is seen impartially, as expressing one same Consciousness, then whatever happens is understood as perfect grace.

guru

Spiritual teacher, as the living expression of Truth through which a disciple realizes her or his true nature.

Guru Purnima

The day traditionally prescribed for renewing a disciple's dedication to the guru. It is a full moon (*purnima*) day, sometime in July-August each year. Exactly when is calculated through the lunar calendar.

happiness

What things are wanted for; the principle of value that motivates all our physical and mental acts. In a state of happiness, the false sense of separated ego dissolves in a feeling of oneness with experience. But no such state is happiness itself. For in the course of time, each such state or feeling of happiness becomes unsatisfying to the mind, which then goes on to look for something else.

Happiness itself is what the state or feeling expresses: the underlying oneness of the knowing Self with the experience that it knows. Each state of happiness is simply a return to one's real Self, where there is truly no duality between what knows and what is known. Happiness itself is just that truth of non-duality. See *Advaita, Sat-Chit-Ananda*.

Heart

Depth of mind: where understanding is intuited, and there is no seeming "me" to understand anything. Understanding becomes complete when spontaneously intuited in the depth of Heart, with no trace of any object "me" to bring in limitation and partiality.

horizontal and vertical

The word "horizontal" is used for the chains of cause and effect that take place in time and space. Thus horizontal causation takes place along the surface of our space-time picture of the world. This picture appears on the ground of Consciousness. All the patterning in the picture is "horizontal": contained entirely in the apparent surface. It does not affect the unconditionded ground immediately beneath it.

By contrast, the arising of appearances — from underlying Consciousness — is called "vertical." Such vertical arising is instantaneous. It is completely contained in the present, at every moment of time. Thus Consciousness is vertically expressed: in the whole world picture that appears on it, and in every part of this picture. There is no distance involved in this vertical expression. The same ground of Consciousness is immediately present everywhere: beneath each part or point of the picture, and beneath the picture as a whole.

"I-Am"

People habitually think: "I am so-and-so" or "I am this" or "I am that." Common to all such particular manifestation is the universal sense of presence: "I-Am." This is the universal sense of "I" that all particular persons share. It is the initial identification of underlying Consciousness, as a generic or universal ego: on the way to being identified with a particular ego, differentiated from other objects and egos, in the multiplicity of the world. "I-Am" is thus a concept of final transition, towards the pure "I" that underlies both the particular and the universal. *See* Self.

"I-I"

Ramana Maharshi's way of describing the pure "I" as the non-dual Reality of the whole world. In reality, each thing is only the pure "I." So where there seem to be two things, there is only "I-I" — the same "I" repeated twice. This repetition amounts to only "I." Similarly the entire multiplicity of the universe is only a seemingly prolonged repetition of the same "I"; thus reducing the whole world to that pure "I."

illusion

Misperception or mistaken appearance. It seems to occur when appearances are somehow mistaken to show something other than Consciousness, though in truth they reflect and consist of nothing but Consciousness. See *maya*, Divine hypnosis, What-is.

intellect

In order to clarify understanding, one has to examine what one currently thinks and believes, so as to remove the mistaken assumptions that are obscuring the inherent clarity of Truth. The search for Truth thus starts with the questioning and analysis of intellect. But the enquiry is reflective: directed back into the basis from which thoughts and beliefs arise. As the enquiry gets deeper, it progressively clarifies the Truth; until no concepts and thoughts remain to obscure the meaning that they represent. Then the questioning intellect has dissolved back into its own basis of understanding, which turns out to be pure, unconditioned Consciousness.

involvement

Getting caught in the complications of a world constructed from the partial objects of ego's limited perception, instead of remaining free in the simplicity of pure Consciousness, which is one's own nature.

jnana

Knowledge. At first, it is seen as knowing objects (physical or mental); but examination shows that such "knowledge of objects" is not really knowledge at all. What we call "knowledge of objects" is only perception and conception, only sensual and mental activity that produces perceived and conceived appearances. Knowledge is not really the production of appearances by body and mind. Instead, it is what lights perception and conception and the appearances that they produce. Thus it is pure Illumination: the unconditioned Consciousness that continues unaffected and unchanged through all experience. That is true *jnana* or knowledge. It underlies both thought and feeling. There, head and heart are reconciled.

See Consciousness.

Jnaneshwar

A great Advaitin sage, regarded as an early founder of the Maharashtrian literary tradition. He symbolizes the unity of *jnana* (knowledge) and *bhakti* (devotion); for he was both a keenly analytical philosopher and a moving poet, who wrote both analytic and devotional works, in simple and moving language that was accessible to ordinary people. Jnaneshwar's classic, *Amritanubhava*, is translated by Ramesh in his book *Experience of Immortality*.

jnani

Literally "a knower" or "one who knows." The word is often used to describe an enlightened sage. But it is also used sometimes to describe someone who follows the path of *jnana* (knowledge), as distinguished from the paths of *yoga* (meditation) and *bhakti* (devotion).

karma

Action. It is experienced over the course of time, involving both its causes from the past and its effects upon the future. The word "*karma*" is used both for particular actions and for the whole process of action that keeps going on and on, with past actions leading to what is done now, and present action leading to further actions in the future. In this endlessly repeated cycle of cause and effect, the ego is involved because it desires results. But all egos, all desires and all actions express Consciousness, which continues uninvolved with all these expressions that arise from it. Instead of chasing results, if the ego stands back in its own source of Consciousness, all involvement immediately ends.

karma yoga, karma marga

The path of action, described in the *Bhagavad Gita*. The approach is not to give up action; but instead to carry it out wholeheartedly, with full absorption in the practical work to be done, yet cultivating an attitude of non-attachment to the results. See *karma, sannyas,* mind (third paragraph).

knowledge

See *jnana*.

kundalini

In Tantric yoga, the creative energy latent within a person is conceived as a serpent called "*kundalini*." Unaroused, it lies coiled at the base of the spine; but it may be aroused to rise up through the spine towards the pinnacle of experience at the top of the head. In the course of this rise, it may produce extraordinary displays of power and energy. The deliberate arousing of *kundalini* is a potentially dangerous and involving practice that is quite unnecessary for enlightenment.

leela, lila

Divine play. In Hinduism, this "Divine play" is a way of conceiving how Consciousness is spontaneously expressed in all the phenomena of nature and in all happenings in the world.

maha

Great. Often used as a prefix.

mahabhogi

Great enjoyer. ("*maha*" means "great," "*bhogi*" means "enjoyer")

mala

Garland or rosary; both for decoration, and for listing or counting (as in a rosary of prayer beads).

manifestation

Everything that appears: the whole apparent universe and all that it contains. Also the arising of appearances from Consciousness. All arising and appearances are nothing but Consciousness; for they each take place in it, and they do not have even a moment's existence away from it.

manolaya

Dissolving or absorption of mind. ("*Manas*" is "mind," "*laya*" is "dissolving or absorption.") When seen from the level of appearance, such dissolution is only temporary; for appearances keep alternating with disappearances. The mind keeps coming up with new appearances, following the dissolution of previous ones.

manonasha

Destruction of mind, including the latent tendency of ego to see things from the level of appearance. When the destruction is complete, it becomes permanent. For even if the mind and all its experiences reappear, they are known from underlying Consciousness. From there, they are mere appearances, which are nothing but Consciousness. They have no effect whatsoever on the pure Consciousness that is their sole reality.

mantra

Chanted words or sounds directing mental energy. Literally "*mantra*" means a "mental device." When a chant is used as a *mantra,* the mind does not enquire into the meaning of words, but is instead focused by the shape of sounds so as to produce an effect on mood (rather like listening to music). The effect is reinforced by repetition. Thus a *mantra* is designed to concentrate mental energy towards special states of experience or qualities of character or other intended results.

maya

Artistry of show, which attracts attention and interest. But when attention remains stuck in the resulting appearances, they become a veil of deceptive illusion: concealing the very source of interest which they truly show, and from which their attractiveness and artistry comes. In the concept of "*maya*," all perceived phenomena are thus taken as a show of nature's artistry.

At the surface of our minds, the show produces a seeming veil of tricky and deceptive appearance. But if one reflects back, into underlying Consciousness, that Consciousness itself turns out to be the real source of all our interest, the one reality that is truly shown by the amazing artistry of nature's unendingly intricate order.

"me"

The "I," mistakenly viewed as an object in the world: thus producing the fiction of a separated, personal ego.

meditation

The practice of directing attention. When meditation deepens, it becomes spontaneous, without the interfering thought of a meditator who is doing the directing and achieving something from it. Not everyone is suited to meditation. It can be useful if it happens; but its deliberate cultivation is not necessary for enlightenment, and can even be an obstacle on the way. See *yoga*.

mind

Consciousness appearing in the form of objects, through a changing stream of perceptions, thoughts and feelings that come and go in the course of experience. As this stream functions, limited objects of attention are thrown up, one after another in the course of time.

Where there is ego, there is involvement: through identification with a doer who is part of the changing stream and who thus carries out acts of perception, thought and feeling. This involved aspect is called the *"thinking mind,"* because it keeps thinking of itself and its achievements, thus distracting attention from the task at hand.

But where mind gets absorbed in work, it stops calling attention to itself, and it is thus dissolved in Consciousness. Then actions rise directly and spontaneously from Consciousness, without the distracting involvement of a grasping ego that keeps getting in the way. This undistracted, uninvolved aspect is called the *"working mind."* Here work arises spontaneously, as action towards objectives, while the mind remains anchored firmly in Consciousness, where ego and objects are all dissolved. *See* thought.

nadi

Channel. Refers both to physical channels, like veins, arteries and nerves, and to mental channelling, in subtle currents of psychic energy and thought.

neti-neti

"Not this, not this." *"Neti"* is a compound of *"na,"* meaning "not," and *"iti,"* meaning "this that is said or conceived." Thus *"neti-neti"* describes a progressive removal of all conception from Truth. In what one takes to be true, anything found conceived in it must be understood as an extraneous element, which compromises plain Truth. Thus questioning the compromising element in one's own standpoint, one comes to a new stand. Again, anything found conceived here is extraneous to Truth. So the process goes on, progressively, until a final Truth is reached where no trace of conception remains.

nirvana

Literally: "blown out, extinguished." Refers to enlightenment, as the complete extinction of ego.

Nisargadatta Maharaj

Ramesh's final guru. He was a renowned *jnani* who lived in Bombay from 1897 to 1981. His teachings are presented in Ramesh's book *Pointers from Nisargadatta Maharaj* (Chetana, Bombay 1983) and in Maurice Frydman's *I Am That* (Chetana, Bombay 1973).

non-duality
　See *Advaita*, dualism.

Noumenon
　The reality associated with pure Knowing. By contrast, phenomena are the appearances associated with perceiving, through body and mind. There are many phenomena; but the Noumenon is one alone.

om tat sat
　A *mantra* describing non-dual Truth, where appearance and Reality are ultimately the same.

　The sound of the word "*om*" has three components, represented by the letters 'a', 'u' and 'm'. These correspond to the three states of waking, dream and deep sleep, respectively. Thus, as the word is pronounced, it proceeds from the seemingly outward objectivity of the waking world, through the inner appearances of the dreaming mind, to the undisturbed peace of deep sleep where all waking and dream appearances dissolve into the immaculate light of pure Subjectivity — which each of us really is. In short, "*om*" represents the manifestation of appearances, dissolving back into their final Source.

　"*Tat*" means "That," referring to the Reality beyond these physical and mental appearances which our bodies and minds perceive.

　"*Sat*" means "Reality" or "Truth," as it actually is, unaffected by our differing and changing views of it.

　"*Om tat sat*" could thus be translated as: "All that appears, in the waking, dream or sleep states, is that Reality."

　To quote Ramesh: "All there is, is Consciousness."

peace
　The underlying unity of Truth is usually obscured by the conflicts and differentiations of physical and mental activity. When differences and conflicts come to rest, they are dissolved in the underlying unity which shines there on its own, as peace.

phenomenality
　The world of physical and mental appearances. *See* Noumenon, *prakriti*.

pool of Consciousness
　Consciousness conceived as a "pool" into which different experiences are absorbed, and from which they rise. In particular, when people die, their various memories and experiences are sometimes conceived as going into a "pool of Consciousness" from which future persons may later remember them. *See* rebirth.

prakriti
   Nature: from *"pra-"* meaning "prior" or "underlying," and *"kriti"* meaning "activity." Thus *"prakriti"* refers to nature as the underlying principle of all activities, including all external happenings in the universe and all the perceiving and conceiving activities of body and mind. Through these activities of nature, all phenomena and appearances are produced, in everyone's experience. Thus nature is the objective or "known" principle that underlies all experience, producing everything that appears. Consciousness is the subjective or "knowing" principle, illuminating all appearances and disappearances. Both principles are always together, underlying everything. In fact, they cannot be distinguished. There is no way of telling them apart. They are only different aspects of the same ultimate ground of Reality, which all appearances truly show. When looking out to the changing world of objective phenomena, that Reality is called "nature." When looking back in, to the source of knowing illumination, the same Reality is called "Consciousness."

predestination
   When viewed from outside time, all past, present and future events may be conceived together, existing simultaneously in the timeless present. From this conceptual position, the future is included in the timeless present and is thus predestined. *See* Present Moment, destiny.

Present Moment
   Since the past and future are always experienced in the present, they do not really exist outside it. In actual experience, there is only the present, without any outside past or future to limit it on either side. The time-bound present that we perceive is only a limited appearance, caused by inadequate conception. The real present is timeless, containing all experience. This timeless present is described by the capitalized phrase: the "Present Moment."

programming
   Genes and inheritance at birth, plus subsequent conditioning. Together, they pattern the responses of body and mind to received inputs, thus playing their part in carrying out the destiny of a body-mind organism.

puja
   Ritual of devotional worship towards a deity or a guru.

Ramana Maharshi
   Advaitin sage (1879-1950), who settled at Tiruvannamalai in Tamil Nadu, India. He recommended the path of Self-inquiry; and was famous for the profound sense of silence that was conveyed by his very presence, which had an effortlessly calming and clarifying effect on those who came to him.

rebirth
    Since the individual person is just a fictitious creation of ego, so is rebirth. There may be memories of experiences in previous lives, but this does not mean that such past-life experiences are rightly identified as having happened to a personal "me" that is present now. They happened to a past body and a past mind, neither of which is the same as the body and mind that remember now. It is only the false ego that identifies these past and present bodies and minds as "me," thus creating the false impression of a personal "me" which has continued through time. In fact, the personality of body and mind keeps changing all the time. The only thing that continues through time is Consciousness, which is completely impersonal. Neither birth nor death apply to it. See *samsara*.

sadhana
    Spiritual practice, striving or work. To the extent that there is emphasis upon a personal doer, who makes the effort and achieves results, such work reinforces the ego and is thus counterproductive. So *sadhana* cannot rightly be done with any personal achievement in mind; but only towards impersonal Truth, where mind completely dissolves.

    Traditional *sadhanas* are meditation (*yoga*), inquiry (*jnana*), devotion (*bhakti*) and selfless service (*seva*). Different persons are suited to different kinds of *sadhana*.

sage
    One who has realized ultimate Truth and is established there.

sahaja sthiti
    The "natural state," in which a sage is permanently established. In that state, there is not even a trace of ego left to disturb the natural spontaneity of experience. No matter what appears, it is effortlessly understood as nothing else but Truth.

    Like the plain Truth it shows, the understanding of the *sahaja* state is not in the least affected, not even for a moment, by all the many deceptions and confusions of changing appearance.

samadhi
    State of absorption. The word is often used to describe the trance states of mental absorption that result from meditation or otherwise from deep thought or feeling.

    When a sage passes away from the body, the word "death" is not used, but instead the term "*mahasamadhi.*" This only means "great *samadhi*": implying a final absorption of the sage's apparent, transient life into the undying Truth of life for which it stands. And the word "*samadhi*" is thereafter used to describe the sage's memorial, where the body's remains are disposed.

sampradaya
   Traditional lineage, in which knowledge has been passed down through a continuing chain of teachers and disciples.

samsara
   Literally: "course, passage, passing through a succession of states." Philosophically used to describe the course or flow of changing experience.
   Seen individually, *samsara* refers to the course of experience that an individual undergoes, including death and rebirth. In fact, *samsara* is permeated through and through with birth and death; for these occur not only at the end and beginning of body's life, but also at every moment — as a previous state of experience dies and a new one is reborn.
   Seen universally, *samsara* refers to the course of events and happenings throughout all space and time. This includes the whole changing universe of physical and mental experience.
   Since Reality is essentially changeless, the flow of *samsara* is essentially illusory. *See* What-is, rebirth.

samskara
   A tendency or predisposition or trait of character resulting from past actions and experiences. A person's *samskaras* are thus the elements of conditioning through which past actions affect the body-mind organism and its present and future actions. In the course of time, these *samskaras* accumulate so as to develop the conditioned personality and its space-time journey through the world. The conditioning is seen most obviously to accumulate in this life; but it may also be conceived to accumulate from previous births, and to go on accumulating in future births as well.

sannyas
   Renunciation. In the traditional institution of *sannyas*, there is a formal renunciation of normal relationships and activities in ordinary society. But such traditional *sannyas* is only a dispensable form. As the *Bhagavad Gita* says, body and mind cannot truly renounce their relationships and activities. They can only be prevented from one particular relationship or one particular activity by diversion to another. As the *Bhagavad Gita* points out, such physical and mental prevention is not really renunciation. The essence of renunciation is not to prevent any relationship or activity, but instead to remain unattached no matter what relationship or activity may engage body and mind. This means detachment from the body and mind that are habitually identified as one's own Self. In the end, the only thing to be given up is this false sense of identity. That alone means detachment from all physical and mental things.

sannyasi, sannyasin

Renouncer. One who gives up the unreality of the world, in search of Truth. This does not mean that body or mind give up the world; but rather that the true *sannyasi* gives up falsely identifying with body and mind, through which the world appears. See *sannyas*.

Sat-Chit-Ananda

Existence-Consciousness-Happiness. *Sat* is pure Existence, the principle of Reality that confronts all action and life. *Chit* is pure Consciousness, the knowing principle that lights all perception and thought. *Ananda* is pure Happiness, the motivating principle that inspires all value and feeling. The three are only different ways of looking at one single Truth. See *yoga*.

satguru

The real *guru*. The term is often used to denote a teacher of ultimate Truth, as opposed to one who teaches only some relative ability. Ramesh uses the term to describe the "*guru* within": meaning that inner principle of Truth which is expressed, for a disciple, in the person of the guru.

satsang

Association in Truth. Meeting with someone who embodies the ultimate Reality.

seeker

Someone identified with a personal ego, looking for the ultimate Truth that the ego obscures.

seeking

Trying to find something that one thinks is missing. This is inevitable wherever ego identifies with a partial personality consisting of body and mind, for body and mind are always lacking something.

Seeking comes to a final end only when the true goal of all seeking is realized as one's own Reality, which is always fully and immediately present, throughout all experience.

Self

What everyone calls "I." The word "I" is used for many things: for a body ("I am fat," "I walk"); for bodily organs of sense ("I see," "I taste"); and for mind and mental faculties ("I intend," "I think," "I feel"). However, these many things are called "I" only by identifying them as the knowing subject, as the subjective centre that knows one's experience.

When the body is identified as "I," it is because this body is taken to know the world that appears around it. But when it is seen that the body is just a physical object, through which the senses know, then identification shifts inward, to the senses. And when the senses are seen as objective organs or faculties, through which perceptions come into the mind, then identification shifts again, to the mind.

But what about seeing the mind as an objective faculty? What happens when the mind is seen as an objectively functioning process, which produces the changing appearances of perception, thought and feeling? Then it turns out that the knowing subject is pure Consciousness, which continues at the background of experience, illuminating the changing appearances that come and go at the surface of mental attention.

Beneath the limited and varying surface of mental appearance, that pure Consciousness is unlimited and always the same. It does not change with time, nor does it differ at all from person to person. It is the real "I," to which a person refers when saying: "I know" or "I am conscious."

Whenever body, senses or mind are identified as "I," they are falsely taken to be the knowing subject of experience, thus producing the fiction of a personal ego, whose limited actions, perceptions, thoughts and feelings are confused with knowing. This personal ego or "me" is a false self, which does not exist at all. The actions, perceptions, thoughts and feelings of body and mind are only objective activities. Body and mind do not know anything in themselves.

Only Consciousness knows. And it does not know by putting on any activity, but by its own unaffected nature of pure Illumination. As knowledge in itself, its very being is to know, to shine with knowing light. That alone is the real Self, which everyone calls "I."

Self-inquiry

Philosophical questioning into the nature of one's own Self. Not to be confused with psychological exploration of personality. The aim of Self-inquiry is not to explore the changing appearances of personality, but to ask what is the underlying Reality of the Self that they seem to show. *See* Self.

seva

Service. One of the traditional means to enlightenment, by service directed selflessly towards an expression of Truth, in particular towards a deity or a guru.

Shankara, Adi

An eighth or ninth century philosopher, who established *Advaita* Vedanta at a central position in the Hindu tradition. In the course of a short but eventful life, he travelled widely over India, articulating *Advaita* philosophy rather more fully than others before him, in the scholastic language and concepts of his times.

siddhi

Accomplishment. The word has come to be commonly used for various psychic powers which attract popular attention, but often inflate the ego and thus become obstacles to the ultimate accomplishment of enlightenment.

silence

Peace, undistracted by the noisy clamoring of ego and ego's objects for attention. Consciousness is silent knowing, unmixed with ego or objects.

"Soham"

"I am That." Concise statement of non-duality, affirming the identity of the knowing Subject "I" with the complete Reality ("That") of known objects appearing in the world. See *Advaita*.

Source

Origin from which physical and mental appearances arise. It may be approached subjectively: by reflective inquiry, back to the inner source of Knowledge from where perceptions, thoughts and feelings rise. Or it may be approached objectively: by penetrating questioning (beneath the surface of appearance) into the underlying source of Reality from which nature manifests the world's phenomena. See *prakriti*.

the three states

Waking, dream and deep sleep.

In the waking state, objects are seen to appear in an external world outside the mind. So there seems to be a duality of inner and outer: with a mind somehow inside a body, looking at an outside world.

In the dream state, all objects are seen to be made of perception, thought and feeling, inside the mind. So nothing is outside. There are only appearances that come and go within the mind, illuminated by Consciousness.

In the deep sleep state, there is no outside nor inside, for all appearances vanish. That disappearance is illuminated by pure Consciousness, shining on its own. It is the light of which all appearances are made, and into which they have all dissolved. It shines there by itself, unseen by sense or mind.

thinking

In general, the functioning of mind. In particular, the functioning of ideas, as mental objects that are thought about.

In the general sense, the mind's functioning can be natural and spontaneous, with the mind absorbed in the task at hand — as described in Ramesh's phrase, the *"working mind."*

In the particular sense, thinking implies the involvement of ego with objects of thought: "I think that..." Then the mind sticks out like a sore thumb and complicates things by distracting itself with its own functioning — as described in Ramesh's phrase, the *"thinking mind." See* thought, mind.

thinking mind
See thinking, mind.

thought
In the functioning of mind, thought occurs somewhere between feeling and perception. Perceptions are interpreted by thoughts, which in turn arise through feelings of intuition. Thus, thought does not originate in body or mind, but arises through intuition from underlying Consciousness. In effect, each thought is an input from beyond both body and mind, which later on produce their outputs, as they react with their conditioning.

At the time it actually occurs, each thought or each reaction of body and mind is entirely in the Present Moment. Body, mind, incoming thoughts, outgoing reactions are all expressions of Consciousness, appearing at different moments of time. Their only relationship is that they express the one Consciousness, which is itself completely uninvolved.

Involvement only occurs through ego's false identification as a personal doer, consisting of a physically doing body and a thinking (or mentally doing) mind. The ego thus claims to carry out actions and think thoughts that involve it in time and tie it up in time-bound cause and effect. And yet it cannot do without its contradictory claim to be somehow independent. Without such independence, it would simply disappear. This is its inherent frustration.

In fact, all thoughts and actions are only momentary expressions of Consciousness. They cannot tie anyone down. The ego and all its apparent involvements are also momentary expressions of Consciousness, which remains completely independent. The independence that ego cannot do without is its own true nature, in which its seeming acts and thoughts are all completely dissolved.

Tiruvannamalai
A small town in Tamil Nadu, India, about five hours by bus from Madras or Bangalore. It is next to the sacred mountain Arunachala, where Ramana Maharshi lived. His ashram is built at the foot of the mountain. *See* Ramana Maharshi.

Totality
Through our bodies and minds, we see things partially. In each of our physical and mental perceptions, something always remains unseen. So each object or event that we see is only an apparent piece of matter or happening, in a much larger universe. Even if we try to conceive of the whole universe, the details get left out. So we are left only with a partial conception, or a

partial picture, in which a lot is left missing. No perception, no conception, no physical or mental picture can ever be total. What appears at the surface of physical or mental attention is always incomplete. It does not tell the whole story. It is not fully real.

And yet we do take into account what is missing at the apparent surface. We do so on the basis of understanding, which stems from the background of experience, beneath the narrow appearances of body and mind. There, in that underlying background, knowing is silent. There is no distraction generated by some little "me," making noisy claims about its incomplete experiences. There is only the silent understanding of pure Consciousness, in the timeless centre of the Heart, continuing unaffected beneath all changing experiences.

This silent knowledge of understanding stands outside time, while every partial experience appears and disappears before it. So it leaves nothing out. All our perceptions and conceptions express it, and are absorbed back into it. It is the one Totality, the complete Reality of every physical and mental thing seen through our bodies and minds in the entire world.

To quote Ramesh: "Understanding is all."

understanding

See Heart, Totality.

Upanishads

Philosophical texts at the end of the *Vedas*. They consist of concise statements which raise fundamental questions and are thus liable to different interpretations. Many schools of Indian philosophy acknowledged the authority of these statements, interpreting them in different ways. See Vedanta, *Vedas*.

Vedanta

Literally: "the end of the *Vedas*" or "the culmination of knowledge." ("*Veda*" means "knowledge.") Vedanta is thus a name given to schools of philosophy that are meant to explain the final knowledge expressed in the concise statements of the *Upanishads* (texts occurring at the end of the *Vedas*).

Some schools of Vedanta are dualistic or maintain a qualified dualism, in order to allow for the "I" and "Thou" of religious worship.

The school of *Advaita* Vedanta is non-dualistic. It maintains that worship and devotion start from a dualistic level, but reach their end in a non-dual Truth where no separation remains. The same Truth is approached through philosophical inquiry, questioning its way back to the basis of knowledge on which our pictures of the world are built. See *Advaita*.

Vedas

The founding texts of the Hindu tradition. They are regarded as sacred revelations, from which all knowledge may be found. The *Vedas* start as mythical, religious and ritual texts; but they end finally with the *Upanishads*, which are philosophical.

vertical

See horizontal and vertical.

vipassana

Literally: "discernment, clear seeing."The term is used for a form of meditation (developed in Theravada Buddhism) where mental and physical appearances are witnessed as coming and going, without becoming involved with them. The aim is to arrive at a clear knowledge that all appearance keeps on changing. Thus one is meant to give up all futile attachment to what keeps passing away; so that one finally comes to a position of unshakable calm and clarity, quite undisturbed by anything which may occur. This is said to be the main meditation that helped the Buddha to enlightenment.

waking

See the three states.

What-is

Reality, shown in common by all differing and changing views of it. Through our limited bodies and minds, we see particular appearances from different points of view. Appearances change and differ, depending on our perspectives. Reality is just that which does not depend on our particular views. It is always the same, no matter how we look, and no matter what appears. It is thus shown universally: by all past, present and future appearances, everywhere in the physical and mental universe. And it is shown individually: by each particular moment of everyone's experience.

At each moment, a particular appearance is perceived, through body and mind. The appearance differs and changes, along with body and mind. But Reality does not. Beneath the passing appearance of the moment, only Reality is truly present, beyond all change and time. So, beneath appearances, the present is always timeless, showing all Reality.

And that Reality is indistinguishable from Consciousness, for both are always present together, throughout experience, underlying all appearances. "Reality" and "Consciousness" may be two words, but what they describe is one and the same.

To quote Ramesh: "All there is, is Consciousness."

working mind

See mind, thinking.

yoga

Literally, "union." The path of *yoga* is that of practical exercise and meditation, expanding the limited powers of body and mind towards unity with all Reality. The way to Truth was traditionally divided into three main paths: *yoga* (meditation), *jnana* (knowledge), and *bhakti* (devotion). These three paths correspond to *Sat* (Existence), *Chit* (Consciousness) and *Ananda* (Happiness): regarded as three aspects of the Truth. See *Sat-Chit-Ananda*, meditation.

Yogavasishtha

An *Advaita* Vedanta classic, describing how the young Lord Rama was taught by the sage Vasishtha.

PUBLICATIONS BY NETI NETI PRESS

INTRODUCTION TO THE TEACHINGS OF RAMESH S. BALSEKAR

Gentle Hammer, Friendly Sword, Silent Arrow This book encapsulates the *Advaita* Vedanta teachings of Ramesh S. Balsekar. The first part—Gentle Hammer—features a series of aphorisms, each of which sums up one element of his teaching. Once the seeker's ego has been weakened by this gentle but persistent hammering, the Friendly Sword is ready to finish the job. This second part consists of Ramesh's answers to 24 key questions put to him by the editor, Madhukar Thompson, at a seminar given in the idyllic surroundings of Kovalam Beach, Kerala, India. The third part—Silent Arrow—is a reprint of "The Search for God-Truth-Reality," an article that Ramesh contributed to "The Mountain Path," a bi-yearly magazine published by the Sri Ramanashram. In this article, Ramesh manages to condense his entire teaching into a few pages. It is written with such precision and profound insight that, while reading it, the reader is led to experience silence—the highest form of teaching. The pithy aphorisms, the brevity of the question-and-answer extracts and the zen-like clarity of the article make this book an ideal introduction to Ramesh's teaching.

Enlightenment: An Outbreak In an absorbing series of interviews and intimate conversations, Ramesh S. Balsekar and five of his enlightened disciples describe their spiritual search and its culmination in enlightenment. The role of the guru in this process, and the nature of their post-enlightenment experience are explored. Full of fascinating insights and touching personal anecdotes, this book will appeal to anyone who is even remotely interested in spirituality.

Six First-Hand Accounts Of Enlightenment Occurences

MAY OR MAY NOT HAPPEN

Enlightenment May Or May Not Happen "The whole problem is that the individual seeks enlightenment as an object which can bring happiness, or the cessation of unhappiness. But so long as there is a 'me' seeking enlightenment, enlightenment cannot happen." This book, and its sequel ***Enlightenment? Who Cares!***, document the teachings of Ramesh S. Balsekar, as expressed in response to questions regarding the spiritual search and related issues. In conversations recorded during his daily teaching sessions, Ramesh repeatedly affirms the impersonal nature of life and seeking. As the spiritual search progresses, the seeker's identification with the fictitious "me"-entity weakens until there is no one left to care whether enlightenment happens or not. "When you come to that stage, it is likely that enlightenment will happen at any time." A series of humorous cartoons accompany the transcripts, underscoring key aspects of the teachings they illustrate.

Enlightenment: Never Found—Never Lost This book documents the teachings of Papaji (Sri Harilal Poonja) using material drawn from extensive recordings of his *satsangs* held in Lucknow, India. Illustrated by a series of humorous cartoons devised by the editor, Madhukar Thompson, the book charts his experience as a disciple of Poonjaji. The dramatic "love affair" between the guru and the disciple eventually comes to an explosive end, but it also provides many precious insights into the guru-disciple relationship and the true nature of freedom.

Teachings en Route to Freedom Throughout history, India has produced an extraordinary range of religious traditions and, even today, innumerable spiritual teachers can be found there. This book documents Madhukar Thompson's encounters with a wide range of gurus: Osho Rajneesh, U.G. Krishnamurti, Annamalai Swami, Ranjit Maharaj, Tulku Urgyen Rinpoche, Choekyi Nyima Rinpoche, Dadaji, Lakshmana Swami, Harish Madhukar, Andrew Cohen, Gangaji, Giridhar and Kiran whom he sought out in his quest for enlighten-ment. It presents a compilation of remarkably diverse spiritual teachings as expressed in conversations which were recorded over a period of 17 years.

Of Jewels, Pigs and Freedom This is a selection of 14 full-color cartoons inspired by the teachings of Papaji (Sri Harilal Poonja), as featured in the book *Enlightenment: Never Found – Never Lost*. Devised by Madhukar Thompson who spent two years in Lucknow as one of Poonjaji's closest disciples, the clarity and humor of these postcards reflect the powerful experience of *satsang* with this remarkable guru.

Zorba 'n Buddha Your Way to Freedom In this set of 14 full-color postcards, Madhukar Thompson takes a light-hearted, even mischievous, look at the world of Osho. His lengthy experience as one of Osho Rajneesh's disciples enables him to present an insider's view, pointing up the humorous aspects of a neo-*sannyasin*'s life of celebration and meditation, and the controversial teachings of this notorious guru.

Enlightenment by Airmail and **Enlightenment à la Carte** Selected highlights of the lively and light-hearted cartoons which illustrate *Enlightenment May or May Not Happen* and *Enlightenment? Who Cares!* are gathered together into these two postcard collections. Each collection consists of a set of 20 detachable full-color cartoon postcards whose humor vividly highlights the wisdom of Ramesh's *Advaita* Vedanta teachings. Send them off to amuse and "enlighten" your relatives and friends!

The Seeker and His Search
Meditation
Enlightenment
Master!

Each of these postcard collections contains 10 detachable full-color cartoons devised by Madhukar Thompson. Their inspiration has been distilled from his experiences during two decades of spiritual search, and while each collection focuses on a different theme, their common purpose is to highlight the funny side of spirituality. They will be enjoyed by full-time, part-time (and even flexi-time!) seekers everywhere.

These titles may be ordered directly from Neti Neti Press or Pacifica. For further information, e-mail, write, call, or fax to:

India

*Neti Neti Press
8 Sheetal Apts.
Kawedewadi
Koregaon Park
Pune - 411001
Tel/Fax: 91-20-603338
E-mail (neti_neti@yahoo.com)
www.neti-neti.org*

Germany

*Neti Neti Press
Kiefernweg 10
64319 Pfungstadt
Tel/Fax: 49-6157-3471*

USA

*Pacifica
P.O. Box 120
Haiku
Hawai, 96708
Tel: 1-888-740-1270
Fax: 1-808-575-2072
E-mail: mohanmaui@hotmail.com*